The Battle of Hanover Court House

ALSO BY MICHAEL C. HARDY
AND FROM McFARLAND

*The Fifty-Eighth North Carolina Troops:
Tar Heels in the Army of Tennessee* (2010)

*The Thirty-Seventh North Carolina Troops: Tar Heels
in the Army of Northern Virginia* (2003; paperback 2009)

The Battle of Hanover Court House

Turning Point of the Peninsula Campaign, May 27, 1862

MICHAEL C. HARDY

McFarland & Company, Inc., Publishers
Jefferson, North Carolina, and London

The present work is a reprint of the illustrated case bound edition of The Battle of Hanover Court House: Turning Point of the Peninsula Campaign, May 27, 1862, *first published in 2006 by McFarland.*

Library of Congress Cataloguing-in-Publication Data

Hardy, Michael C.
　　The Battle of Hanover Court House : turning point of the Peninsula Campaign, May 27, 1862 / Michael C. Hardy.
　　　　p.　　cm.
　　Includes bibliographical references and index.

ISBN 978-0-7864-6920-8
softcover : 50# alkaline paper

　1. Hanover Court House, Battle of, Hanover, Va., 1862.
2. Peninsular Campaign, 1862.　I. Title.
E473.6.H37 2012
975.5'46203 — dc22　　　　　　　　　　　　　　2006006088

British Library cataloguing data are available

© 2006 Michael C. Hardy. All rights reserved

No part of this book may be reproduced or transmitted in any form or by any means, electronic or mechanical, including photocopying or recording, or by any information storage and retrieval system, without permission in writing from the publisher.

Cover photograph: Captured Confederate cannon in the camp of the 17th New York (Library of Congress)

Manufactured in the United States of America

McFarland & Company, Inc., Publishers
　Box 611, Jefferson, North Carolina 28640
　　　www.mcfarlandpub.com

To the memory of the families who lost sons, husbands, and
brothers as a result of the battles of Hanover Court
House and Slash Church. It is especially in honor of
the Robnett family of Alexander County, North Carolina: to
lose three out of four sons in one day is too terrible to imagine.

Table of Contents

Preface	1
1. "Give Me Liberty, or Give Me Death!": Hanover County	5
2. "But You Must Act": McClellan and the Peninsula Campaign	11
3. "Preserve a Firm Front to the Enemy": McDowell, Johnston, and Fredericksburg	33
4. "Charge — Charge Them, Brave Boys": The Battle of Kinney Farm and Hanover Court House	45
5. "Pop! Pop! Bang! Bang! for About an Hour": The Battle of Peake's Turnout	67
6. "Every Room a Sickening Contrast to the Splendid Furniture": Hospitals	93
7. "Morning Came, and Stiff and Sore We Rose": The Day After	99
8. "Our Boys Are Yet Cheerful, and Feel Confident of Success": Richmond	111
9. "I Take Exception": The Battle in the Press	115
10. "We Have a Hard Road to Travel": The Battle in Perspective	129
11. "It Still Should Not Be Forgotten": The Battlefield Today	137
Appendices	
A. Order of Battle	141
B. Fitz John Porter's Official Report	145
C. Lawrence O'Bryan Branch's Official Report	149
D. Casualties	153
Notes	179
Bibliography	195
Index	201

Preface

"The fight of to-day was in the highest degree sanguinary," confided a member of Battery C, First Rhode Island Light Artillery in his diary, "and will be conspicuous among the battles of the peninsula." Unfortunately, an anonymous member of the Confederate army, writing to the *Wilmington Weekly Journal* on June 5, 1862, made a more accurate prediction: "This battle will never be faithfully chronicled." And he was almost right. It would take more than 100 years for anyone to show an interest in the battles that swirled around Hanover Court House, the Kinney farm, Peake's Turnout, and Slash Church.

Through the spring of 1862, George B. McClellan's 100,000-man Army of the Potomac sat poised at the gates of Richmond, seemingly ready to strike a fateful blow to the Confederacy at any moment. If things were not bad enough, an additional 40,000 men under the command of Irvin McDowell were just to the north, at Fredericksburg. It was between these two forces that Confederate general Lawrence O'B. Branch found himself in late May. Branch and his command, mostly North Carolinians, save for the Forty-fifth Georgia, were in the vicinity of Hanover Court House, protecting the railroads that were vital to the Confederate supply system. An advance by either Federal force would prove disastrous to Branch's force.

On May 26, McClellan, believing that he needed to clear the Confederate troops off his right flank and open the way for McDowell, chose to attack. In a disjointed effort, both Branch and his antagonist, Union V Corps commander Fitz John Porter, operated under the influence of misinformation, and McClellan's forces succeeded. Had McClellan or McDowell been able to advance into Richmond on the day after the battle, May 28, the Confederate capital would have been lost. But McDowell was under orders from the president to move large portions of his troops toward the valley, and McClellan was not interested in a tactical movement into Richmond, preferring to rely on siege tactics. Never again would McClellan take his army on the offensive during the summer of 1862, and the battles around Hanover Court House and Peake's Turnout were the high tide of McClellan's Peninsula campaign.

A writer today must stand in awe as he ponders the massive amounts of literature concerning the American Civil War. Yet, history has not often considered the May 27 battle. *The Seven Days: The Emergence of Lee*, written by Clifford Dowdey and published in 1964, devotes two paragraphs, about 200 words, to the "little-known 'Battle of Hanover Court House.'" Joseph P. Cullen's 1973 work, *The Peninsula Campaign 1862*, makes no mention whatsoever of the action. The first serious look at the battle occurred in 1992 when Stephen W. Sears published *To the Gates of Richmond: The Peninsula Campaign*. Sears devotes about four pages to the battle, and even includes a map of the action. This was followed in 1997 by an excellent essay on the battle written by Robert E. L. Krick. The essay, complete with maps and illustrations, appeared in Volume 2 of *The Peninsula Campaign of 1862: Yorktown to the Seven Days,* edited by William J. Miller. Finally, in 1999, Jerry J. Coggeshall used the subject in his master's thesis, entitled "Hanover Court House: The Union's Tactical Victory and Strategic Failure," for Old Dominion University. The book by Sears is likely where most readers might have come in contact with the battle of Hanover Court House and Peake's Turnout. However, due to the dearth of coverage this action has received, even those well-read in Civil War scholarship may never have heard of the battle by any of its many names.

Choosing a title for this study has been a challenge that I have been pondering for a long time. The battles actually took place at Kinney Farm, with the Confederates falling back through Hanover Court House and Peake's Turnout, where the rest of the Confederate forces first advanced and later fell back through toward Ashland. For many Federal soldiers, the action was nearly always called only the battle of Hanover Court House. Many of the Confederates also called the battle by this name in their letters home and in published casualty lists. Colonel Lee, in his official report, referred to the action as the battle at Lebanon Church. Slash Church, where General Branch established his headquarters the night before the battle, has also been used as the battle's sobriquet from time to time. But, when it came time to adorn their flags with their battle honors, both the Northern and the Southern soldiers chose to paint "Hanover."

As is often the case, this book is the product of a line of research that originally began with another project. In the mid-1990s, I undertook to write a book on the Thirty-seventh North Carolina Troops. As I researched that book, it became apparent that a full-length work was needed on the battles of Hanover Court House and Peake's Turnout. Many of the people and institutions that I acknowledged in that work are, more or less, the same ones that I find myself indebted to with this book.

First and foremost, I would like to thank all of the descendants of the men who fought — and of those who died — for the little pieces of information that they have preserved, handed down, and passed along to me.

David Ward, of Canton, Connecticut, graciously photocopied newspaper clippings from his own files and sent them to me. This saved me many countless hours trying to track down these sources.

Diane Jones, historian at Slash Church, kindly gave me a tour of Slash Church and the countless historical sites in Hanover County.

Preface

Eric Wittenberg generously allowed me to view a chapter from his upcoming study on the Sixth Pennsylvania Cavalry.

Mostly importantly, I would like to thank Robert E. L. Krick, who first guided me through the records of the Richmond National Battlefield Park and later read and made comments on the manuscript.

I would also like to thank the folks of the Branch-Lane Brigade Discussion Group, a wonderful group of people, mostly descendants, who routinely meet online (and on a battlefield once a year) to discuss the actions of the Tar Heels of the Branch-Lane brigade.

Lastly, I would like to thank my readers: Clay Kearney, of Orlando, Florida, a descendant of a member of the Thirty-seventh North Carolina Troops; Daphne Baird, of Odessa, Missouri, for her intrepid proofreading; and Elizabeth Hardy, who cares for this story and these people as much as I do.

1

"Give Me Liberty, or Give Me Death!": Hanover County

Located in the Tidewater section of Virginia, an area where the rivers are influenced by the ebb and flow of the ocean tide, Hanover County was already immersed in history well before the American Civil War began. When European adventurers and settlers arrived in the early 1600s, they found that a powerful native chieftain by the name of Powhatan had established a confederation of 9,000 Algonkin-speaking peoples from 30 different tribes. The Powhatan Confederacy controlled much of the James, Pamunkey, and Mattaponi Rivers. It was Powhatan and his nation that the early Jamestown colonists relied upon during their first harsh winter. Also during this period of time, America crowned its first hero, Captain John Smith, one of the seven council members of the new Jamestown Colony. Smith was part of a hunting group in present-day Hanover in December 1607 when the party was ambushed by Indians. Smith was taken prisoner, and according to legend, saved from execution by Pocahontas, daughter of Powhatan. Pocahontas later married another leader of the new colony, John Rolfe. Captain Smith would go on to create the first map of the area in 1612. Things would not be peaceful for long: before the year 1630 violence erupted in two Anglo-Powhatan Wars, with peace coming in 1632.[1]

In 1654 New Kent County was created and encompassed much of Hanover. It would be 66 years before the government carved an additional county from New Kent. This new county was formed on November 26, 1720, and named Hanover in honor of King George I, who was the elector of Hanover in Germany. The new county was bordered on the north by the North Anna and the Pamunkey rivers, on the west by Louisa County, on the south by Goochland and Henrico counties, and on the east by New Kent County. The area in the eastern portion of the county is low and marshy, while the western section has semimountainous hills. Two of the most important trading centers in the Virginia colony were located in the new county: Newcastle and Hanovertown. Newcastle was proposed as the new capital of Virginia when the original capital, located in Williamsburg, burned in 1749. In 1779, when the decision was finally made to move the capital, Hanovertown, rather

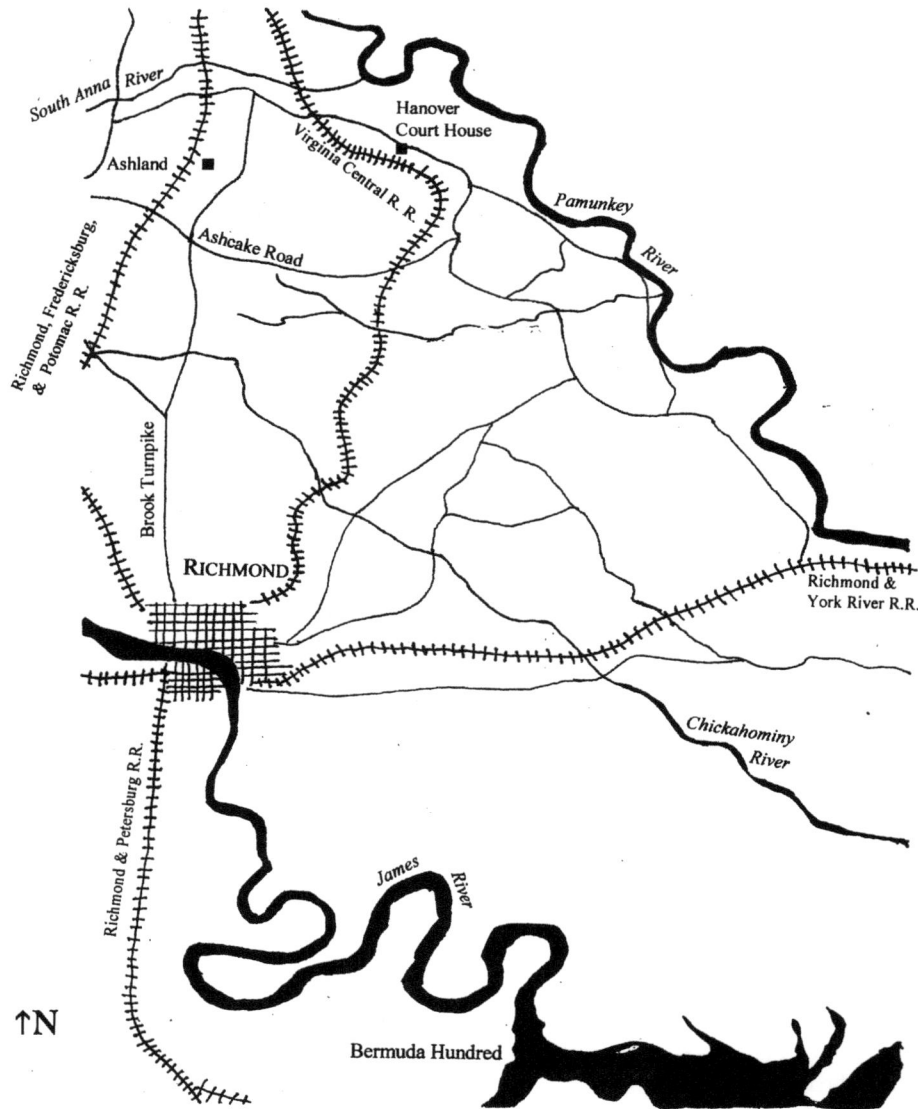

Eastern Virginia in 1862.

than Newcastle, was proposed as a potential site, and lost to Richmond by only a few votes. [2]

The county has had more than its fair share of distinguished citizens. Patrick Henry, who uttered one of the most famous lines in American history: "Give me liberty, or give me death," was born in Hanover in 1736. Henry practiced law, managed a tavern, was a member of the Continental Congress, and had the distinction of being the Commonwealth of Virginia's first governor. John Paul Jones, a British-born sailor of fortune, spoke words almost as famous as Henry's when he informed an English sea captain during a naval battle in 1779: "I have not yet begun to fight"; he was staying in Hanover County at The Grove before he joined the Continental Navy. General Thomas Nelson, Jr., a signer of the Declaration of Independence, the commander of the Virginia troops during the siege of Yorktown, and a delegate to the Constitutional Convention, had a home in the northwestern portion of the county. Dolley Payne Madison's parents were from Hanover County. She was born in Guilford County, North Carolina, but the family moved back to Hanover when she was nine months old. She later married James Madison, the fourth president of the United States. Dolley was noted for her graciousness and charm as she entertained guests at the White House during both Thomas Jefferson's tenure in office and her own husband's administration. Wilson Cary Nicholas, commander of the Washington's Life Guard and governor of Virginia from 1814 to 1816, also lived in the county. During the American Revolution, some of the major participants of the war spent time in or passed through Hanover County. Those names now synonymous with history include George Washington, the Marquis de Lafayette, Lord Cornwallis and his chief cavalry officer, the infamous Banastre "Bloody Ban" Tarleton. It was in Hanover County, at Merry Oaks Tavern, that the Continental Army had its beginnings.[3]

"The Mill Boy of the Slashes," a nickname for young Henry Clay, also called Hanover County home. He was born at Clay Springs in 1777, and lived in Hanover until the age of 14, when his family moved to Richmond. After obtaining an education in law, Clay moved to Kentucky in 1797. He would go on to serve as one of America's greatest statesmen, earning a new nickname, "The Great Pacificator." Clay served in the United States House of Representatives, the United States Senate, and made an unsuccessful bid for the presidency. Some say that Clay's 1850 Missouri Compromise averted the Civil War for another decade. Clay titled his estate just south of Lexington, Kentucky, Ashland; the residents of Slash's Cottage renamed their town Ashland in honor of Clay. Another important performer on the stage of American history who spent time in the county was John Marshall. In 1783, he married Mary Willis Ambler in Hanover County. The man that Marshall would beat by a few votes for the position of chief justice of the Supreme Court of the United States also resided in Hanover County. Spencer Roane, a judge of the Virginia general court, lived at Spring Garden. Also in the 1780s, Bishop Francis Asbury, known as the "Apostle of American Methodism" visited the area and in 1786, started one of the first Sunday schools in America in Hanover County. This Sunday school later became St. Peter's Methodist Church.[4]

One of America's greatest agriculturists, Edmund Ruffin, moved to Hanover County in 1843. Born into a leading Tidewater family in Prince George County, Virginia, in 1794, Ruffin earned acclamation as the greatest agricultural reformer in the Old South. He purchased an estate in Hanover County in 1843, named it Marlbourne, and proceeded to transform the estate using the methods that he had outlined in his *An Essay on Calcareous Manures* (1832). Ruffin retired from management of his estates in the 1850s and turned his energies toward politics. By 1856,

The tavern where Patrick Henry lived and worked (author's collection).

he had become one of the leading prosecession voices in the country, advocating slavery as a necessary institution. He traveled all over the country trying to persuade the people of the South that their hopes lay in a separate nation. It was Ruffin who, on April 12, 1861, in Charleston, South Carolina, fired one of the first shots of the war at the Federal garrison in Fort Sumter.[5]

Hanover County would make some major contributions in the war for southern independence that Ruffin helped start in 1860 and 1861. Confederate general Williams Carter Wickham, born in 1820 in Richmond, Virginia, and a great-grandson of Gen. Thomas Nelson, moved with his family to Hanover County in 1827. After attending the University of Virginia, he returned to Hanover and practiced law. In November 1859, Wickham formed the Hanover Light Dragoons, a mounted militia company. He was also elected to the state senate that same year. Wickham was selected to represent the area at the Virginia convention on secession and voted against it. But, once his state seceded, he threw his fortunes in with those of his kinsmen. Wickham, while a captain in the Fourth Virginia Cavalry, participated in the battle of Manassas, and in September 1861 was commissioned a lieutenant colonel of the Fourth Virginia Cavalry. On May 4, 1862, during the battle of Williamsburg, Wickham was severely wounded in the side by a saber stroke during a cavalry charge. He returned home to Hanover County to recover from his wounds before returning to further service and promotion in the field.[6]

At least 1,138 other men from Hanover County took up arms in defense of the state of Virginia. They formed regiments such as the Patrick Henry Rifles, the Ashland Grays, the Hanover Grays, the Ashland Artillery, and the Morris Artillery.

Possibly even more important than the soldiers or the area's agrarianism were the roads and railways that ran through the county. In the eighteenth century, the major road connecting northern Virginia with Williamsburg and Richmond ran through Hanover County. A stagecoach route used this road heavily, bringing both passengers and freight, such as the mail, from north to south, and vice-versa. Taverns were built along the road to accommodate travelers. One such lodge was the Hanover Tavern, built near the courthouse. The tavern's guest books record such patrons as Edgar Allan Poe, John Marshall, Charles Dickens, and P. T. Barnum. Since the area in and around Hanover County had no navigable waterways, in 1835 the Richmond, Fredericksburg, and Potomac Railroad was chartered by the State of Virginia. By 1860, this line stretched from Richmond, through Hanover County and Fredericksburg, to the Potomac River. A year after the Richmond, Fredericksburg, and Potomac Railroad was chartered, a second line was established: the Louisa Railroad. The first train ran on the Louisa Railroad in December 1837. The railroad reached Gordonsville in 1840 and Shadwell in 1849. In 1850, the Louisa Railroad was renamed the Virginia Central Railroad, and in 1852, the line had extended through Charlottesville and on toward the Blue Ridge Mountains. [7]

Both of these lines were vital to the new Confederacy. The Richmond, Fredericksburg, and Potomac ran north and south, and was able to shuttle supplies and war materials from Richmond to Fredericksburg and points north during the early days of the war. The Virginia Central Railroad connected the Tidewater section of the state with the Piedmont and mountains, and brought supplies essential for the Confederate army from the valley area. One Union general termed the Virginia Central "the one great line of the enemy's communications between Richmond and Northern Virginia." [8]

Despite its inherent beauty and historical significance, Hanover County, Virginia, would soon bear witness to some of the most bloodcurdling struggles of a civil war.

2

"But You Must Act": McClellan and the Peninsula Campaign

If Federal army commander George B. McClellan had any indication of the history of the region in and around Richmond, Virginia, he failed to mention it to his wife in a letter he wrote when his steamer landed at Fortress Monroe on the afternoon of April 2, 1862. The Pennsylvania-born McClellan, a West Point graduate, had brought his Army of the Potomac down the Potomac River and into the Chesapeake Bay for an assault against the Confederate capital in Richmond. McClellan's force was the largest amphibious operation that the world had ever seen. The 389 vessels, of all shapes and sizes, were employed in the transport of 121,500 men, 14,592 animals, 1,224 wagons and ambulances, 44 artillery batteries, and an enormous amount of war munitions from the Washington, D.C., area to Fort Monroe.[1]

Richmond, Virginia, was the capital of the recently established Confederate States of America. A group of 11 Southern states, once a part of the United States, had broken away, established a separate nation, and had chosen Richmond to be its capital. The United States government did not believe the rogue states had the right to leave the Union, and war had broken out between the northern and southern sections of the country.

In addition to serving as the ceremonial capital of the new country, Richmond was also the industrial nucleus of the South. With a population of 37,910 people in 1860, Richmond was the 25th largest city in the United States. Sixty-two percent of the population was white, and more than one-fifth was foreign born, with Irish Catholics and German Lutherans the most prominent immigrant groups. Baptists, Methodists, and Presbyterians dominated the religious makeup, with the Episcopalians at the top of the social establishment. There was also a significant Jewish minority. Eighteen percent of the resident African-Americans were freemen, and the majority of African-Americans held skilled jobs. The city's four largest financial institutions had combined assets greater than $10 million. There were 14 foundries and machine shops in the town, along with four rolling mills, six companies that manufactured iron railings, a nail works, and 50 general iron and metal works. Joseph R. Anderson's Tredegar Iron Works was the second largest foundry in the United States. There were also 12 flour and meal mills, including the world's largest. Richmond also had the world's largest tobacco market, and was the largest importer of Brazilian coffee in the world. The area was serviced by five railroads: the Richmond and Danville; the Richmond and Petersburg; the Virginia Central; the Richmond and York River; and the Richmond, Fredericksburg, and Potomac. There was heavy barge traffic on the James River canal system and oceangoing vessels could dock just below the city. Richmond also boasted four major newspapers, several theaters and public halls, and four large schools: the Medical College of Virginia; Richmond College; the Richmond Female Institute; and the Virginia Mechanics Institute. The war with the North brought powder mills, armories, laboratories, government offices, and troop encampments. Richmond provided over 7,300 troops for the Confederacy, including 40 companies of infantry, artillery, and cavalry. For the Confederacy to survive, Richmond had to survive.[2]

Born in 1826, George McClellan had served in the Mexican War, and was later sent to the Crimea by the United States War Department to observe the French and British battling the Russians. After returning from his trip to Europe, McClellan resigned from the army, first serving as chief civil engineer and vice president of the Illinois Central Railroad and later president of the Ohio and Mississippi Railroad, a position he occupied at the start of the war. He was now in command of the largest army of the United States. McClellan was given the task of taking Richmond and destroying the Confederate army that protected the capital. Taking charge of a Federal force that had been defeated during the first large-scale land battle of the war in July 1861, the general had reorganized, resupplied, and drilled his men into an effective fighting force. Furthermore, McClellan began construction on a line of forts to better protect the capital. These fortifications would allow McClellan to leave the capital with a small garrison and take the field against his foe. But as the leaves grew golden and fell off the trees, the northern populace became impatient. They wanted the rebellion crushed.[3]

Not long after taking command, McClellan began developing different strategies for forcing the Confederacy to capitulate. In August and September 1861, McClellan considered the Occoquan-Cedar Run plan. Based largely upon McDowell's campaign against the Confederates in July, the Occoquan-Cedar Run idea called for the Federal force to cross the Occoquan River below the town of Alexandria, Virginia, proceed south through Maple Valley, then divide the column into small forces, due to the poor roads, and advance to Brentsville on Cedar Run. This movement would force the Confederates out of their entrenchments, sever their lines of communication, and lead them into an open battle with the Federals. This plan of action had several supporters, most notably, Abraham Lincoln. McClellan believed that he could launch this campaign by December 25.[4]

Another plan was floating around the headquarters of the Army of the Potomac. As early as May 1861, McDowell had presented to Secretary of the Treasury Salmon P. Chase the idea of moving a force by water to the Peninsula between the James and York Rivers and marching on to Richmond. It is believed that after McClellan took command of the army, McDowell shared this idea with his new commander. By mid–January, McClellan had totally disregarded the Occoquan-Cedar Run plan. He felt that the right flank of his army and his supply line would be too much exposed to attack by attempting such a turning movement. Plus, the Confederates occupied a strong defensive position.[5]

Instead, as McClellan outlined in a letter to Edwin Stanton, he wanted to seize the strategic offensive. By selecting the best piece of ground and readying impregnable field fortifications, he could force the Confederates to attack him. Maintaining a tactical defense was the best way of securing a victory over his foe.[6]

In mid–November, McClellan began to receive intelligence on the Confederate forces on the Peninsula

Maj. Gen. George B. McClellan, Commander of the Army of the Potomac, and his wife, Mary Ellen (courtesy the Library of Congress).

between the York and James rivers. The area was lightly defended and the Union possessed naval superiority, allowing it to control the waterways. The general's first intentions were to land a force at Old Point Comfort, near the Union-controlled Fort Monroe on the tip of the peninsula, then advance a force up the peninsula on the opposite side, away from the Confederate fortifications at Yorktown. Once in the rear of the town, the Federal forces would be able to besiege the historic spot with a small force, while the remainder of the force advanced toward Richmond. By early December, McClellan changed the spot for the deployment of his army from Old Point Comfort to Urbanna, a little tobacco port located on the Rappahannock River and east of Richmond. The roads from Urbanna to Richmond were traversable during all seasons; the countryside had an early spring and sandy soil, with thin vegetation; and his force could be easily supplied from the Chesapeake Bay. From Urbanna, the army would march to the town of West Point, located on the York River, and cut off the army holding the lower peninsula from the army in Manassas. There was a great possibility that the Confederates on the Peninsula would be forced to make a hasty retreat, opening themselves to attack and destruction. It would then require only a two-day march by the Federals to be in Richmond, well before the Confederates had time to act. When the Confederates did react and start toward their capital, McClellan would be able to fight them in the open and on ground of his own choosing. The war would end with one great Napoleonic battle.[7]

The Army of the Potomac's commander soon began to share his strategic plan with others, usually his close friends, including Generals Fitz John Porter, Andrew Porter, and William B. Franklin; John A. Dahlgren, commander of the Washington Navy Yard; Secretary Chase; and Rear Admiral Louis M. Goldsborough. At approximately the same period of time, the United States Congress formed the Joint Committee on the Conduct of the War. After the military failures of Bull Run and Ball's Bluff, powerful Republican members of Congress created the committee and began to investigate the actions of high-ranking officers with the armed forces, mostly Democrats whom they believed were not prosecuting the war as aggressively as possible. The committee met in the basement of the Capitol, and the day after its organizational meeting, called McClellan to come before them. But before McClellan could fulfill his obligations, he was stricken with typhoid fever.[8]

Commanding General of the Army of the Potomac and General in Chief of the United States Armies George B. McClellan lay incapacitated, some feared gravely sick, at the start of the second year of the war. He had no second in command, and the armies of the United States lay dormant as winter set in. Lincoln repeatedly tried to see his general, but was repeatedly turned away. On December 31, five members of the Joint Committee visited Lincoln, demanding action. Three members returned on January 5, demanding that McClellan be replaced, wanting Irvin McDowell to take his place.[9]

Five days later, on January 10, Lincoln, under this pressure from members of Congress, summoned Generals Irvin McDowell and William B. Franklin, along with Secretaries Salmon P. Chase, William H. Seward, and Assistant Secretary of War Thomas A. Scott, to a "war council." Lincoln, in conferring with the army commanders in the West, Maj. Gen. Henry W. Halleck and Brig. Gen. Don Carlos Buell, discovered that they had no orders from McClellan and that their commands were stagnating. Lincoln opened the meeting by providing an overview of the diplomatic, political, economic, and military problems facing the government. Lincoln, in a humorous tone, stated that "If General McClellan did not want to use the army, he would like to *borrow* it, provided he could see how it could be made to do something." Lincoln then asked the generals present what they would do with the Army of the Potomac if they were in command. McDowell responded that he would keep Washington, D.C., as a base of operations, and attack the Confederate supply lines, forcing the Confederates out of their positions at Manassas Junction and Centreville and to a fight out in the open. This strategy was to President Lincoln's liking, and would protect Washington. General Franklin, who was privy to some of McClellan's plans, informed the president that an advance on Richmond via the lower Chesapeake River was a better approach. Lincoln dismissed the meeting, asking McDowell and Franklin to gather information about the condition of the army and to consult each other on their proposals. The next meeting was scheduled for the evening of the next day,

January 11. At this gathering, Secretary Montgomery Blair was present, and argued against a direct assault on the Confederates at Bull Run. Secretary Chase spoke almost prophetically when he argued that what was needed was a "moral ... victory over the enemy in his present position. It would be just as great as one elsewhere ... and the danger lay in the probability that we should find, after losing time and millions, that we should have as many difficulties to overcome below as we now have above."

Lincoln still wished for more information and called for another meeting the next day at 3 o'clock.

Someone, possibly Stanton, informed McClellan of the meetings, and the general arrived at the White House unannounced on January 12. The still-ailing general gave Lincoln the outline for his Urbanna strategy. At the end of McClellan's conference with Lincoln, the president asked him to attend a meeting at the White House the next after-

Abraham Lincoln, president of the United States of America, and his cabinet (courtesy the Library of Congress).

noon, but did not inform him about the meeting to take place in a few hours. When the other officers and cabinet members arrived that afternoon, they were told that McClellan was well and then notified about the meeting scheduled for the next afternoon. Present at the meeting on the 13th were Lincoln; Generals McDowell, Franklin, Montgomery C. Meigs, and McClellan; along with Secretaries Chase, Seward, and Montgomery Blair. General McClellan simply stated that there were too many Confederates at Manassas to attack, but when pressed for details regarding his own strategy, McClellan refused. He believed that to share this information would be a breach of security and would undermine his authority. His refusal alienated some powerful and patriotic members of Lincoln's cabinet. Ironically, the very next day, January 14, McClellan granted an interview with a reporter from the *New York Herald*, disclosing in detail many particulars about upcoming campaigns.[10]

Still nothing happened, and the president grew weary of waiting for McClellan. On January 27, Lincoln issued "President's General War Order, No. 1." Lincoln designated George Washington's birthday, February 22, 1862, as a "day for a general movement of the Land and Naval forces of the United States against the insurgent foes." The Army of the Potomac was one of the "land" forces that Lincoln targeted. A second order, "President's Special War Order, No. 1," followed on January 31, 1862. It stipulated that "all the disposable force of the Army of the Potomac, after providing safely for the defense of Washington, be formed into an expedition, for the immediate object of seizing and occupying a point upon the Rail Road South Westward of what is known as Manassas Junction, all details to be at the discretion of the general-in-chief, and the expedition to move before, or on, the 22nd day of February next." That same morning, McClellan appeared at the White House and asked Lincoln if the orders were "to be regarded as final," or could he submit his objections in writing. Lincoln agreed. He was finally going to see in-depth plans for the subjugation of the Confederacy from his general.[11]

Due to the pressure of the office, Lincoln's secretary of war, Simon Cameron, resigned in early 1862. He was replaced by Edwin Stanton. McClellan considered the new secretary of war one of his closest supporters. Stanton was described as "irascible, with a nature which was a singular blend of a habit of blunt speech and a fondness for devious intrigue ... he had a talent for savage criticism — a man who could plunge into sudden pessimism so deep as to resemble abject panic, but who could also drive for a chosen goal with uncommon ruthlessness." McClellan wrote to a friend on January 18: "Stanton's appointment was a most unexpected piece of good fortune, & I hope it will produce a good effect in the North." Stanton, on the other hand, since taking office, had been urging Lincoln to either force McClellan to action, or to get rid of McClellan. One of Stanton's plans was to send McClellan "west" with a number of troops and personally take command in that theater of war. The general was unaware that if he had indeed gone west, Stanton planned to pressure Lincoln to appoint a new commander for the Army of the Potomac. McClellan gave the idea of going to the western theater some consideration. On January 26, the general had written Stanton: "My mind is more & more tending in that direction, tho' not fully committed to it. But there should be no delay in ascertaining precisely *what we can do* should it prove advisable to move in that direction."[12]

On February 3, McClellan presented his 22-page report to Lincoln, outlining his Urbanna strategy. Lincoln responded the same day with a short note, asking McClellan questions about his strategy and at the same time voicing his objections to McClellan's plan. Lincoln wrote:

> 1st. Does not your plan involve a greatly larger expenditure of time, and money than mine?
> 2nd. Wherein is a victory *more certain* by your plan than mine?
> 3rd. Wherein is a victory *more valuable* by your plan than mine?
> 4th. In fact, would it not be *less* valuable, in this, that it would break no great line of the enemy's communications, while mine would?
> 5th. In case of disaster, would not a safe retreat be more difficult by your plan than by mine?

Lincoln hit the crux of the matter in his fourth question. McClellan's Urbanna strategy would cut the less valuable Richmond, Fredericksburg, and Potomac Railroad, and possibly capture Richmond, a certain blow to the morale to the Confederates, and an international embarrassment. But the strategy left open portions of the Virginia Central which ran into Gordonsville and the Richmond and Danville Railroads. The latter linked with the Southside Railroad that ran into Richmond. Both the Southside and the Virginia Central linked with the Orange and Alexandria Railroad. This line became the Virginia and Tennessee south of Lynchburg and eventually reached Chattanooga, providing one of the most important railway links in the entire Confederacy. McClellan's responses to Lincoln's concerns are unknown.[13]

McClellan had failed to move any of his forces by mid–February, and many politicians were beginning to complain loudly about the Confederate blockade of the upper and lower Potomac River. By late February, McClellan was ready to build a bridge across the Potomac near Harpers Ferry, in an attempt to reopen the Baltimore and Ohio Railroad to the Ohio Valley. Federal engineers constructed a small pontoon bridge across the river on February 26, and portions of Maj. Gen. Nathaniel P. Banks's division crossed over into Virginia. A large bridge was to be constructed on canal boats sent over for the project. This new bridge would allow the movement of wagons, artillery, and other heavy equipment over the Potomac, and McClellan planned to move on to Winchester. The canal boats were scheduled to pass through the Chesapeake and Ohio Canal, and when they reached the Potomac, they were to pass through a lock into the river. When the canal boats arrived, it was discovered that they were six inches too wide to fit in the locks—no one had bothered to measure either the locks or the boats. McClellan telegraphed the War Department that he was "scaling down" his plans and that he would leave only enough troops on the Virginia side of the river to protect the men rebuilding the railroad. When Lincoln asked Stanton what all this meant, Stanton replied: "It means that it is a damned fizzle. It means that he doesn't intend to do anything."[14]

On March 8, Lincoln called McClellan to the White House for a meeting. Lincoln, most likely still distraught from the death of his son just days earlier, told his general that there were those who were dissatisfied with McClellan's performance, thought that McClellan was a traitor, and believed that his design was to take the Army of the Potomac down the Chesapeake and leave the capital unprotected and open to capture. McClellan was outraged, demanding that Lincoln retract the statement. Lincoln merrily stated that he was passing along the views of others. McClellan did not need to look far for those dissatisfied with his performance up until that point. Horace Greeley, the editor of the *New York Tribune,* was charging McClellan with seeking a compromise with the South. Congressman John A. Gurley, from Ohio, where McClellan had served as a major general of the Ohio Militia, told guests at Washington dinner parties that McClellan was a traitor. Brig. Gen. James S. Wadsworth wrote to lawyer and poet William Cullen Bryant, an abolitionist and key founding member of the Republican Party: "Is it possible to account for all of [McClellan's] errors on the theory of incompetence alone? Is there not in some high quarters a plan for putting down this Rebellion by some other means than by whipping the Rebels?" Even Lincoln was disappointed, and members of the president's cabinet were amazed that the president had not sacked McClellan. McClellan soon returned to his own headquarters, where his generals had gathered, and there McClellan asked them to decide two questions: whether the Army of the Potomac should move from Washington to the lower Chesapeake, and what should be done about the Confederate batteries blocking the lower Potomac River. The generals, by a vote of eight to four, thought that the move to the Chesapeake was a good idea. On the second question, seven of the five generals agreed with McClellan that the Confederate batteries were insignificant to the Army of the Potomac's plan of operation. McClellan and the other 12 generals were called to the White House where they presented their views to a dismayed president.[15]

After they left, Lincoln issued three orders. The first stated that "no change of base of operation of the Army of the Potomac shall be made without leaving in and about Washington such a force ... [that] shall leave said city entirely secure." A council of generals had estimated that this force needed to be 40,000 men. McClellan promised the president that the capital would be protected, and the Peninsula campaign was born. Also on that day, Lincoln took the initiative and ordered the organization of the Army of the Potomac into four corps. McClellan and Lincoln had talked about this plan, but McClellan wanted to wait for its execution until "some little experience in ... battle should show what general officers were most competent...." Lincoln disagreed: an army made up of a dozen divisions was too large to effectively command. The four corps were the I Corps, under Maj. Gen. Irvin McDowell; the II Corps, under Brig. Gen. Edwin V. Sumner; the III Corps, under Maj. Gen. Samuel P. Heintzelman; and the IV Corps, under Maj. Gen. Erasmus D. Keyes. Three of the four new corps commanders—McDowell, Heintzelman, and Sumner—had voted against McClellan's Urbanna movements, and Keyes had approved the idea only if the Confederate batteries on the Potomac were destroyed first. The troops near the upper Potomac would constitute a provisional fifth corps, under Nathaniel Banks, and the troops around Washington, D. C., were assigned to James S. Wadsworth. McClellan had preferred another for the post: William B. Franklin. Wadsworth was neither a military man nor friendly to McClellan. Wadsworth was a lawyer, studying first at Harvard, then Yale, and finally reading law under Daniel Webster. At the start of the war he became a member of the Union Defense Committee of the city of New York and soon thereafter became a major general in the state of New York. At Bull Run, he was a volunteer aide on the staff of General McDowell, and on August 9, 1861, was commissioned a brigadier general in the United States Army and assigned a brigade of New Yorkers in McDowell's division. Wadsworth often denounced General McClellan for being inactive.[16]

Lincoln's third order was a crushing blow to McClellan. The president removed McClellan as general in chief, effective March 11, 1862, a move supported by Lincoln's cabinet. McClellan was summoned to Washington and failed to report. He learned the next day, through a newspaper, that he had been "demoted" from supreme army commander to the commander of the Army of the Potomac. Lincoln wanted McClellan to concentrate on the Confederate army in the east, while McClellan believed that the stripping of his powers would not allow him to coordinate his attacks in Virginia. William Dennison, governor of Ohio, was chosen to deliver the news to McClellan, and after Dennison left camp, McClellan wrote a letter to the president, thanking him for his consideration and pledging to "work just as cheerfully as ever before...."[17]

As soon as President Lincoln had issued his orders and McClellan began to gather his troops, a problem arose. Before a single regiment, or artillery battery, or cavalry troop could embark, the Confederate soldiers around Manassas, led by Gen. Joseph E. Johnston, vanished. The 55-year-old Johnston, a Virginia

Gen. Joseph E. Johnston, commander of the Confederate forces in Virginia (courtesy the Library of Congress).

native and also a West Point graduate, had been friends with McClellan prior to the war. Johnston commanded all of the forces in Northern Virginia and had occupied a 50-mile line from Dumfries in the east to Leesburg in the west. In an effort to consolidate his forces which had been thinly stretched across Northern Virginia and to be in a position to defend Richmond, Johnston chose to withdraw his army behind the Rappahannock River.[18]

The war was not going well for the Confederates. They had won several early victories, such as Fort Sumter in April 1861; Big Bethel Church, Virginia, in June; and First Bull Run in July. The Confederate strategy for the first year was to disguise the South's weaknesses—their lack of cannons, long arms, and powder—long enough so that a "combination of home production and imports through the blockade" would allow them to go on the offensive. This aggressiveness on the part of the Confederacy had kept large portions of the Federal armies inactive during the winter of 1861–1862. The Confederate armies had even succeeded in erecting batteries on the Potomac River, effectively blockading Washington as far as its water approaches were concerned. But since that time, the South had lost ground with defeats at Mill Springs, Kentucky; Forts Henry and Donelson in western Tennessee; Pea Ridge, Arkansas; and Nashville, Tennessee, the first Confederate state capital to fall under Federal control. Furthermore, sections of the coast along North Carolina, South Carolina, and Georgia had also fallen, providing bases for Federal incursions both into the Confederate interior and further south. To further compound the South's problems, their armies were undergoing a massive reorganization that was potentially destructive and extremely demoralizing. Many of the one-year terms of enlistments of the men who made up the Southern armies were due to expire. To combat this, regiments that reorganized for three years or the war were allowed to hold elections for new field officers. Many of the men saw this as an opportunity to do away with strict disciplinarians, and the army lost many good, effective officers.[19]

"We have Sangster's Station & Fairfax Court House," McClellan telegraphed to Lincoln and Stanton on March 9. "I am arranging to move forward to push the retreat of rebels as far as possible." Word had arrived from all over Northern Virginia that the Confederates had spiked their guns, destroyed munitions that could not be removed, and retreated. The Confederate movement caught McClellan by surprise, and on March 10 he moved the entire Army of the Potomac toward Manassas. But the chance for the Federals to catch the Confederates was gone. This was McClellan's type of victory: bloodless. McClellan inspected the Confederate works, and discovered that several of the embrasures contained the notorious "Quaker guns"—logs that had been shaped and painted black to resemble cannons. McClellan suffered mightily at the hands of the press. An article from the *Philadelphia Inquirer* was reprinted around the nation. It read, in part, "'QUAKER GUNS IN THE REBEL FORTIFICATIONS."

> The fortifications look, *at a distance*, formidable.... We rode up to them, and found them merely dirt trenches and sand forts. They have been evidently laid out by an engineer who understood his business, but have been constructed by men who merely wanted to put in time. *There has never been a single heavy gun mounted in them. Embrasures have been made and logs of wood run out in all of them....*

Yet another newspaper journalist, this one belonging to *New York Tribune*, wrote on March 15

> Utterly dispirited, ashamed and humiliated I returned from this visit to the Rebel stronghold.... For seven months we have waited, organized a powerful army, until its drill and equipment should be so complete that we might safely advance against the "Gibraltar" of rebellion.... And now ... we see that our enemies, like the Chinese, have frightened us by the sound of gongs and the wearing of devil's mask.

The great guns that had kept the Army of the Potomac immoveable all fall and winter were incapable of firing a single round. McClellan's "chief of the secret service," Allan Pinkerton, had reported these "Quaker" guns six weeks prior to the Confederate departure, but the general chose to follow his own plan and not attack the Confederate entrenchments. Despite his growing loss of favor among politicians, the press, and even his own soldiers, McClellan remained obliviously optimistic, declaring in a letter to a friend, "My movements gave us Manassas with the loss of one life—a gallant cavalry officer—history will, when I am in my grave, record it as the brightest passage of my life that I accomplished so much at so small a cost."[20]

While Johnston and the Confederates took up their new positions closer to Richmond, McClellan was obligated to fall back upon the plan he considered "the worst coming to the worst." On March 13, he held a council of "high officers" at Fairfax Court House and chose to alter his plans for the campaign. His new design was to land his force at Fortress Monroe, a position already in Federal hands. The Union stronghold was 75 miles southeast of Richmond on the end of a peninsula. A major Union force here would allow the Union forces to maneuver with their flanks, rear, and lines of communication in absolute safety. On March 17, the lead elements of the Army of the Potomac, Brig. Gen. Charles S. Hamilton's division of the III Corps, got underway, bound for Fortress Monroe.[21]

McClellan continued to face problems among the politicians in Washington. On the very day that the Army of the Potomac set sail, a vote narrowly failed to pass the Senate to censure the general and dismiss him from the service. At the same time, Stanton offered command of the Army of the Potomac to Ethan Allen Hitchcock, a retired regular army officer with 40 years of service, who was commissioned major general of volunteers in February 1862 and assigned to staff duties under Stanton. Hitchcock passed on the opportunity. "Now-what is to come of this? I want no command. I want no departments.... On the whole, I am uncomfortable. I am almost afraid that Secretary Stanton hardly knows what he wants, himself," Hitchcock wrote. Just a few days prior to this, Stanton appeared before the Joint Committee on the Conduct of the War, criticizing McClellan and stating that eight of McClellan's commanders should have been dismissed after the embarrassment at Manassas.[22]

But there was still the problem of the protection of Washington. Lincoln had ordered that a sizable force be left to protect the capital. One of his principal concerns was that Confederates could leave a small force in the works around Richmond to occupy McClellan's attention while the remainder of the Confederate army marched north to sack Washington. McClellan's predecessor as general in chief, Winfield Scott, had little concern about the safety of Washington. "I have not the slightest apprehension whatsoever for the safety of the government," was the aged Scott's opinion. It was McClellan, in a letter dated August 8, 1861, and addressed to President Lincoln, that pricked the president's fears for the capital. McClellan wrote: "The Vital importance of rendering Washington perfectly secure, and its *imminent danger*...."[23]

Lincoln's fears regarding the Federal capital were not unfounded. Twice Joseph Johnston argued for just such an operation, leaving "an adequate force to garrison Richmond and drive with the remainder of the army 'rapidly across the border, and make an active campaign beyond the Potomac, striking Baltimore and Washington, if not Philadelphia and New York, before McClellan could take the works around the Confederate capital.'" Even McClellan, not long after taking command in Washington, was issuing orders to brigade commanders in the Harpers Ferry area, warning them that a crossing by a Confederate force in their arena was a likely probability.[24]

By the time of his movements in the spring of 1862, McClellan considered the politicians' concerns for the safety of Washington unfounded. These were the apprehensions of "unmilitary persons...." The general believed that the best defense of Washington was his offensive campaign against Richmond. On April 1, General McClellan fired off a dispatch to Stanton outlining the disposition of the forces he had left behind to guard Washington. Before the dispatch had reached Stanton's office, McClellan boarded the steamer *Commodore* and set sail for Fortress Monroe. According to the general's communication, he left 55,456 from his "own army," along with the 19,022 men in Washington under General Wadsworth, for a total of 74,478 men. General Wadsworth, the commander of the forces in Washington, waited until McClellan was en route before raising concerns over the orders left by McClellan. McClellan wanted Wadsworth to send "4,000 troops from Washington to Manassas ... as fast as they report to you" and "a regiment of infantry to Budd's Ferry, to relieve Hooker's division...." McClellan sent a second dispatch, ordering Wadsworth to send two cavalry regiments "to report to General Abercrombie at Warrenton Junction." In response, Wadsworth telegrammed General Sumner: "I find no regiments really fit to move or go into the field." Stanton became concerned, and sent to the adjutant general, Brig. Gen. Lorenzo Thomas, and Major General Hitchcock the president's war order of March 8, detailing the number of troops he wanted left behind; the report of the council held at headquarters at Fairfax Court House, dated March 13; the president's instruction to McClellan, dated March 13; the report of McClellan, dated April 1; and the communiqué of Wadsworth "as to the forces in his command." Stanton asked the generals to examine the documents and "to report to me whether the President's order and instructions have been complied with in respect to the forces to be left for the defense of Washington and its security...." After looking over the documents, Thomas and Hitchcock concluded that "the requirement of the President ... has not been fully complied with." McClellan's 74,000 men existed largely on paper. He had assigned a scant 26,761 men for the defense of Washington. And large numbers of these men, in the words of General Wadsworth, were "new and imperfectly disciplined" or "in a very disorganized condition." When Lincoln was informed of the discrepancies in McClellan's dispatch, "he was justly indignant." Lincoln had not only the safety of Washington to be concerned about, but international opinion, and even his own political career.[25]

To McClellan's credit, he had envisioned an adjustable force for the protection of the Federal capital. Many of the Federal forces that he included in his report but that Lincoln's examiners did not were mobile forces within a day's march of the capital. Had some attack of Washington been organized by the Confederates, these forces, veteran men for the most part, could have quickly consolidated in the defenses of Washington, or upon the flank of the enemy.[26]

Regardless, President Lincoln was quick to act. On April 3, he instructed one of the corps that had belonged to the Army of the Potomac to stay behind in front of Washington. The I Corps, under the command of Maj. Gen. Irvin McDowell, the general who had commanded Union forces on the field at the battle of Manassas the previous July, was ordered to remain behind. McClellan fired off a telegram to the president, begging him to "reconsider the order detaching the first Corps" and believing that "the success of our cause will be imperiled by so greatly reducing my force." The next day he wrote to his wife: "the order detaching McDowell's Corps ... is the most infamous thing that history has recorded ... the idea of depriving a General of 35,000 troops when actually under fire!" Many on McClellan's staff believed that McDowell had used McClellan's absence to get his corps withheld from McClellan's command.[27]

The president's actions should not have been a surprise to McClellan. On paper, his army numbered over 100,000 men. Furthermore, other Union generals were winning victories with much smaller forces. Stanton was quick in recognizing these men, mostly likely in hopes of spurring McClellan on. These official thanks went out to Henry W. Halleck, for successes in the West; Generals Franz Sigel and Samuel R. Curtis for their victory at Pea River, Arkansas; Generals Don Carlos Buell and Ulysses S. Grant for the victory at Shiloh; and to John Pope for his capture of Island Number 10 in the Mississippi River. Furthermore, President Lincoln issued a proclamation recommending that places of worship should offer prayers of thanks for the victories.[28]

Lincoln's worries about the capital still had merit. A sizeable force under Maj. Gen. Thomas J. "Stonewall" Jackson, the hero of Bull Run, was operating in the Shenandoah Valley west of Washington. The Shenandoah Valley was critical to the Confederate States for both military and economic reasons. Militarily, the valley provided a screen for eastern Virginia, moving Federal troops away from Richmond. A movement by the Confederate soldiers traveling north up the valley placed the Southern armies near Washington or Baltimore. Economically, the valley was an important source of subsistence, supplying the Confederate armies with edibles for the majority of the war. Stonewall Jackson believed "that if this valley is lost Virginia is lost."[29]

A Federal army under the command of Banks had moved into the valley in February 1862. Jackson's force was outnumbered by General Banks's command, but Jackson "was instructed to endeavor to employ the invaders of the valley, but without exposing himself to the danger of defeat, by keeping so near the enemy as to prevent him from making any considerable detachment to reinforce McClellan, but not so near that he might be compelled to fight." The Federal army began to encircle the Confederate force on March 7. Jackson abandoned his headquarters at Winchester on March 11, and his small force fell back to Mount Jackson. The Federals made only a halfhearted attempt to follow the Confederates. On March 16, Banks was ordered by McClellan to move his command to Manassas, leaving a couple of cavalry regiments to occupy Winchester. Jackson, correctly deducing that Banks was uniting his force preparatory to a move to reinforce McClellan, set out after the Federals on the morning of March 22. On March 23, General Jackson's weary soldiers, now numbering only 2,700 infantrymen due to the strenuous march, met a portion of the Federal army at Kernstown. The Confederates believed that they were attacking only a small portion of Banks's men, but they soon found themselves battling a division of three brigades under the command of Gen. James Shields. Jackson's small band was forced to retreat after three hours of combat. Yet, what appeared to be a tactical failure for Jackson constituted a strategic victory for the overall Confederate strategy in early 1862. The Federal authorities believed that Jackson's force was much larger than it really was. Shields's division was tied up for three weeks pursuing Jackson's Confederates before being ordered on to Fredericksburg. General Banks and his single division were ordered to stay in the valley to contain Jackson. The Confederates in the valley spent most of April resting and reorganizing.[30]

President Lincoln had already removed one of McClellan's divisions prior to detaching McDowell's corps. This division belonged to Brig. Gen. Louis Blenker, contained 10,000 men, and was sent to shore up things in Gen. John C. Fremont's command in the mountains west of the Shenandoah Valley. Fremont was a southerner, born in Charleston, South Carolina, in 1816, and was well known prior to the war as one of the leading explorers of the West. He had also been the first Republican Party candidate for the presidency in 1856. Fremont was commissioned major general in May 1861, and sent to Missouri in an attempt to keep that state in the Union. Fremont's issuing of a proclamation freeing all slaves in the area he commanded was quickly repealed and Fremont was relieved of duty. But Fremont had powerful friends in Washington, and Lincoln created a new district for the general to command. The Mountain Department, essentially comprising western Virginia and eastern Tennessee, was created in March 1862. Lincoln confessed to McClellan that he had bowed to political pressures in creating the department. It was the hope of the administration that Fremont might advance into eastern Tennessee and cut the railroads, the South's only direct east-west line.[31]

Lincoln's patience with McClellan was quickly waning. He wrote to his young general on April 9:

> Your dispatches complaining that you are not properly sustained, while they do not offend me, do pain me very much.... I think it is the precise time for you to strike a blow. By delay the enemy will relatively gain upon you — that is, he will gain faster, by *fortifications* and *re-enforcements,* than you can by re-enforcements alone. And, once more let me tell you, it is indispensable to *you* that you strike a blow. *I* am powerless to help this.... The county will not fail to note — is now noting — that the present hesitation to move upon an entrenched enemy, is but the story of Manassas repeated. I beg to assure you that I have never written you, or spoken to you, in greater kindness of feeling than now, nor with a fuller purpose to sustain you.... *But you must act.*

But there were still objectives that Lincoln could complete. To help protect Washington, the president ordered General McDowell and his I Corps to proceed to Fredericksburg. The I Corps arrived on April 18, and after an intense, brief skirmish, occupied the town.[32]

Lincoln's removal of McClellan as general in chief was well justified, but it did create a problem. Now, instead of several small forces in Virginia reporting to McClellan, forces that the general could have used in conjunction with each other to overwhelm the Confederates, there were now six different commands, all reporting to the War Department. Corps commander Keyes wrote to Senator Ira Harris on April 7, 1862, a letter that undoubtedly found its way to Lincoln:

> The plan of campaign on this line [Warwick River] was made with the distinct understanding that *four* army corps should be employed. Today I have learned that the 1st Army Corps have been withdrawn altogether from this line of operations. The greatest master of the art of war said that "If you would invade a country successfully, you must have one line of operations and one army under one general." But what is our condition? The State of Virginia is made to constitute the command, in part or wholly, of some six generals, viz: Fremont, Banks, McDowell, Wool, Burnside, and McClellan.[33]

Now back to his earlier role as general, rather than general in chief, McClellan's own campaign was proceeding ever so slowly. After landing at Fortress Monroe, he rapidly set out toward the Confederates at Yorktown, believing that it would take only a couple of days and that he would be able to give the Confederates a good "drubbing." What he found was a Confederate force in front of him that was well entrenched. Maj. Gen. John B. Magruder had erected a line of fortifications that stretched across the entire Peninsula. It was the strategy of the Confederate high command to keep the Federals as far down the Peninsula, and away from Richmond, as it could for as long as possible. Many of these fortifications had followed the lines of Cornwallis's 1787 defenses. Plus, Magruder had built a pair of dams on the Warwick River, flooding much of the area the Federal force had to maneuver through to reach the Confederate lines. McClellan's maps, made by an aide to Brig. Gen. John E. Wool, who held command at Fortress Monroe, showed the Warwick River running parallel with the James River, and not across the Peninsula. McClellan's soldiers also found numerous swamps and tangled woodlands. The roads, according to his maps, were not made of sand and did not drain well. As soon as the spring rains hit, they became "pure gumbo mud," causing undue hardship on men and animals. The Confederates only had 12,000 men, but Magruder skillfully placed these soldiers at the most visible points, and had others that routinely marched in sight of the Federals, creating the illusion of a much larger army. The ruse worked, and McClellan, not wanting to lose men in frontal attacks against strong works, called for a siege.[34]

Magruder's theatrics had provided just what the Confederate army needed: more time. When Robert E. Lee had assumed the duties of military advisor to President Jefferson Davis in late March 1862, just a month earlier, there had been seven individual Confederate forces in Virginia under six commanders. Maj. Gen. Benjamin Huger was in command of the Department of Norfolk, with 13,000 troops, along with the naval facilities that were vital to the Confederates. Maj. Gen. John B. Magruder, who was to so effectively create an illusion of superior force, commanded the Army of the Peninsula, with 12,000 troops. He was charged with protecting Richmond from any advances from the east, including the Federal-controlled Fortress Monroe. Gen. Joseph E. Johnston's force along the Rappahannock River was the largest, numbering approximately 37,000 troops, and the best organized of the commands. In the Shenandoah Valley, Thomas "Stonewall" Jackson commanded 5,000 men and was technically a part of Johnston's command, but was isolated from Johnston by the mountains. West of Staunton, further into the mountains, was a small force under the command of Brig. Gen. Edward Johnson with 2,800 troops. Near Lewisburg, guarding the road into the Kanawha Valley, were 1,500 men under the command of Brig. Gen. Henry Heth. Further to the south, in Russell County, was Brig. Gen. Humphrey Marshall, with 1,500 soldiers protecting the Virginia and Tennessee Railroad. Elsewhere across the Confederacy other troops were scattered. On taking the office of Davis's military advisor, Lee was forced to send men, approximately 10 percent of the Confederate forces in Virginia, to North Carolina to protect the Wilmington and Weldon Railroad, a vital link between the Deep South states and Virginia. As April turned into May, Johnston, Davis, and Lee all worked toward mobilizing and concentrating the scattered Confederate regiments and brigades into an effective fighting force and toward an aggressive strategy to destroy the Federal forces. Furthermore, the time it would take McClellan to mount his siege guns and dig entrenchments would further allow the Confederates to manufacture or import much-needed materials of war.[35]

Overestimating the size of the Confederates he faced was practically an art form for McClellan. Prior to the war, the general became acquainted with Allan Pinkerton of the National Detective Agency based in Chicago. Pinkerton, who helped foil a possible attempt on Lincoln's life as the president-elect traveled to Washington, joined McClellan first in Ohio, and later with the Army of the Potomac, as McClellan's "chief of the secret service." The detective engaged in both espionage and counterespionage throughout the war, but in late 1861 and 1862, he was responsible for information regarding the size of the Confederate forces in Northern Virginia. Once Pinkerton learned what McClellan wanted in his reports, he did not fail his chief. Pinkerton reported in October 1861 that the Confederates in Virginia numbered

Jefferson Davis, president of the Confederate States of America (courtesy the Library of Congress).

126,000 men, in 184 regiments. A month later he informed McClellan that the Confederates near Manassas and Centerville, which had numbered 98,400 men in October, now numbered, conservatively, 116,430. In contrast, Confederate returns in January 1862 actually showed only 24,882 effectives. By March, Pinkerton reported 115,500 men, 300 field guns, and 26 to 30 siege guns in Northern Virginia. All of this data McClellan passed on to Lincoln and Stanton, numbers the general used to support his clamor for additional troops.[36]

Meanwhile, Joseph E. Johnston arrived from north of Richmond with a large portion of his army. These soldiers were sent down toward the Yorktown lines to contain the Army of the Potomac. Johnston wanted to quickly withdraw back toward Richmond.

It took McClellan 30 days to erect his big guns — massive 200-pound Parrott Rifles and mammoth 13-inch mortars, among others, to combat what had begun as a mere handful of Confederate soldiers. All the while McClellan's men huddled in the rain and mud, contracting sicknesses and diseases that decimated troops faster than bullets and mortar rounds in the battlefield. McClellan wrote to his wife on May 3, "The task is a difficult one, yet I am sure we have taken the right way to accomplish our purpose...." That night, just hours before McClellan had scheduled his immense weapons to open fire on the entrenched rebels, General Johnston quietly pulled his men out of their fortifications and moved his army back toward the colonial capital at Williamsburg. When the Federals awoke on the morning of May 4, the Confederates were gone. McClellan estimated that an assault on Confederate lines with the siege would have cost the lives of 10,000 Federal soldiers. One Federal commander, disgruntled with McClellan's hesitancy, believed that the loss of those men "would have been much less than that caused by the sickness attending a siege — on our left the men lived in low swampy places that put nearly half of them on the sick list."[37]

The Confederates slowly retreated up the Peninsula, fighting rear-guard actions at Williamsburg on May 5, and at Eltham's Landing on May 7. Johnston stopped along the banks of the Chickahominy until he learned of the evacuation of Norfolk and the destruction of the C.S.S. *Virginia*, on May 10 and 11, respectively. These two events turned Johnston's flank by water, and the Confederates prepared to fall back again. Johnston's withdrawal back toward the environs of Richmond came not from an unwillingness to fight McClellan, but from an attempt to draw the Federals as far as possible from their base of supplies, opening their lines of communication and supply to an attack. Furthermore, the position that Johnston chose between the Chickahominy and Pamunkey rivers was close enough to Richmond to keep his own army supplied; was not close to any navigable bodies of water for the Federal Navy; and was densely forested, to some extent negating the Federal army's sizable numerical advantage. Possibly even more important were the low-level bottomlands that stretched along the banks of the Chickahominy. Even in dry weather there were bogs with which to contend. The spring of 1862 was unusually wet, and the bottomlands surrounding the river were frequently flooded, not only causing the Federal delays but ushering in even more sickness as well. Even as Johnston continued to retreat, the Confederate high command continued to bring reinforcements from other states in an attempt to improve the odds. In mid–April, Anderson's brigade had passed through the capital, and in early May, Branch's North Carolina brigade also arrived.[38]

Events in western Virginia were somewhat quiet. In mid–April, Stonewall Jackson's command in the Shenandoah Valley was forced to withdraw up the valley, and General Banks informed his superiors that the Confederates in the valley were on their way to Richmond. On May 1, Shields's division was detached from Banks's corps and ordered to report to McDowell in Fredericksburg. This would bring the I Corps to 41,000 men. General McClellan had repeatedly badgered the War Department for reinforcements, grossly exaggerating the number of Confederates he faced. Stanton wrote to McClellan on May 18:

> Your dispatch to the President asking for re-enforcements has been received and carefully considered. The President is not willing to uncover the capital entirely, and it is believed that even if this were prudent, it would require more time to effect a junction between your army and that of the Rappahannock by the way of the Potomac and York rivers than by a land march. In order, therefore, to increase the strength of the attack upon Richmond at the earliest moment, General McDowell has been ordered to march upon that city by the shortest route. He is ordered—keeping himself always in position to save the capital from possible attack—so to operate as to put his left wing in communication with your right wing....

Lincoln, by ordering McClellan to make contact with McDowell, and by ordering that McDowell had to maintain his stance between the Confederate capital and Washington, D.C., limited the mobility of the Army of the Potomac. McDowell estimated the trip would take four days and drew up plans to combat the 12,000 to 15,000 Confederates between himself and McClellan. McDowell's advance was slated to begin on May 26.[39]

Soldiers from Brig. Gen. Silas Casey's division of Keyes's corps arrived at Bottom's Bridge on the Chickahominy River on May 20. The Confederates burned the bridge and the trestle of the Richmond and York River Railroad not far away, but did not contest the crossing of the Federal soldiers, a move that baffled McClellan. Additional troops from Keyes's corps forded the river the next day and established the left flank of the Army of the Potomac at Seven Pines.

Construction began on two new spans at the site of Bottom's Bridge on May 22, and the structures, 120 feet long, were completed by the next evening. According to one engineering officer, 79 regiments, almost 1,000 wagons, and several artillery batteries had crossed these two new brigades by the evening of May 24. Construction also began on a new railroad trestle. Federal engineers found a sawmill nearby, and soon had its machinery humming, milling lumber for the new bridge. Rails were brought up from the Federal supply depot, and on the evening of May 27, the first train loaded with supplies streamed across the reconstructed trestle over the Chickahominy and into Savage's Station three miles away.[40]

On May 22, Lincoln, Secretary Stanton, and Commander John Dahlgren embarked for a visit with McDowell at Fredericksburg. McDowell and Col. Herman Haupt, an aide-de-camp and chief of construction and transportation on military railroads, met the president's party at Aquia Creek. They then boarded a baggage car and traveled by train to McDowell's headquarters, located at Chatham. Lincoln met with Brig. Gen. Marsena R. Patrick, acting military governor of Fredericksburg, and then reviewed selected brigades and divisions, riding "along the lines with hat off" as the soldiers gave him a cheer. The next day, Lincoln wrote to McClellan, asking the Army of the Potomac commander to "send a force from your right to cut off the enemies supplies from Richmond, preserve the Rail Road bridges across the two forks of the Pamunkey and intercept the enemies retreat...." By doing this, McClellan could prevent the Confederate army in Richmond "from receiving an accession of numbers of nearly fifteen thousand men...." Lincoln next added that by following his plans, McClellan could secure "a line of Rail Road for supplies in addition to the one you now have." It would almost seem that Lincoln was trying to draw McClellan's army north of Richmond.[41]

While Lincoln was writing to McClellan, the president's plans were falling apart. Lincoln and Stanton had weakened their forces in western Virginia, and had divided the commands. Jackson seized upon this opportunity. On the morning of May 24, Banks's division at Strasburg, in the Shenandoah Valley, began to retreat to Winchester. By noon, Confederate cavalry had engaged their Union counterparts, and by 4:00 p.m., the Confederates had taken a ridge that overlooked the town of Middletown. Jackson's artillery went into position and began to rake the turnpike below that was clogged with Federal cavalry, infantry, and a wagon train. Carnage ensued, and when the smoke from the artillery blocked the view of the Confederate gunners, Jackson ordered his cavalry to charge. Much of the rear of the Federal column was cut off and captured, but a large portion of the column reached Winchester. After a forced march to Winchester during the night, Jackson's Confederates attacked early on the morning of May 25 and drove the Federals from the heights that commanded the town, and from Winchester itself. General Banks ordered his men to retreat toward Williamsport, Maryland, and the north bank of the Potomac River. The Confederates under Jackson now set "poised like a dagger at the north end of the Shenandoah," and, thanks to the hasty retreat of the Federals, were able to resupply themselves with captured stores.[42]

Dread rippled though Washington. Stanton, on May 24, requested the governors of Northern states to "organize and forward immediately all the volunteer and militia force in your state...." Stanton also authorized the War Department to assume temporary control over the railroads to hasten the arrival of these troops. There was a meeting that evening of Lincoln, Stanton, Chase, Seward, Sumner, and several generals. Lincoln described the events, and "said among other things that Banks's men were running & flinging away their arms, routed and demoralized." By the evening of May 26, an estimated 2,000 militia were assembled on Boston Common and were soon on their way to Washington. Stanton believe that the Federal capital was "the only object now worth a desperate throw."[43]

General Jackson became the focus of Lincoln's attention, and the president inaugurated an offensive against the Confederates in the valley. Reports came in from other Federal commanders, placing the size of the Confederate force under Jackson at 40,000. Furthermore, the Confederates at Fredericksburg, some 15,000 strong, had disappeared, and the Federals did not know where they had gone. At 4:00 p.m., Lincoln telegraphed McClellan: "In consequence of Gen. Banks' critical position I have been compelled to suspend Gen. McDowell's movements to join you. The enemy are making a desperate push on Harper's Ferry, and we are trying to throw Fremont's force & part of McDowell's in their rear." At 5:00 p.m., Lincoln telegraphed McDowell at Fredericksburg: "You are instructed laying aside for the present the movement on Richmond to put twenty thousand men in motion at once for the Shenandoah moving on the line or in advance of the line of Manassas Gap R Road. Your object will be to capture the forces of Jackson & Ewell...." Lincoln sent likewise orders to Fremont. McClellan simply replied: "Telegram of four PM received. I will make my calculations accordingly." McDowell promptly replied to Lincoln's missive, writing to Stanton: "The President's order has been received and is in process of execution. This is a crushing blow to us." Lincoln's reply was to thank McDowell for his "alacrity in obeying my order." He continued with: "The change is as painful to me as it can possibly be to you or to any one."[44]

McDowell's reply came at 9:30 p.m. "I obeyed your orders immediately ..." he wrote, almost reaffirming his relationship between himself and the president. "Perhaps" he continued,

> there I ought to stop; but ... I beg to say that co-operation between General Fremont and myself to cut Jackson and Ewell there is not to be counted upon.... Next, That I am entirely beyond helping distance of General Banks; no celerity or vigor will avail so far as he is concerned.... It will take a week or ten days to get to the valley by the route which will give food and forage, and by that time the enemy will have retired. I shall gain nothing for you there, and shall lose much here....

McDowell then informed the president that he had ordered Shields's division to move at daylight, and that a second division would follow that afternoon.[45]

Writing to a friend, McDowell was even more critical of Lincoln's decision to cancel his movement toward McClellan. He wrote on June 17, 1862:

> It is now the middle of the third week since I was at Fredericksburg with a splendid little army of 41,000 men, 100 pieces of artillery, and 14,000 horse — fully equipped, admirably organized, and as a general thing well disciplined and well officered! We were all in high spirits. For this army which had been assembled quietly, was the *next morning* to march down and join the army before Richmond under McClellan. I had been held back by peremptory written orders from the President not to cross the Rappahannock. And even for a while, to make bridges over the River!! But he had given his consent, had issued his orders that I might go as soon as Shields' division should join. It had joined. The wagons were all loaded, the orders given, and we were to march the next day! When came the orders breaking us up and sending us over to the valley after Jackson!
>
> I telegraphed the President that the order was a crushing blow to us all. That I could not get to the valley in time to affect Banks' position. His case would be disposed of one way or the other before I could arrive! ...
>
> But they were alarmed over the safety of Washington! Then came this extraordi-

nary forced march over the Piedmont and Blue Ridge mountains to Front Royal, in which I estimate we had 4,000 men broken down.[46]

"I get more sick of them every day," McClellan wrote to his wife, regarding politicians, on May 25, "for every day brings with it only additional proofs of their hypocrisy, knavery & folly.. ." McClellan wrote the president that Jackson's actions were only a ploy to prevent reinforcements from reaching the Army of the Potomac. Lincoln replied that every Confederate soldier occupied elsewhere was one less soldier McClellan had to fight. "A scare will do them good, & may bring them to their senses," McClellan continued to his wife. The move actually caught McClellan in a precarious situation, with the Chickahominy separating his army.[47]

Jackson's valley campaign might have been modest in size, but his thrashing of Banks produced the desired effects. While no men were removed from McClellan's command, large numbers of soldiers were diverted from the Army of the Potomac and sent to try to entrap the Confederates. In addition to depriving McClellan of troops, Lincoln and Stanton had now poised McClellan in a dangerous position. Lincoln's order to extend his lines had left McClellan's right exposed, and that same order had removed some of the mobility of the Army of the Potomac.[48]

The Confederate commanders in Richmond knew little about the struggles between McClellan and Lincoln over McDowell's corps. Both Lee and Davis viewed the possibility of an overland advance from the north as seriously as McClellan's army to the east. If McDowell's 40,000 plus men could link up with the 100,000 or more that McClellan had, the Confederate army around Richmond stood little chance. To combat this threat, Lee and Davis created the Army of the North. This army was composed of the brigades of Field, Anderson, and Gregg, with Brig. Gen. Joseph R. Anderson in command. This force was stationed in and around Fredericksburg. Added to this was Branch's brigade which was stationed at Gordonsville, and acted as a floating reserve between Anderson at Fredericksburg, and Jackson and Richard Ewell in western Virginia.

3

"Preserve a Firm Front to the Enemy": McDowell, Johnston, and Fredericksburg

Joseph E. Johnston probably received orders from his Richmond commanders sometime on the evening of April 8 to transfer the rest of his army, two divisions of infantry (with artillery) and a cavalry brigade, to Richmond and the Peninsula. While there had been some doubt about the intentions of the Federals prior to the first of April, the Confederate high command was now sure about McClellan's purposes. It took Johnston about two days to organize the forces to be left behind. Stonewall Jackson, now with 8,500 men, continued to operate in the Shenandoah Valley, with instructions to keep in contact with General Ewell's division in case he needed reinforcements. Richard Ewell's division, some 7,500 men, was to guard the "middle Rappahannock," looking for opportunities to strike isolated Federal commands, and to reinforce Jackson if he called. Last, Johnston left the brigade of Brig. Gen. Charles W. Field, with 2,300 men, to guard Fredericksburg.[1]

Field's brigade was composed of the Fortieth, Forty-seventh, Fifty-fifth, and Sixtieth Virginia regiments, and the Twenty-second Virginia Battalion. Also assigned to his command was the Ninth Virginia Cavalry. Fredericksburg, the boyhood home of George Washington, was a thriving community before the war. The town could boast of a population of more than 3,000 and was a major shipping port. In 1860, Fredericksburg had five churches, two newspapers, four taverns, a dozen schools, and at least 100 small businesses. Added to this, the town was on the rail line that ran to Richmond, less than 30 miles away. General Field positioned his cavalry regiment in an arc above Fredericksburg, stretching from "Sackett's Mill, Aquia Church, Potomac Creek, &c., to the river below Fredericksburg," and charged them with watching for a Federal advance.[2]

At about the same time Johnston was withdrawing his forces and sending them to contend with McClellan to the east of Richmond, Edwin Stanton, the secretary of war for the United States, sent orders to Maj. Gen. Irvin McDowell, at

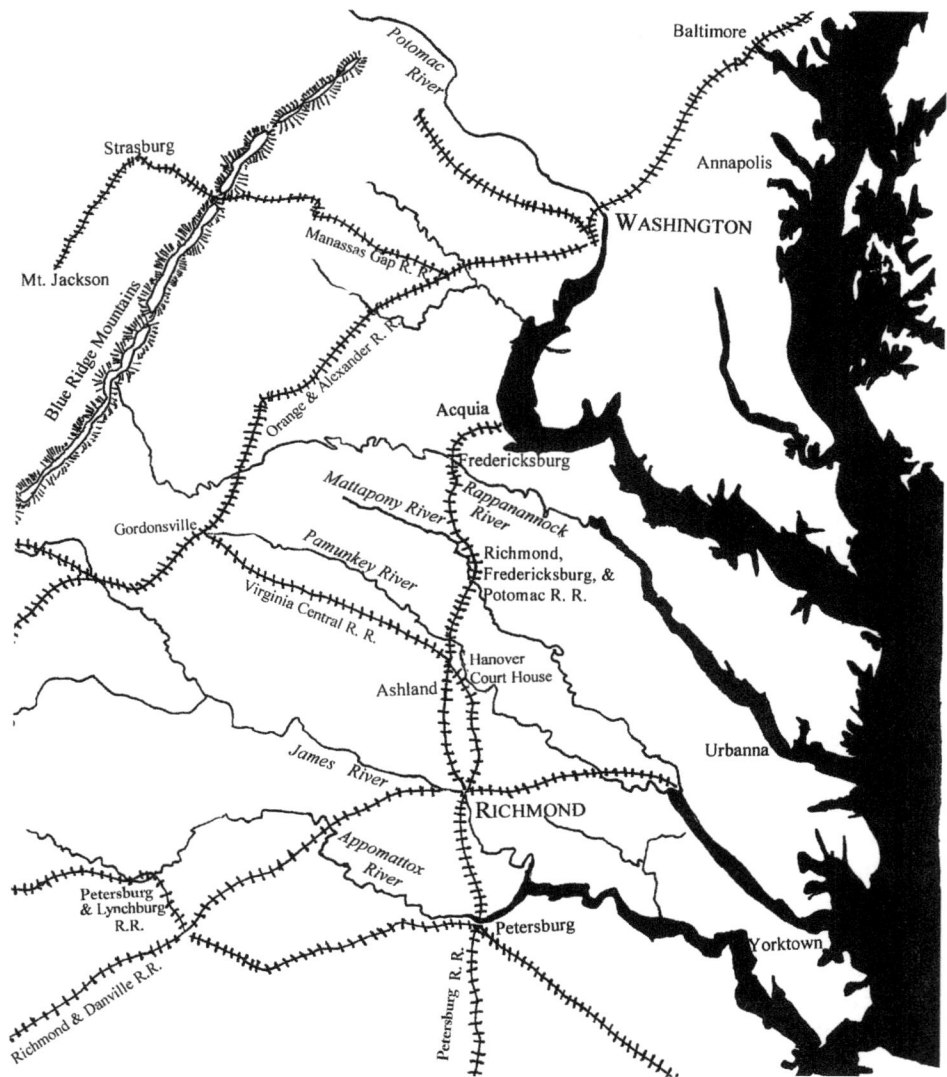

Hanover and Henrico Counties

Manassas. McDowell, in command of the newly created Department of the Rappahannock, was entrusted with the defense of Washington, D. C., and was to "make no movement throwing your force out of position for the discharge of this primary duty." Various groups of Federal soldiers, both authorized and unauthorized, made reconnaissance toward Fredericksburg in the following days. One such authorized party, sent out by Brig. Gen. John J. Abercrombie, reported on April 16 that Confederates were "throwing up entrenchments," but no bridges at Fredericksburg. The party also relayed that the Confederates in Fredericksburg were under the command of "General Smith" and numbered 5,000 or 6,000 men.[3]

That same day, McDowell issued orders for the seizure of Fredericksburg. Brig. Gen. Christopher C. Augur was to take his brigade of King's division, Gibbon's battery, a section of Gerrish's battery, eight companies of First Pennsylvania Cavalry, and eight companies of the Second New York Cavalry, along with "two days' subsistence in the haversacks, four days' in wagons, and beef on hoof" and "proceed ... to Fredericksburg." McDowell was especially concerned about the three bridges that crossed the Rappahannock River and desired "with reference to ulterior operations that these bridges be saved."[4]

For several days, General Field had been reporting to his superiors an increase in activity around Fredericksburg. On April 15, he sent two telegrams to Gen. Samuel Cooper, describing the landing of troops on the Rappahannock. The following day, he reported seeing "five gunboats pass[ing] down the Rappahannock by Urbana...." Most of these reports were met with little interest in Richmond.[5]

A column of Federal soldiers set out early from Catlett's Station on the morning of April 17. They were only 18 miles from Catlett's when they encountered their first Confederate pickets. General Augur desired to capture the picket post to keep his movement to Fredericksburg a surprise, but was "only defeated in capturing it by a little girl from a neighboring house discovering our men creeping through the woods and signaling them to the picket." Next, Augur heard of a Confederate cavalry camp at Brick Church, some five miles away. On nearing the camp, Augur sent the First Pennsylvania Cavalry and a battalion of the Second New York Cavalry forward with orders to attack. The regiments charged, "and the camp and its forage and a few horse [were] captured." The Confederates retired about a mile, and the Federals, after covering some 26 miles, halted for "some hours." Word came in during the night of an "ambuscade" awaiting the Federals on the main road. Two local citizens, loyal to the Union, also came in during the night and informed Augur of a "by-road" in which the Federals could come out between the Confederates and the bridges across the river.[6]

Since word had arrived of the Federal advance, General Field had busied himself preparing a reception. Two companies of the Fortieth Virginia were sent across to reinforce four other companies and the Ninth Virginia Cavalry. The rest of the Fortieth Virginia Infantry was positioned near the Falmouth Bridge. Pegram's battery went into position commanding the same bridge, with the Fifty-fifth Virginia in Fredericksburg, within supporting distance of Pegram. The Fifth Alabama Battalion was charged with firing the bridges, already prepared, and Captain Lewis, of the C.S. Navy, was responsible for the destruction of the shipping.[7]

After contesting the advance of the Federal cavalry with only four Confederate companies, Lt. Col. William H.F. Lee, of the Ninth Virginia Cavalry, chose Greeve's [Grove] Church, one mile from Falmouth, as the place to make his stand. He was reinforced by a battalion from the Fortieth Virginia and a squadron of cavalry under Captain B.B. Davis. The infantry was posted across the road and erected a barricade, with cavalry on the right, left, and in the rear. At 2:00 a.m., on April 18, Good Friday, portions of the First Pennsylvania Cavalry and Second New York Cavalry set out toward the presumed rear of the Confederate line. That line was actually constructed south of the intersection of the main road and the byroad that the Federals traversed. Col. George D. Bayard, of the First Pennsylvania Cavalry, chronicled the cavalry's actions:

> To Lieut. Col. Owen Jones, First Pennsylvania Cavalry, with four companies — F, E, K, and M — of the same regiment, I assigned the duty of seizing the bridge, rushing across it, cutting down the heavy gates which were reported on the opposite side, and throwing out pickets in advance, purposing to cross myself with the Second Battalion of the [Second New York Cavalry] leaving to Lieutenant-Colonel [Judson] Kilpatrick, with the remaining battalion of his regiment [Second New York] the duty of holding Falmouth. As soon as I learned that we had come upon the pickets of the enemy I ordered Colonel Jones forward at full gallop. He rapidly went up the hill in front, and when he reached the top was met with a heavy fire of infantry from all sides. The night was dark and the hill on both sides of the road were covered with brush, yet the colonel pushed on under this fire until he found barricades across the road.

The cavalry and infantry under Lee "waited in silence until they came within 20 yards of the barricade, when the infantry poured a deadly fire into and repulsed them." Companies E and K of the First Pennsylvania, "fled back to camp without having either horse or man injured.... [T]he greater portion of Companies F and M were rallied in rear by Colonel Jones."[8]

Colonel Bayard was "determined if possible to have the hill" and personally led forward a battalion of the Second New York. "We charged," Bayard wrote,

> up the hill within 25 yards of the barricades, when they poured upon my column a galling fire, when the companies retreated. I finally rallied them, but as I knew nothing of the enemy's force, except that both infantry and cavalry were in my front, stationed behind impediments placed in the road, and as from the heaviness of the fire it appeared to be quite a heavy force, I decided to withdraw my command. Lieutenant-Colonel Kilpatrick, with his battalion, I gave the post of rear guard, with orders to cover my retreat, and to his coolness and good judgement I am much indebted...."

Colonel Lee examined the ground when morning broke and found "4 dead bodies and several wounded ... 7 or 8 dead horses in one place."[9]

Even with a minor victory over the Federal cavalry, General Field chose to withdraw his men. Field had hoped that the "numbers" of the Federal foe "might not be too great for me to resist him successfully on the other side." But with a force of "not more than 2,200" effectives, there was little Field could do but pull back. He "ordered the bridges to be burned, the shipping cotton, &c., burned, and every preparation made to retire from the town." At sunrise, General Augur advanced with his whole command, "prepared to fight," but except for a few pickets he saw very little of the Confederates. By 7:30 a.m., the Federals had arrived at Fredericksburg.[10]

As the Federal soldiers approached the town, they were greeted by a woman waving, of all things, a skull and crossbones flag. One local citizen, Helen Bernard, wrote that "The enemy are in possession of Falmouth ... & what is to follow who can say? We are not frightened but stunned and bewildered waiting for the end....

It is heartsickening to think of having our beautiful valley that we so loved and admired all overrun & destroyed by our bitter enemies...." Mayor Montgomery Slaughter and a delegation of citizens, many conspicuous men, surrendered the town on April 19, and gained a promise from Union officers that personal property would be respected.[11]

General Lee, on April 19, wrote to Field, expressing his regret at the evacuation of Fredericksburg. He next asked Field for a report on the number of the enemy, their approach, and the time they were first discovered. Field replied to Lee's questions the following day. He also reported, in a separate dispatch, a reconnaissance by William H.F. Lee. He described seeing no less than 5,000 troops, and inquired of local citizens, who "estimate [the Federals] variously from 5,000 to 13,000." Furthermore, when asked for terms with the citizens of the town, General Augur declined, deferring until the arrival of General McDowell, "whom he expected to arrive to-day (19th) at Aquia Creek with a large force." Lee also reported tugs in the river trying to pass the obstructions placed by the Confederates. Next, Field sent a small reprimand to his superiors. He wrote: "I beg leave to add that I believe there is a much larger force of the enemy in my front than the commanding general had any conception of, and that he meditates an advance upon Richmond from this point in force." In a dispatch to Ewell on April 21, General Lee expressed his concern and bewilderment. He first reported the loss of Fredericksburg, the occupation of Falmouth by Augur's command, and the supposed landing of McDowell. Lee wrote that he did "not know where the forces said to be approaching Fredericksburg are drawn from, unless from those attributed to Banks's column." He also proposed to Ewell, if "practicable ... strike a speedy blow at General Banks and drive him back" in an effort to alleviate some of the pressure on Fredericksburg.[12]

Orders went out on April 21 to Field. He was instructed to "preserve a firm front to the enemy," observe the Federals' strength and movement, and to convey any information to Richmond. Another dispatch was sent, this one to General Jackson in the valley. Lee advised Jackson of the loss of Fredericksburg and the arrival of McDowell. Next, Lee confirmed his reevaluation of the situation. "I have no doubt an attempt will be made to occupy Fredericksburg and use it as a base of operations against Richmond," he wrote. Lee than confessed that the "present force there is very small, and cannot be re-enforced except by weakening other corps." Lee wanted Jackson to use Ewell to attack Banks, or to send Ewell to act as a buffer between Fredericksburg and Richmond.[13]

McDowell was anxious to establish a permanent base at Fredericksburg. He reported to Stanton that the Confederates, some 12 miles south of town, were in small numbers, and that there were many stores, including 1,000 barrels of flour, in the town which he wished to save. The president denied the request and ordered McDowell to "get your bridges and transportation all ready and wait further orders." McDowell and the majority of his command were stuck on the northern bank of the river.[14]

No greater opportunity for the capture of Richmond would present itself than the third week of April 1862. If Fremont and Banks could keep Jackson and Ewell's force distracted, and with McClellan holding the attention of Johnston to the east, McDowell should have been able to cross the river, sweep aside the insignificant brigade of Field, and march into Richmond, only 30 miles away.

In Richmond, Lee was still pressing Jackson for activity against Banks, or for Ewell and Field to unite against McDowell at Fredericksburg. General Lee's top priority was to prevent any reinforcements from reaching McClellan. The Confederate line just south of Fredericksburg was extremely weak, so Lee began to gather what reinforcements he could and sent them to General Field. Until that time, Field was ordered "to preserve a firm front to the enemy, to keep yourself accurately advised of his strength and movements, and to communicate anything of importance that may occur at once to this office." Lee sent two regiments and a light battery "probably over 1,000 men" from Richmond. On April 25, Lee ordered Joseph R. Anderson and his brigade to Fredericksburg. Anderson, the proprietor of the Tredegar Iron Works in Richmond, had a mixed brigade, composed of the Thirty-fourth and Thirty-eighth North Carolina Troops, the Forty-fifth and Forty-ninth Georgia, the Fourth Louisiana Battalion, McIntosh's Pee Dee Battery, and Crenshaw's Virginia Battery. Anderson's orders were to assume command, try to block the Rappahannock River, and to limit the baggage of his command in an effort to be more mobile. Likewise, Lee also ordered Maxcy Gregg's South Carolina brigade, comprised of the First, Twelfth, Thirteenth, and Fourteenth South Carolina Regiments, and Davidson's Letcher Battery to report to Anderson. Anderson named his new division the Army of the Rappahannock which, by April 28, contained at least 12,000 men.[15]

Word came quickly to McDowell of the Confederate reinforcements. The general informed Stanton at 11:30 p.m. on April 30 of the arrival of Anderson and his artillery. Anderson continued to shift his men around and reconnoiter the Federals. McDowell was also receiving reinforcements and thought that by May 2 he should have "nearly 20,000 effective men on the Rappahannock, with a broad bridge of boats, a pontoon bridge, and a steam ferry-boat to cross the river." On May 4, McDowell received word of the evacuation of Yorktown and the withdrawal of the Confederates toward Richmond. He urged Stanton to let him cross his men over the river and "operate on the enemy's extreme left...." McDowell constructed a pontoon bridge on May 2 and then sent a regiment of cavalry out to survey the roads that led south out of Fredericksburg on May 5.[16]

Confederate brigades continued to be called out of other Southern states to reinforce the armies in Virginia. Lee wrote, in a letter to Gen. Theophilus Holmes, commanding in North Carolina, that "such is the pressure in Virginia that it is imperatively necessary to concentrate our forces to enable us successfully to meet the heavy columns of the enemy." With no sign of activity on the part of General Burnside in North Carolina, Lawrence O'Bryan Branch was ordered on May 5 to move his brigade by rail and report to General Ewell at Gordonsville. Branch could then reinforce Anderson at Fredericksburg; Ewell, who was near Gordonsville; or Jackson, who was moving to attack the lead elements of Fremont's men. Branch's brigade was composed of the Seventh, Eighteenth, Twenty-eighth, Thirty-third, and Thirty-seventh North Carolina Troops, and Latham's battery. Lee hoped that Ewell, with Branch's support, could attack Banks's line of communications.[17]

Affairs along the Rappahannock quickly escalated. Stanton believed that since the evacuation of Yorktown, "a considerable force has been sent toward the Rappahannock and the Shenandoah to move on Washington." General Ewell reported to Robert E. Lee at the same time that "there have been two or three skirmishes, one pretty sharp, yesterday...." That same day McDowell wrote to Stanton that he also believed that major Confederate reinforcements were on their way from Richmond to face him and to join Jackson in the Shenandoah Valley. McDowell in turn also sent for reinforcements, although he believed that "it is highly probable that they may attack me before I shall have force enough to attack them." On May 10, the day the Confederates evacuated

Brig. Gen. Lawrence O'Bryan Branch (author's collection).

Norfolk, McDowell sent three more regiments across the river into Fredericksburg, and reported that "Guerrilla parties have shown themselves on this side of the river ... in small parties." Peter H. Watson, the assistant secretary of war, writing in regard to McDowell's dispatch about "guerrillas," rebutted "like pirates and buccaneers they are common enemies of mankind, and should be hunted and shot without challenge wherever found." Again Watson telegraphed McDowell on May 11, wanting to know why McDowell did not conduct a "spirited demonstration" on the Confederates across the river and "destroy the Mattapony and Pamunkey Bridges?" Or, the assistant secretary recommended, "could not Gordonsville and Charlottesville be easily reached by a sudden dash ... and the railroad bridges either held or broken so that they could not be used by the enemy either retreating or advancing." McDowell politely replied that he was under orders not to advance, and even if he did, he could not go far due to his lack of supplies for his men. South of Fredericksburg, Anderson was also clamoring for reinforcements and for additional supplies, including bread and ambulances.[18]

On May 12, General Branch was ordered to "take command of all troops assigned to" Ewell's "division which may be at Gordonsville." The 41-year-old

Lawrence O'Bryan Branch had almost no military training. As a child, the North Carolinian had been taken under the care of his uncle, Governor John Branch, after the death of his parents. When Governor Branch was appointed secretary of navy by President Andrew Jackson, Lawrence went to Washington, D.C., where Salmon P. Chase became his tutor. The young Branch matriculated at the Bingham School, the University of North Carolina, and in 1838 graduated with distinction from the College of New Jersey, now Princeton University. After reading law in Tennessee, Branch removed to Florida where he gained admittance to the bar. He unsuccessfully tried to enter the political sphere, and later served as an aide to General Robert Reid during one of the Seminole Indian Wars. Branch married North Carolina native Nancy Haywood Blount in 1844, and in 1848, moved back to North Carolina where he practiced law. In 1854, he was elected to the United States House of Representatives, where he served until 1861.[19]

When the war came, he enlisted as a private in the Raleigh Rifles, but was quickly appointed as the state quartermaster general, with the rank of major general. Branch served in this capacity until September 20, 1861, when he resigned and accepted the command of the Thirty-third North Carolina Troops as their colonel. On November 16, 1861, Branch was promoted to brigadier general in the provisional Confederate Army and assigned to one of the departments on the coast of North Carolina. Branch lost his first battle at New Bern in March 1862, fighting against odds of three to one. On March 17, 1862, a second North Carolina brigade was created, and Branch was selected as its commander.

Gordonsville, Virginia, was a strategic location between Fredericksburg and the Shenandoah Valley. At Gordonsville the Virginia Central Railroad and the Orange and Alexandria Railroad converged. A Confederate force here could cooperate with either the Confederate forces in Fredericksburg or with Jackson and Ewell in the valley. A force here could also prevent the Federals from disrupting communications between Jackson and Richmond. Branch's brigade should have numbered 5,000 men, but sickness, the casualties endured at New Bern, and other absentees brought the strength of the brigade down to just 2,735 men and 199 officers.[20]

General Ewell sent a missive to General Lee on May 14, explaining orders from Jackson for his command to "follow Banks down the valley." Ewell also ordered "part of the forces at Gordonsville to cross the ridge for Luray." Those orders to Branch read: "If you can procure transportation I wish, in obedience to the instructions from General Jackson, that the troops at Gordonsville should move into the valley via Madison Court House and Fisher's or Blue Ridge Turnpike Gap to Luray. I have such contradictory information about the supplies in the section ... that I don't think you ought to start with less than five days' rations...." Ewell instructed Branch to leave at least two regiments "to protect our present line." He then pressed upon Branch to limit his equipage, adding that "the road to glory cannot be followed with much baggage."[21]

"This is a very wet day.... We have no tents in camp except for the officers," wrote one private in Branch's command. It was still raining on May 16 when the brigade left "Camp Rapidan" that night. After covering 12 muddy miles, the brigade received orders from Ewell to halt. One possible reason was a letter sent from Anderson to Ewell, in which Anderson proposed to unite their forces and attack McDowell before Banks could reinforce the Federals at Fredericksburg. Unbeknownst to the Confederates, Lincoln, "in consultation with Stanton and the War Department bureau chiefs," had finally decided to order McDowell to join McClellan. Lincoln telegraphed McDowell on May 15, asking how many troops he had. "Thirty-thousand one hundred and twelve officers and men for duty. At Belle Plain and Aquia Creek as guards, and unloading stores, repairing railroad and wharf &c., one thousand three hundred and sixty one, officers and men," was McDowell's response.[22]

Both Stanton and Lincoln sent orders to McDowell at Fredericksburg on May 17. Stanton ordered McDowell, once he was joined by Shields's division, to "move upon Richmond by the general route of the Richmond and Fredericksburg railroad, cooperating with the forces under General McClellan now threatening Richmond from the line of the Pamunkey and York Rivers." Stanton then ordered McDowell to "hold yourself always in such a position as to cover the capital of the nation against a sudden dash of any large body of rebel forces." Lincoln's orders to McDowell at Fredericksburg were confusing. McDowell "retained separate command of the forces" he currently had, but "while co-operating with Gen. McClellan" he was to "obey his orders, except that you are to judge, and are not to allow your force to be disposed otherwise than so as to give the greatest protection to this capital which may be possible from that distance." McClellan was quick to point out that Lincoln's orders violated the Articles of War, as McClellan was senior to McDowell.[23]

By noon on May 17, General Branch and his brigade were on the move again toward the Blue Ridge Mountains. They had covered 13 miles, again in the rain, before a short rest, then moved another three miles west when a message arrived to return to Gordonsville. The Tar Heels spent the night "at the foot of the Blue Ridge in a Large Clover field and had plenty of wheat straw to lay on," according to a member of the Thirty-seventh North Carolina. General Branch wrote to his wife: "This foolish ordering and counter-ordering results from rivalry between Gens. Jackson and Ewell. It is very unfortunate...." Orders finally arrived on May 19 from General Johnston. Branch would immediately proceed to Hanover Court House. Branch took the time to write to Ewell, disclosing to the general his orders from Johnston. The brigade retraced its steps to Gordonsville, where Branch had sent his quartermaster to procure transportation as soon as he had received his orders from Johnston. In Gordonsville, the Twelfth North Carolina joined Branch's brigade as it traveled east. Flatbed rail cars were waiting for the brigade at Gordonsville on the morning of May 21, and the regiments loaded themselves and what little equipment they had for their trip to Hanover. By dark, they had made camp in the mud around the historic courthouse.[24]

McDowell was able to report on the morning of May 19 that he had completed his bridge over the Rappahannock and would be prepared to move south as soon as Shields's division arrived. The different regiments were ordered to turn in their large camp tents and obtain shelter tents, one-half of a tent for each man, in their stead. By the 20th, McDowell had his railroad in operation between Aquia and Fredericksburg and even farther. Shields's division had finally started to move, but was not expected "before to-morrow night — possibly not before the day after." McDowell telegraphed McClellan on May 22, informing him that he expected to move toward McClellan's army on May 24. But, on May 23, reports started filtering in to the War Department in Washington. The guards at Front Royal had been forced back to Middletown and the telegraph had been cut to Strasburg and Front Royal. McDowell was ordered by Assistant Secretary Watson, in lieu of an absent Stanton, to make "no movement ... until [the] arrival of the Secretary of War. He gives the order."[25]

General Johnston sent further orders to Branch on May 22. Branch was to serve as a connection between Johnston's army east of Richmond and General Anderson's army, near Fredericksburg, and to protect the railroads. Furthermore, if Branch was "too strongly pressed, or you hear of a battle, join us." The following day, more directives came from Johnston. He wrote: "Since my last dispatch addressed to you.... [T]he enemy's positions have been changed. They are now nearer to the Chickahominy. Do not, therefore, consider Hanover Court-House your station, but be governed by circumstances in placing your troops.... In the event of a general engagement within your reach, in the absence of other orders, attack the enemy's flank, if you can."[26]

Slash Church, where General Branch had his headquarters (author's collection).

In the Shenandoah Valley on May 23, the Federals at Front Royal had been routed, and on May 24, Jackson attacked the Federals under General Shields. This attack stopped McDowell's movement toward Richmond before it got started. By that evening, orders came for McDowell to send 20,000 men toward the valley and Jackson's force. Both McDowell and McClellan, who had begun to prepare for the arrival of the I Corps, protested the movement.

On May 24, portions of the Federal army occupied Seven Pines and Mechanicsville, only five miles from Richmond and southeast of General Branch's position. General Johnston, in Richmond conferring with Lee and Davis that day, worried that Anderson and Branch could be cut off by a swift movement by the Federals; he ordered them to withdraw closer to Richmond. By May 25, Anderson had removed as far south as Hanover Junction. Branch issued commands the same day to regimental commanders, ordering them to remove all excess baggage and the sick to Richmond. The next day, Branch moved his command about five miles to the southwest, and set up his headquarters at Slash Church. General Branch positioned his regiments to help conceal the withdrawal of Anderson at Fredericksburg from the prying eyes and ears of Federal cavalry troopers.

Added to Branch's command was a second regiment, the Forty-fifth Georgia. Also, at least two detachments of Confederate cavalry reported to Branch. The first was commanded by Capt. Beverly B. Douglas, of Company H, Ninth Virginia Cavalry. In Douglas's dispatch, he told Branch of the traffic on the Pamunkey River; the size of McClellan's army, estimated at 120,000 men; and, most importantly, that Federal officers had visited "Mrs. Braxton's (a little below the Old Church in Hanover) on Monday or Tuesday, selecting a place of encampment for a large force ... 8,000 or 10,000 men." Portions of the Fourth Virginia Cavalry were also in the area. They had made their camp at Hanover Court House on May 21, and were picketing the Pamunkey River.[27]

Anderson heeded Johnston's orders, and on May 25, wrote to Branch from Hanover Junction: "I arrived here at 7 o'clock. Head of my column is encamped within 2½ miles, and the extreme rear back, I suppose, 4½ miles farther." Anderson concluded with a postscript: "I marched all night and day, and am pretty tired, and of course my men are more so, and for that reason I want to move them by rail. If you move your camp from the Court-House please inform me before I start my troops." McDowell seemed perplexed at the disappearance of the Confederates in his front. "The enemy left this front by stealth in the night.... They left so hurriedly and so fearful of pursuit as to leave a corpse unburied," he wrote to Lincoln.[28]

General Branch received another communiqué from his commander on May 26, stating that Anderson was transporting his men "down the Richmond, Fredericksburg and Potomac Railroad as far as Kilbey's Mill; will there leave the railroad and proceed to Halfsink." Anderson was ordered to "open communication with you as soon as possible." The letter unfortunately gave no timetable for the movements, and Branch was effectively cut off from reinforcements. With Federal cavalry probing his position from the south, he must have been somewhat nervous as he bedded down at his headquarters in Slash Church.[29]

4

"Charge — Charge Them, Brave Boys": The Battle of Kinney Farm and Hanover Court House

Those cavalry troopers probing Branch's line belonged to the newly created V Corps under the command of Brig. Gen. Fitz John Porter. Born in Portsmouth, New Hampshire, in 1822, he was the son of Capt. John Porter of the United States Navy. Two other family members also served with distinction in the navy. David Porter, Fitz John's brother, rose to the rank of commodore, and his nephew was Admiral David Dixon Porter. Fitz John entered West Point in 1841, and graduated in 1845, ranking eighth in a class of 123. Some of his classmates included Edmund Kirby Smith, Thomas J. Wood, Barnard E. Bee, and Gordon Grander.

After graduation, Porter was assigned to the Fourth United States Artillery and sent to Mexico. During the war with Mexico, Porter was wounded once, and brevetted to the rank of captain, then major, for gallant and meritorious conduct. For the next 15 years, Porter served throughout the United States: as a cavalry instructor at West Point, at Fort Bradley, and with Albert Sidney Johnston during the Utah expedition. In November 1860, Porter was sent to Charleston, South Carolina, to inspect coastal defenses, and in February 1861 to Texas where he saved a large portion of the regular army from surrender after Texas seceded. In April 1861, Porter was selected to superintend the protection of the railroad between Baltimore and Harrisburg. Finally, on May 14, Porter was commissioned colonel of the Fifteenth United States Infantry, and a few days later, at the request of McClellan, he was promoted to brigadier general of volunteers.

In early August 1861, Brig. Gen. William T. Sherman was transferred to the western army, and Porter took command of Sherman's brigade. The brigade was composed of the Second Maine; the Thirteenth and Forty-first New York; the Ninth and Fourteenth Massachusetts; and the Fourth Michigan Infantry regiments, along with Battery E, Third United States Artillery; and Troop I, Second United States Cavalry. It would not be long before Porter was given command of a division, with three brigades under the commands of Brig. Gen. John H. Martindale, Brig. Gen.

George W. Morell, and Brig. Gen. Daniel Butterfield. On March 13, 1862, Porter's division was assigned to the III Corps, under the command of Brig. Gen. Samuel P. Heintzelman.

On March 17, the largest amphibious operation the modern world had ever seen got underway. Porter's division boarded the transports at Alexandria on March 22, and landed at Fortress Monroe the next day. On April 4, McClellan started his grand campaign, and Porter's division led the advance upon Yorktown, going through the old battlefield at Big Bethel Church. When the Union advance stalled in front of the Confederate entrenchments at Yorktown, McClellan called for his heavy cannons, and named Porter "director of the siege." After a month of operations, in which Porter's command "continually in the trenches, and most faithfully and cheerfully, under all circumstances, frequently most trying, performed their laborious and dangerous duties," the Federal army was on the eve of opening their batteries, and the Confederates slipped out and retreated back toward Williamsburg. On May 8, Porter's command once again boarded transports and embarked at Yorktown for West Point, an attempt to cut off the Confederate army on its retreat. But the Federal army moved slowly, and it was May 13 before Porter reached Cumberland.[1]

In an effort to make his army easier to control, as well as to ensure the promotions of Porter and Franklin, whom he wanted as corps commanders from the beginning, McClellan began to petition the War Department to reorganize his existing command structure. On May 9, he received a response from the secretary of war that allowed him to "temporarily suspend [the] organization in the army now under [his] immediate command, and adopt any you see fit until further orders." McClellan opted to create two new corps on May 18: the V Corps, which he placed under the command of Porter, and the VI Corps, under the command of Brig. Gen. William B. Franklin. Franklin's division of the I Corps had joined McClellan in late April. The command of Porter's old division went to Brig. Gen. George Morell.

George Webb Morell, born in 1815 in Cooperstown, New York, graduated from the United States Military Academy in 1835, and was assigned to the engineering department. He resigned from the army in 1837 and was both a civil engineer, working with the railroads, and a lawyer. In May of 1861, Morell became a quartermaster in the New York State Militia, with the rank of colonel. On August 9, 1861, he was promoted to brigadier general and commanded a brigade in Porter's division. When the V Corps was created, Morell advanced to division command. His division consisted of three infantry brigades, four batteries of artillery, and a regiment of sharpshooters. The first brigade was commanded by Brig. Gen. John H. Martindale and was composed of the Second Maine, the Eighteenth and Twenty-second Massachusetts, and the Thirteenth and Twenty-fifth New York Infantries. Col. James McQuade commanded the second brigade, containing the Fourteenth New York, Ninth Massachusetts, Fourth Michigan, and Sixty-second Pennsylvania. The final infantry brigade was commanded by Brig. Gen. Daniel Butterfield and consisted of the Sixteenth Michigan; Twelfth, Seventeenth, and Forty-fourth

New York; and Eighty-third Pennsylvania. Batteries C and E, Massachusetts Light Artillery; Battery C, First Rhode Island Artillery; and Battery D, Fifth United States Artillery, were under Morell's command and were led by Capt. Charles Griffin. Another graduate of West Point, Griffin was from Ohio and had commanded a battery of regulars at Bull Run. Also attached to the division were the First United States Sharpshooters under Col. Hiram Berdan. General Porter considered Morell a trusted confidant, and thought him possessed of a "bright, clear mind, familiar with his duties and always true to them, though not initially very active or passing."[2]

Porter's second division was under the command of Brig. Gen. George Sykes. Born in Delaware in 1822, Sykes graduated from West Point in 1842. He was an old army officer, spending nearly 20 years in the infantry. He was commissioned a brigadier general on September 28, 1861, and commanded the infantry reserves of the Army of the Potomac prior to being assigned command of a division of regulars in Porter's new corps. Sykes' new command was composed almost entirely of regulars. The First Brigade, under Lt. Col. Robert C. Buchanan, included the Third and Fourth United States Infantry; the First Battalion, Twelfth United States Infantry; and the First Battalion, Fourteenth United States Infantry. The Second Brigade was led by Lt. Col. William Chapman and was composed of the Second and Sixth United States Infantry; the First Battalion, Eleventh United States Infantry; and the First Battalion, Seventeenth United States Infantry. Leading the Third Brigade was Col. Gouverneur K. Warren. There were only two regiments in this brigade: the Fifth New York Infantry, and the First Connecticut Heavy Artillery, serving as infantry. The artillery was under the command of Capt. Stephen H. Weed, and contained Batteries L and M, Third United States Artillery; and Battery I, Fifth United States Artillery. The artillery reserve was also attached to Porter's V Corps. The reserve was commanded by Col. Henry J. Hunt and contained 22 batteries in six brigades.[3]

Rounding out Porter's command were several detachments of cavalry, including the Fifth and Sixth United States Cavalry and the Sixth Pennsylvania Cavalry. All three regiments were under the command of Brig. Gen. William H. Emory, a Marylander. Emory was also a West Point graduate, and had risen to the rank of lieutenant colonel of the Third United States Cavalry prior to the war. He was promoted on March 17, 1862, and commanded one of the brigades in the cavalry reserve for the Army of the Potomac. The Sixth Pennsylvania Cavalry, also known as Rush's Lancers, was recruited in mid–1861 by Richard H. Rush, of Philadelphia. Rush was also a graduate of the military academy and a member of the famed class of 1846. The Sixth Pennsylvania was originally armed with lances, "nine-foot-long wooden" poles each "tipped with an eleven-inch-long steel blade." These weapons were based upon a Austrian design. They weighed about eight pounds and each had a scarlet pennant on the top.[4]

Rush moved his Lancers from Yorktown on May 9, and made camp at Old Church, about 15 miles southeast of Hanover Court House. On May 20, Brig. Gen. George Stoneman personally led a reconnaissance composed of the Sixth United States Cavalry and the Eighth Illinois Cavalry from Old Church, which, along with commissary stores, horses, and mules had fallen into Federal hands the day before, toward New Bridge. Skirmishing with Confederate troopers resulted in a few Federal casualties. May 21 found Professor Thaddeus S.C. Lowe aloft in his balloon, 500 feet above the Chickahominy, observing Confederates across the landscape. On May 22, Rush's cavalry was detached from their brigade by order of General McClellan, and commanded to "make a reconnaissance around and about the Pamunkey River...." McClellan was trying to ascertain just how many Confederates were between the Army of the Potomac and McDowell's corps. After Branch's command was found in and around the courthouse, Porter ordered Colonel Rush to destroy all of the ferries and bridges along the Pamunkey. The Lancers continued to probe the enemy, and on the 23rd fought a brief skirmish with Confederate cavalry. Again the Federal cavalry went out on May 24. This time, Colonel Rush led a party of 125 men toward Hanover Court House, moving through both "thick wood" and "cultivated meadow." One member of the regiment preserved the events of the day in a letter home: "Our Squaddron drove in a line of the Enemies Pickets, until we came within site of their mane Picket Guard when we Retreated slowly to try and draw them out. But they would not come. They were encamped in a large piece of woods." Once verifying the position of the Confederates, Colonel Rush retired and forwarded his report to General Porter. Rush almost correctly estimated that the Confederates had "not less than 3,000 infantry, six piece of cannon, and 300 cavalry, four regiments of infantry having arrived day before yesterday." As Colonel Rush returned to the vicinity of Old Church, Colonel Warren arrived to take command of the forces around Old Church. Born in New York in 1830, Warren was an 1850 graduate of West Point, and had served in the topographical engineers for the past 10 years. He was commissioned lieutenant colonel of the Fifth New York on May 14, 1861, and colonel on September 11. His force was made up of the two regiments in his brigade, the Fifth New York and the First Connecticut, along with the Thirteenth New York, Rush's Lancers, and Battery C, First Rhode Island Light Artillery. Porter sent Warren orders on the 23rd directing the colonel to advance to Hanover Court House and destroy both the Confederate cavalry and the "small Rail Road bridge over a stream near Hanover" and any other bridges in the area. Additionally, if a train were to arrive while Warren's men were on their expedition, they had orders to seize the conductor, engineer, and "operatives," and to use their discretion in regarding whom to arrest and whom to release. All mails, correspondence, and papers were also to be confiscated. While at Old Church, a member of the Thirteenth New York recalled camping "in a splendid clover field.... In front of the 'Old Church Hotel' stood a pole from which the *Stars and Bars* floated first. This was cut down, and the beautiful Stars and Stripe (belonging to Co. A,) raised upon it for the first time.... This pole was raised in honor of the rebel victory at Bull Run in July last."[5]

A second reconnaissance was made that day under the command of Maj. Alexander S. Webb, an artillery officer on the staff of Gen. William F. Barry. Webb took a detachment of the Eighth Illinois Cavalry and a piece of Tidball's horse artillery, about 140 men. The party proceeded from Mechanicsville north on the

Ashland road. Webb skirmished with the Confederates and dismantled a portion of the Virginia Central Railroad. The Federals examined the grounds, made maps of the area, and forwarded the maps to headquarters.[6]

For the next two days, the Federals and Confederates continued to test each other. Orders came from Porter to Warren on the 25th. Warren was to

> push mounted parties well to the front and flanks and get all the information you [can]. Tell your parties not to be disturbed by reports of large forces, though to act upon them as a caution. The enemy have an object in keeping up an alarm, or causing a stampede with you, and to do this will magnify their force. The force there is to defend the road not to attack, and you need not to fear any approach in force, but guard against it and post your command to give the enemy a warm welcome.

Porter was right about the Confederates' guarding the road, but on the same day that his orders arrived, the Confederates drove in the Federal pickets, causing Warren to deploy his troops into a line of battle. The next day, both the First United States Cavalry, with Barker's squadron of the McClellan Dragoons, and Rush's Lancers went out on separate reconnaissances. The First Cavalry "drove in the enemy's pickets to within about 3 miles of Hanover Court House," and took one of the wounded pickets as a prisoner. Lt. Col. William N. Grier of the First Cavalry provided more details of the Confederate activities, stating in his report that "General Branch is said to be in command" and that Grier was "inclined to think that 5,000 to 6,000 is ... the maximum number of troops stationed" around the courthouse. Seven companies of the Lancers also probed the Confederates. Company C charged a group of Confederate pickets with their lances, one of the rare occasions during the war when the weapons were actually used. Colonel Rush himself was almost a casualty. As he assisted in the chase of the Confederates, a shot sounded from the woods along the road, and a ball grazed his cheek.[7]

Mrs. Willoughby Newton, who was visiting her daughter-in-law and family at Summer Hill and Westwood, chronicled the arrival of the Federals in her diary. She reported on the 23rd "a squad of their cavalry has been in the Hanover Town lane all day; five or six lancers, with their red streamers, rode slowly by our gate this evening." The following day, Mrs. Newton came face to face with the South's foe. She wrote:

> We were aroused this morning at an early hour, by the servants rushing in, exclaiming: "The house is surrounded by Yankees, and they are coming into the house." I rushed to the window, and there they were. An officer in the front porch, and a squad of cut-throat-looking fellows on the steps; while a number, with their red streamers and lances, were dashing hither and thither; some at the stable, some at the kitchen, others around the servants' quarters and at the barn, while the lane was filled with them.... We dressed as rapidly as possibly. C. and M. had been up all night with L., and were soon ready to go down. They quickly returned, to say that the officer was Colonel Rush, of Philadelphia, and demanded that my little son Edward should be sent down immediately.... The child was aroused from his sleep, and hastily dressed himself, but not quickly enough for our impatient Colonel, who walked to the staircase and began to ascend, when C. called to him, "Colonel R., do you mean to go to a lady's chamber before she is dressed? The boy is in his

mother's room." Somewhat abashed, he stepped back. I soon descended.... There on the mat before me stood a live Yankee colonel, with an aid on either side. I approached; he pointed to W.S., saying, "Is that Edward N.?" "No," said I; "that is my grandson; this is E.N." He said, "I want the boys to go with me."

Rush took the lads and questioned them, and sending them back, called them "little rebels." A day later, Newton again recorded her observations in her diary: "A cry of 'Yankees,' this morning, sent us to the windows; there we saw a regiment of Lancers, one of regulars, one of rifles, and another of zouves, composed of the most dreadful-looking creatures I ever beheld, with red caps and trowsers; also two guns." These soldiers, according to Newton, were "on their way to the Wyoming bridge, which they destroyed."[8]

Part of the force that Mrs. Newton saw undoubtably belonged to an expedition composed of the First Connecticut Artillery (serving as infantry while their siege equipment was back with the wagon train), the Fifth New York, and three guns of the First Rhode Island Light Artillery. Their orders were to drive in the pickets and destroy a bridge over the Pamunkey River, which they accomplished, taking one prisoner and returning to camp by 6 p.m. on the night of May 26.[9]

"I never seen so much business done here before," observed one of the local Virginia citizens in Old Church. With large groups of Federal soldiers in the area, locals came to trade with the soldiers. One New Yorker recalled that "Hoecakes, milk and sweet potatoes are brought into camp by the darkeys in any quantity, and as long as specie last we can live. Strawberries and green peas, too, we can get *for cash.*"[10]

Finally, on May 26, McClellan ordered General Porter to move his command at daylight the next day and clear the Confederates from the area, opening the way for McDowell and his corps. One possible reason for McClellan's order could have been intelligence the general received from a local citizen, a Dr. Pollock, that a force of 17,000 Confederate troops was at Hanover Court House.[11]

Rain was abundant the night of May 26, contributing to the already sodden spring and making many of the roads in Hanover County nearly impassable. General Branch moved his headquarters into Slash Church, already 133 years old by 1862. The church had been built by the Anglicans, but had been taken over by the Disciples of Christ. The area in and around the church was known as the Slashes, due to the terrain that was wet, swampy, and suitable only for growing scrub pines and bushes. Before retiring for the evening, Branch posted cavalry pickets from the Ninth Virginia Cavalry along the roads in the area. Around midnight he sent part of the Thirty-seventh North Carolina Troops, Companies D and E, to picket a road east of Hanover Court House near Taliaferro's Mill. Company B of the same regiment was detailed to guard the two wagons that Branch had brought along, an ambulance and an ammunition wagon. A member of the Eighteenth North Carolina recalled that the entire regiment was sent out to picket "a certain part of the railroad" and the men did "their part well with some grumbling and pretty sharp criticism...." The men in Branch's regiments slept out in the open. One officer in the Twenty-eighth North Carolina recalled that he and his men "all suffered much

4. "Charge—Charge Them, Brave Boys" 51

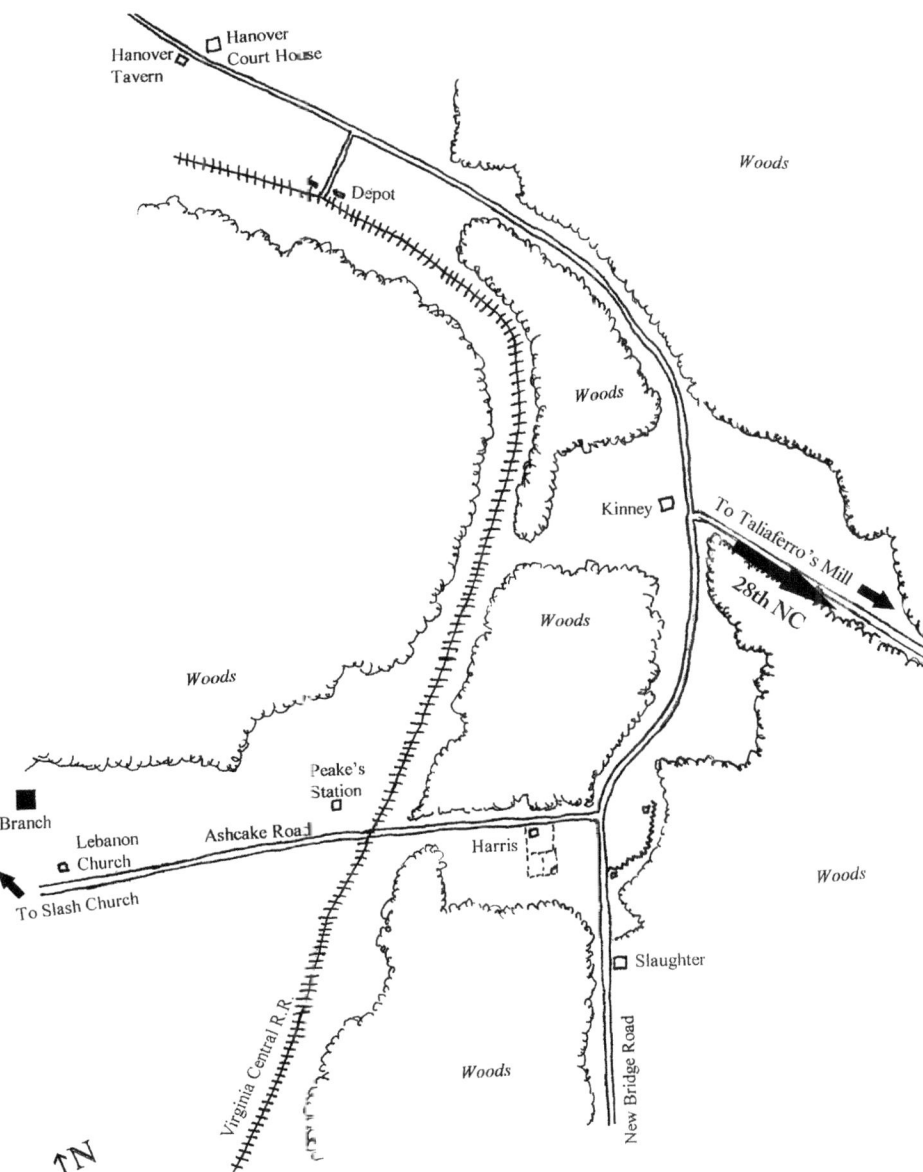

The Twenty-eighth North Carolina moves toward Taliaferro's Mill.

that night as we had no tents neither had we slept in tents but one night in five weeks."[12]

General McClellan was known to play favorites among his officers, and one of these preferred generals, Fitz John Porter, was selected to eliminate the Confederate threat that lay between McDowell and McClellan. Orders came late on the night of May 26 for the men of Porter's V Corps: two days' rations, 60 rounds of ammunition, "40 of the latter to be carried in boxes and 20 in pockets," and light marching order, including a shelter-half for each man. Lt. Amos Judson of the Eighty-third Pennsylvania recalled that "Col. McLane called the commandants of companies together and informed them that an important movement was on foot, and ordered them to have their companies in readiness to march at daylight the next morning." The men were ordered to be up at 3:30 a.m. and on the road by 4:00. Some of the regiments were ordered to leave their knapsacks behind. The Federal soldiers broke camp "in the midst of a heavy rain" and started down "a muddy and tedious road," unable to even boil their coffee. One member of the Forty-fourth New York recalled that he and his comrades were "awakened by the orderly ... the ground floor of our tent was a sheet of mud, and we were half suffocated with the smoke of our morning fire." Their breakfast, according to Oliver W. Norton, Company K, Eighty-third Pennsylvania, consisted of "but crackers and water." General Porter's plan of action was a two-pronged attack on the Confederates, whom he still believed to be in the vicinity of the courthouse. General Morell's division would advance from the south, along the New Bridge Road. Colonel Warren's brigade, located near Old Church, was to advance along a road that ran near the Pamunkey, and "to fall upon [Branch] in flank and rear." Preceding Morell's division were two regiments of cavalry—the Fifth and Sixth United States Cavalry—and a light battery of artillery, all under the command of General Emory. The Sixth Pennsylvania Cavalry covered Warren's brigade. The first battle of the day was against the elements. Even General Porter recalled in his official report that the column traveled through "a pelting storm of rain, through deep mud and water" before contact was made with the Confederates. Another soldier, an artilleryman from Battery C, First Rhode Island Light Artillery, believed that "A Virginia rain of ten hours is about equal to a picket force of twenty-five thousand men in retarding the rapid advance of the grand army." Still another soldier, from the Forty-fourth New York, "found the road one broad mass of plastic mud knee deep.... The long train of artillery rendered this so much worse that, for the first time in any march, I was quite discouraged." There were all too many who were of the same opinion.[13]

The march was difficult on the Federals. General Butterfield mentioned the loss of men in his official report: "The regiments [were] much reduced in numbers by the march...." Likewise, Col. Henry A. Weeks of the Twelfth New York made mention: "that upon entering the action yesterday my command was much reduced in numbers by the severity of the march...." Col. Elisha Marshall of the Thirteenth New York claimed the march was "tedious...." "Officers could not stand it any better than the men, for we had not very heavy loads, and officers and men gave out and lay by the roadside together, unable to go any further without rest," recalled Private Norton in a letter home on May 30. One of the New Yorkers remembered that after two hours "we halted and the mail came up. Many a poor fellow read his home letters that day who before sunset lay gasping in death." A member of the Second Maine recollected halting for a rest at Pole Green Church. While filling his canteen from a creek, Pvt. John O'Connell, of Company I, "met a negro and asked him how far it was to the [railroad]. he answered—[']Youl' *meet de people before you get to the Railroad.*[']"[14]

As the cavalrymen who screened Morell's division advanced, they discovered that the main road was "intersected by other roads every 2 or 3 miles." Each road was picketed by small groups of Confederate cavalry that had to be chased off. The Fourth Virginia Cavalry reported the loss of nine men at Old Church alone. Emory then posted his own detachments to watch these roads. After the cavalry came Colonel Berdan's regiment of Sharpshooters, mostly armed with Colt revolving rifles. Next came Morell's First Brigade, then the Third, and finally the Second. Each brigade had a battery of artillery assigned to it.[15]

Reports arrived at Slash Church that the Federals were advancing toward Taliaferro's Mill, the position of the two companies of the Thirty-seventh North Carolina sent out on picket the previous evening. Some of those reports likely came through the efforts of civilians living in the area. Mrs. Newton, who had witnessed Federal activity in the preceding days, sent one of her sons toward Hanover Court House to retrieve "our letters and papers." If the child met Federal pickets, they would most likely send him back home. But, "if he could reach [Confederate] pickets, he could give the alarm." The child was sent on his way, and the family commenced to worry for his safety. "I got up and went down to the yard," chronicled Mrs. Newton,

> for I could not sit still; but what was my consternation, after a short time had elapsed, to see at the gate, and all along the road, the hated red streamers of our enemy, going towards the Court-House! S. and myself were miserable about W. C. and C. gave us no comfort; they thought it very rash in us to send him — he would be captured and "Fax" (the horse) would certainly be taken. We told them that it was worth the risk to put our people on their guard; but, nevertheless, we were unhappy beyond expression ... what was our relief to see W. Ride in, escorted by fourteen lancers, he and his horse unmolested! The child had gone ahead of the Yankees, reached our picket, told his story, and a vidette had immediately been sent with the information to head-quarters.

With such information in hand, Branch dispatched Col. James H. Lane's Twenty-eighth North Carolina, along with a section of Latham's battery, commanded by Lt. J.R. Potts, "to support the pickets and repel any small body." Branch also sent out the Forty-fifth Georgia, commanded by Col. Thomas Hardeman, "to repair the railroad to Ashcake, where it had been obstructed by the enemy the day before, and watch any approach of the enemy on that road." It is unclear if Branch had information regarding the approach of Federal soldiers in that direction, or if this was simply a precautionary movement. Regardless, the Forty-fifth Georgia was taken away from the fighting for the day. Marion H. Fitzpatrick of Company K wrote to his wife on May 30 that the Georgians were "called out and formed a line of battle several times but did not get a fire."[16]

The Twenty-eighth North Carolina would not be as lucky as the Forty-fifth Georgia. Coming from counties in the central portion of the state, the Twenty-eighth North Carolina Troops was mustered into service on September 15, 1861. James Henry Lane, from Matthews County, Virginia, was the regiment's first colonel. Lane was educated at the Virginia Military Institute, where he studied under Thomas J. Jackson. In 1860, Lane was teaching at the North Carolina Military Academy in Charlotte, and at the governor's call for troops in 1861, he volunteered. He was soon elected major of the First North Carolina Volunteers and participated in the battle of Big Bethel Church in June 1861. When the regiment's colonel, Daniel H. Hill, was promoted to brigadier general, Lane was promoted to lieutenant colonel. After the First North Carolina was mustered out of service, Lane was elected colonel of the Twenty-eighth North Carolina Troops. He was only 28 years old.

Just a few moments after receiving his orders, Colonel Lane mounted his horse, Old Jim, and started off toward the mill. Capt. William Henry Asbury Speer of Company I, Twenty-eighth North Carolina, recalled that "the road was very muddy. Some places almost impossible for the men to travel & one place we had to leave the road." When Colonel Lane's command reached the road to the courthouse, the men turned left. Upon reaching a farm owned by Dr. Thomas Kinney, the regiment halted "till ten men from each company went to Dr. Kinney's well & filled all the canteens full of water." Colonel Lane also took time to confer with cavalry scouts, trying to ascertain the positions of the Federals. The regiment then proceeded east on the road across from the Kinney farm which led to Taliaferro's Mill. After arriving at the mill, the Twenty-eighth halted, loaded their muskets, "and waited there till our scouts reported that the enemy was flanking up." That "enemy" proved to be portions of the two companies of the Thirty-seventh North Carolina sent to picket the area. While Colonel Lane was examining the ground for a suitable defense, word came that Federals were approaching from the rear. Lane turned his regiment around and threw out Company G as skirmishers. One platoon, under Capt. George Johnston, was deployed to the right, while the other platoon, under Lt. Daniel Morrow, was ordered to the front and left.[17]

The Federal column was within five miles of Hanover Court House when the Federal cavalry screen made a dash upon Confederate cavalry pickets, most likely located at the intersection of the New Bridge Road and the Ashcake Road. General Porter ordered a regiment to be sent out as skirmishers. The order passed down through Morell to Brigadier General Martindale, who commanded the First Brigade. John H. Martindale was born in 1815 in Sandy Hill, New York, and graduated from the United States Military Academy in 1835. He served for a brief time in the First United States Dragoons before resigning and becoming a railroad engineer and lawyer. In August 1861, Martindale was commissioned a brigadier general and assigned to command a brigade under Porter, who thought Martindale was "intelligent and active and attentive to his duties when they did not clash with his interests or safety" but "vain, ambitious of advancement and unscrupulous in his means of attaining his ends." Martindale was ordered to "send forward his best regiment to throw out skirmishers." The general replied: "I have no best regiment in my command, they are all alike." Martindale chose the Twenty-fifth New York under Col. Charles A. Johnson and ordered the regiment ahead. They advanced by the right flank, in column, until reaching the intersection of the New Bridge and Ashcake Roads. One soldier, simply identified as "W.E.S" in an article in the *Rochester Union and Advertiser,* recalled that the "roads were in a horrible condition. We had to wade through mud and water knee deep, and were obliged to march as fast as we possi-

4. "Charge—Charge Them, Brave Boys" 55

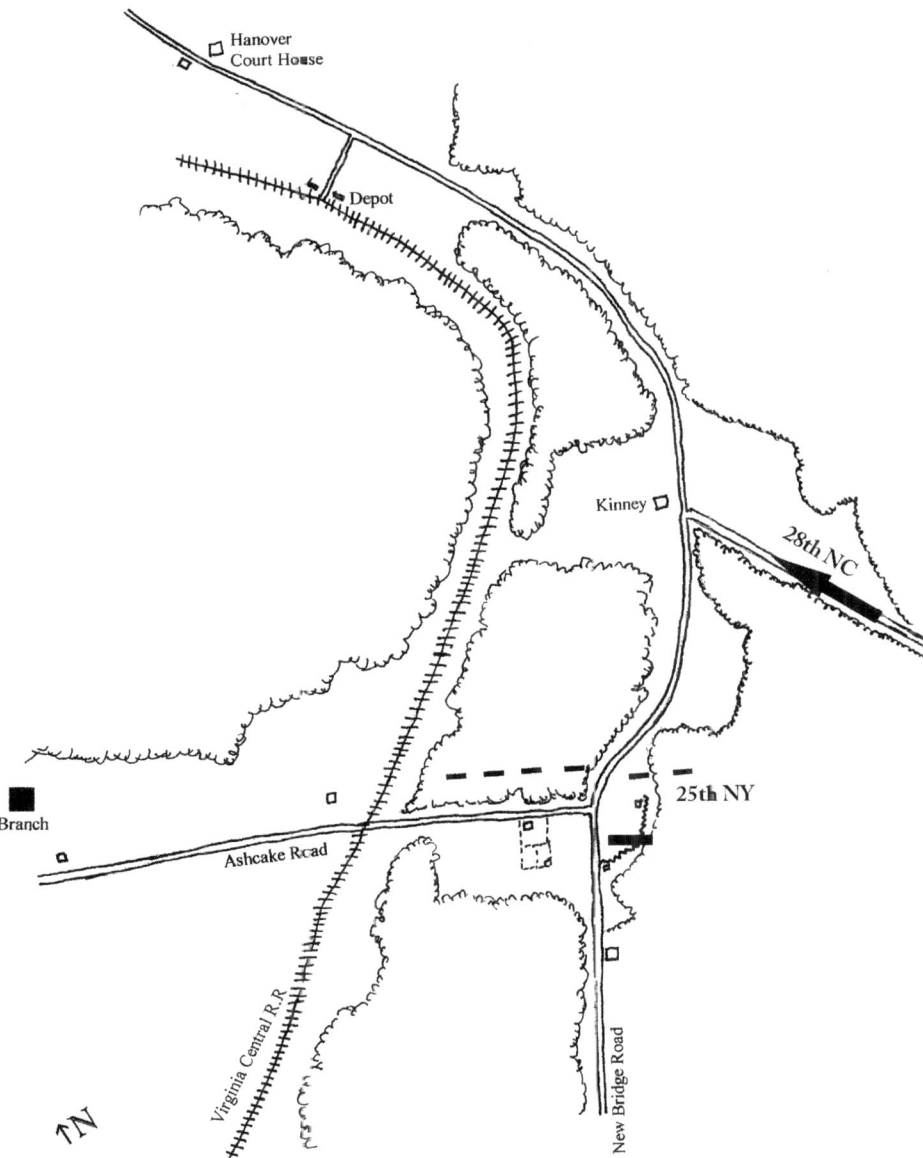

The Twenty-fifth New York deploys; the Twenty-eighth North Carolina returns from Taliaferro's Mill.

bly could." Once they neared the junctions of the New Bridge and Ashcake roads, the regiment, under the personal command of General Porter, was deployed as skirmishers by division. "We were on a narrow turnpike," recalled a member of the regiment. When the orders came, the New Yorkers "dashed down the rails, and our colonel (Johnson), as cool as if on dress-parade, sung out 'Deploy skirmishers!'"

The First Division, Companies B and C, deployed to the right of the road. The Second and Third Divisions, Companies F, K, E, and G, deployed to the left of the road. Companies D, I, A, and H, were ordered off the road into a wheatfield, behind the First Division, as a reserve. The Twenty-fifth New York numbered nearly 400 men.[18]

General Porter was at the junction of the Ashcake and New Bridge Roads when

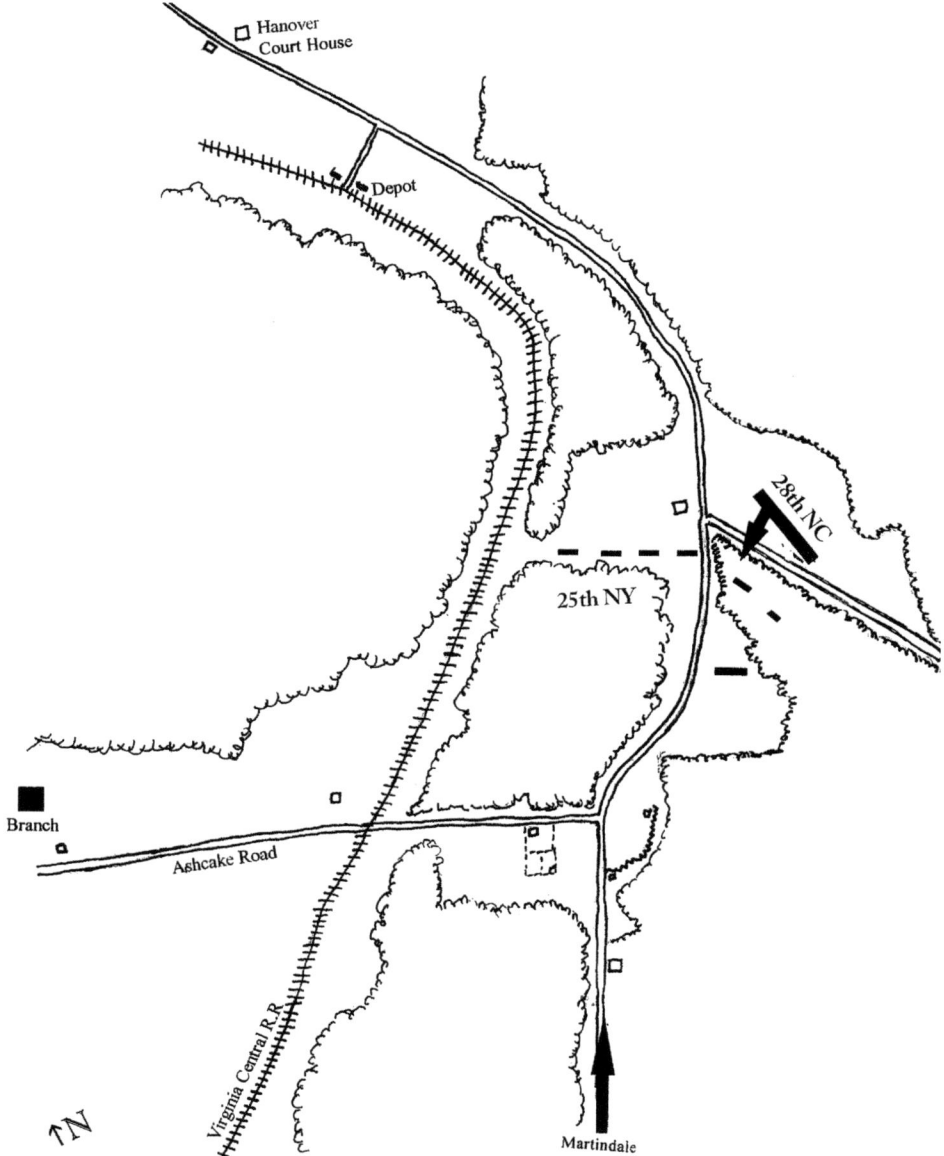

The Twenty-eighth North Carolina attacks and pushes back the Twenty-fifth New York. Martindale approaches from the south.

4. "Charge—Charge Them, Brave Boys"   57

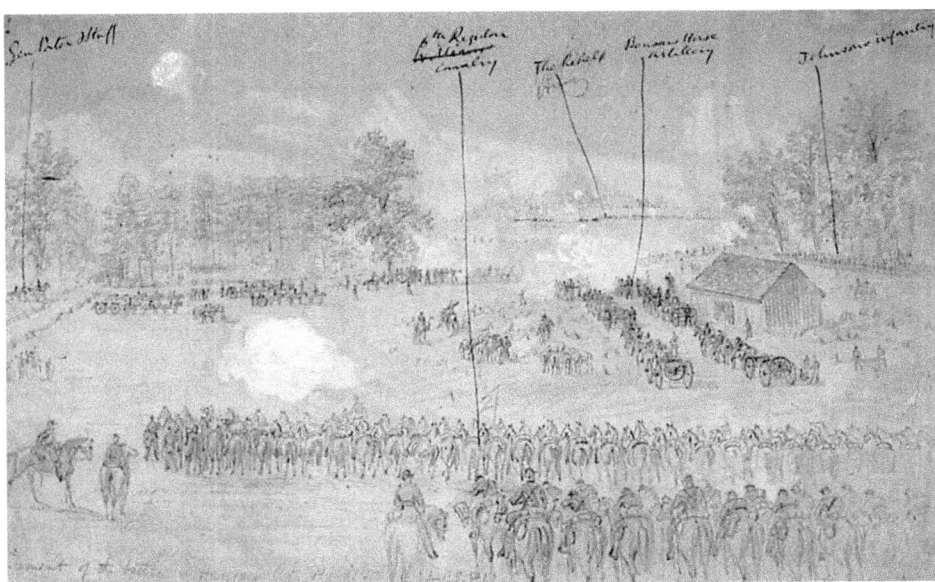

Alfred Waud's sketch of the opening of the battle (courtesy of the Library of Congress).

the rest of Martindale's brigade, which now numbered only two regiments, the Second Maine and the Twenty-second Massachusetts, arrived. Porter ordered Martindale to move down the Ashcake road, destroying the railroad, cutting the telegraph wires, and "driv[ing] back the enemy, should I meet one...." A section of Benson's battery was detailed to go with Martindale.[19]

Colonel Johnson and his New Yorkers continued to slowly advance in skirmish order, moving from wheatfields to wooded thickets. Charles A. Johnson was the great-grandson of President John Adams. He was born in New York in 1826, was a prewar lawyer, and served as a lieutenant in the Tenth United States Infantry from 1847–1848. Johnson first served as a major of the Seventeenth New York before being transferred to the Twenty-fifth New York. About noon, as Johnson and his New Yorkers neared the road just above Dr. Kinney's farm, they ran into the skirmishers from the Twenty-eighth North Carolina. Both sides seemed to be caught off guard: the Federals believed the Confederates were coming from Hanover, and Lane's Tar Heels believed the Federals were coming from the same direction. Once the Twenty-eighth North Carolina reached the fork of the road, the skirmishers of the Twenty-fifth New York fired first and the "balls whistled furiously." Lane ordered his skirmishers to fire and halted the remainder of his regiment, fronted them, faced them by the rear rank, and wheeled the entire regiment, numbering almost 900 men, to the right, catching the skirmishers of the Twenty-fifth New York on the flank. The Twenty-eighth North Carolina fired on the right wing of the Federal skirmishers first, driving them back on their reserve. Next, they turned their attention to the skirmishers on the left side of the road, and delivered another volley. The Twenty-fifth New York's lieutenant colonel, Henry F. Savage, was wounded in the arm while also attempting to reform his men. Surgeon Hiland A. Weed was struck in the thigh and Lt. George E. Fiske "lay dead in the yard under a tree, a shattered musket by his side. A musket ball had passed through his heart."[20]

"Charge—charge them, brave boys!" were Colonel Lane's orders. The men of the Twenty-eighth North Carolina obeyed their colonel, and they "did it most gallantly, many of them, shouting, leaped the ditch and high fence inclosing the field of wheat, while the rest rushed into the yard and around the house." One of the Tar Heels recalled in a letter to Raleigh's *The State Journal*: "We rushed on them, killed from 150 to 200 and captured 70 prisoners. We also took a large number of Springfield guns, three fine repeaters, and five swords." Another member of the Twenty-eighth North Carolina wrote that "the dead lay thick through the woods and in the wheat field through which the boys impetuously charged and a few dead and wounded were to be seen in Dr. Kinney's yard, near his door." Seeing that it was impossible for his force to withstand the Confederates, Colonel Johnson gave the order to retire and to rally on the reserve. Maj. Edwin S. Gilbert of the Twenty-fifth New York recalled that "Lieutenant Thompson lay near the house, and all through the yard and around the house, the dead of both sides covered the ground. The rebels were easily distinguished by their gray clothing. Sergeant Clark lay across the body of a rebel. Captain McMahon and Lieutenant Halpin lay dead near the barn." A member of the regiment later chronicled that Sgt. Harry Clark, a New York City fireman, "was wounded, and the rebels thought to take him a prisoner; he resisted, as it is supposed, for he was found lifeless over the dead body of a rebel, having put his bowie knife through the rebels throat." The remnants of the Twenty-fifth New York fell back and rallied on the newly arrived Federal batteries.[21]

By early afternoon, the rain had stopped, and the heat and humidity became oppressive. Federal artillery, Battery M, Second United States Artillery, under the command of Capt. Henry Benson, arrived on the field. Benson ordered the two sections of the battery to go into position. "One (right) section ... was placed on the road to Hanover Court-House, whilst another, the center section ... was moved to a position in a large field to the left of the road leading to the railroad station. Both soon became engaged with the enemy's infantry. The left section ... was for a time held in reserve." General Porter ordered Benson to move a section of the battery forward and "shell the buildings at the railroad station...." There were Confederates "in a dense woods" in the direction the Federals needed to advance. Benson redeployed the center section, with "one piece in the road and the other in a peach orchard to the left...." The Federal artillery unleashed "a few well-directed discharges of canister and shell (percussion)" and forced the Confederates to retire. These two sections were then redeployed "in a large field to the right of the Hanover road." Benson "directed the fire of the battery ... on the infantry in position in rear of a building...." That building was Dr. Kinney's home.[22]

Colonel Lane's regiment soon began to feel the effects of Benson's artillery. Captain Speer of Company I, Twenty-eighth North Carolina, recalled some of this artillery fire he and his men were subjected to:

4. "Charge—Charge Them, Brave Boys"

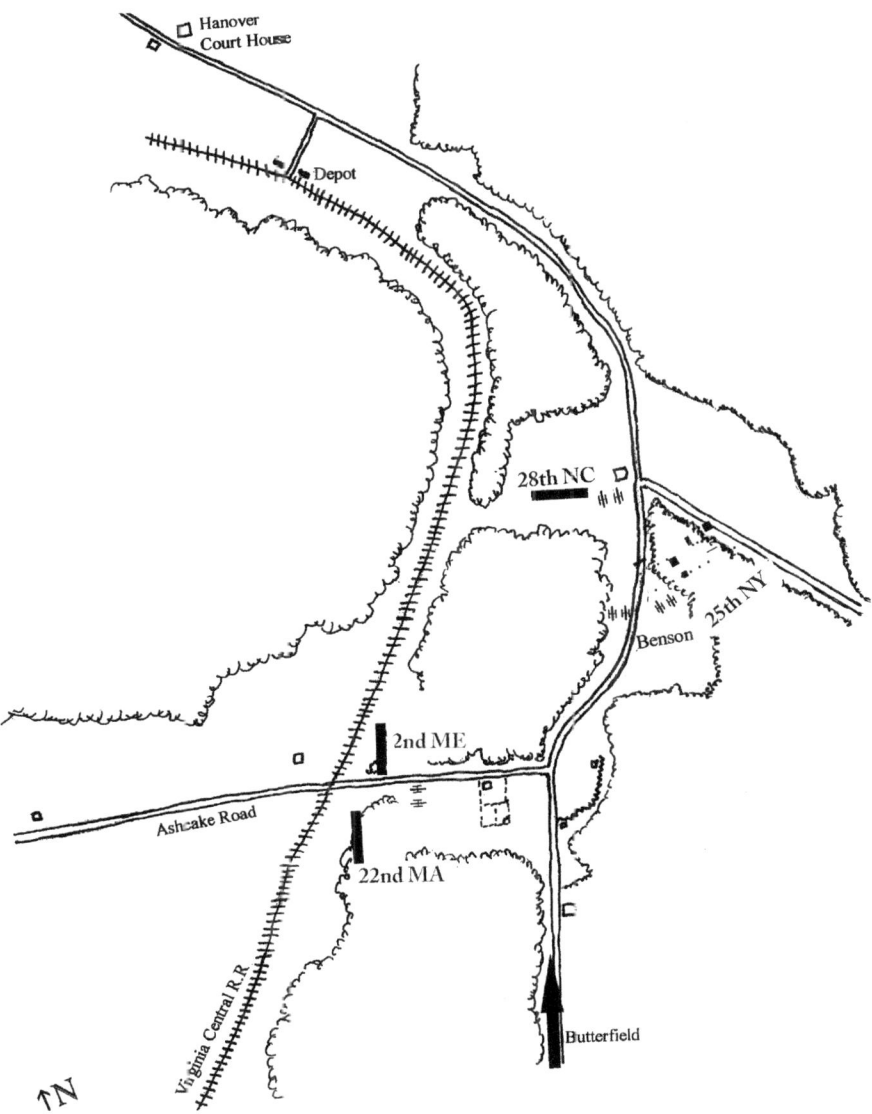

The Twenty-eighth North Carolina reforms near the Kinney House. The Twenty-fifth New York continues to fall back as Martindale's two regiments and a section of Benson's battery deploys along the Ashcake Road and Butterfield's brigade advances up the New Bridge Road.

> As we were marching . . a shell passed so near my head I dodged to one side & came very near falling, the shell striking the flagbearer & a private in Company C just before & knocking both of them down.... While we were maneuvering in the field I seen a shell strike a young Mr. Roberts of Co. A injuring him badly fracturing both of his thighs from which he died. Also I seen two more men of Co. A killed with shells, taking off the top of one of their heads & cutting the other [in two].

Dr. Kinney's home in 2004 (author's collection).

Another member of the Twenty-eighth North Carolina, Jonas S. Cloninger of Company B, echoed Speer when he wrote that "the Yankees ... had bin throwing Balls and Shells at us all the time one bursted in ten feet of me and a Small piece of te Bum hit me on my little finger and knocked the skin off of it...." As the Federal artillery found their range, Lieutenant Potts deployed his own two guns, one brass 12-pounder howitzer and one 10–pounder Parrott, in the road near Dr. Kinney's. Soon, the third section of Benson's battery arrived and the entire battery advanced and redeployed further to the front.[23]

Lane worked hard at rounding up prisoners from the Twenty-fifth New York and reorganizing his own men. Once regrouped, the members of the Twenty-eighth North Carolina, now "heated and excited, threw off their knapsacks, made heavier than usual by the drenching rain of the previous night...." Now that the Confederates were less encumbered, they advanced a short distance to a fence and were ordered to lie down, making themselves less-tempting targets for the Federal artillery, and to await the movements of the new group of Federal soldiers forming 400 yards to the south. At the same time, Colonel Lane sent word to General Branch for reinforcements. The Confederate artillery also redeployed, moving to the rear of the buildings around the Kinney farm. The Federal prisoners were handed over to a detachment of the Fourth Virginia Cavalry and escorted to the rear.[24]

Coming up the road toward the Tar Heels were four regiments under Brig. Gen. Daniel Butterfield and the First United States Sharpshooters under Colonel Berdan. When Butterfield reached Benson's battery, General Porter himself directed the position he wished Butterfield to take. Butterfield deployed his regiments in two lines: the Seventeenth New York and the Eighty-third Pennsylvania in the front line and the Twelfth New York and Sixteenth Michigan in the second line. Skir-

4. "Charge—Charge Them, Brave Boys"

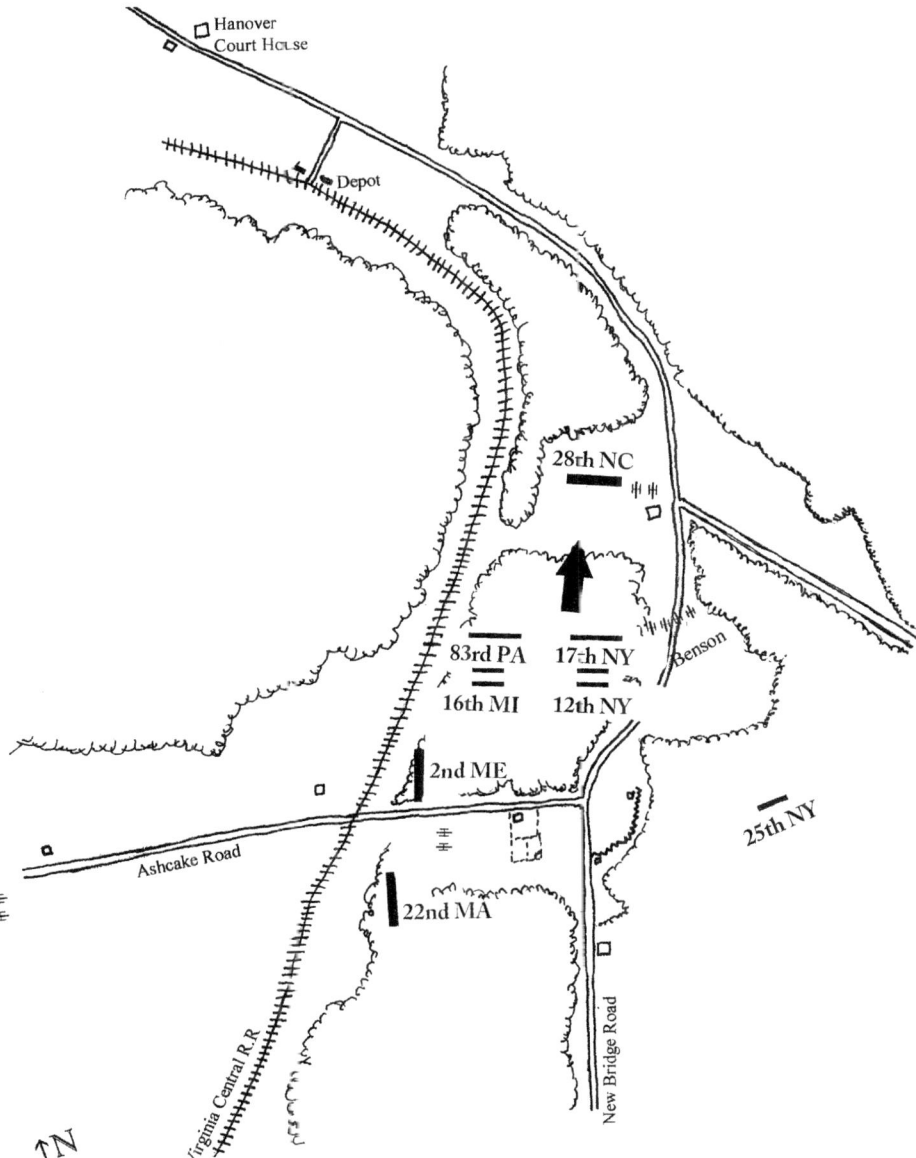

Butterfield's brigade advances and drives the Twenty-eighth North Carolina from the field, back toward Hanover Court House.

mishers were deployed to the front. The Federals "threw off blankets, knapsacks and shelter-tents" and were soon into line. In order to better understand the position of the Confederates, Butterfield "ascended a small tree" and sent portions of his staff to reconnoiter the field and the Confederate line of battle. After making minor adjustments to his own lines, Butterfield called for the advance, personally sounding the notes on a bugle. The skirmishers, belonging to the Eighty-third Pennsylvania and under the eye of General Butterfield, led the way, followed by the battle lines of the Federals. Adj. Thomas E. Morris of the Sixteenth Michigan remembered the events after the war:

> The bugle call[ed] Forward ... and, in perfect order, ranks dressed with all the precision of dress parade or review, the right and left general and color guides taking direction, in exact time, with cadenced step, the lines advance[ed]. The enemy's fire opened at short range, plunging shell and canister in the close ranks. Silently, and in accordance with the orders and directions personally given by General Butterfield ... the lines move[d] grandly on, with no check or falter, the perfect formation never for a moment broken, with eyes directed to the front, every step in exact time, flags flying, the sunshine flashing from thousands of glittering bayonets, and with all the "pomp and circumstance of war," the glorious line swept fearlessly on.

Col. Henry S. Lansing of the Seventeenth New York echoed Morris's thoughts when he wrote in his report, three days after the charge, that his men advanced "in quick time, in line of battle and arms at right-shoulder shift, cheering, exchanging shots with the enemy...." Pvt. Oliver Norton of the Eighty-third Pennsylvania was less "patriotic" than Morris of the Sixteenth Michigan. Writing two days after the battle, Norton noted that he and the other members of his regiment "came out" of the woods and "followed across the field (or fields, for it was cut up by numerous gullies) and in them we took several prisoners. Company K took the first two. They were skirmishing under bushes, and, as I jumped over the fence, I almost stumbled on them. They were instantly disarmed." Sgt. Egbert D. Hulbert of Company K, Eighty-third Pennsylvania, was wounded in the foot, which was later amputated. Pvt. Frank McBride of the same company and regiment was also wounded in the foot, his left, and Cpl. Jacob T. Shriver was mortally wounded.[25]

"It was a grand and glorious spectacle of war," Adjutant Morris continued in his enthusiastic portrayal, "that will never, never be forgotten by any soldier that participated...."

> With his black moustache seeming to be larger and more fierce than ever, his rosy cheeks, his erect and martial figure, our young general [Butterfield] looked the very picture of delight and eagerness, as with his sword he pointed at the glistening line of bayonets and the flash of the enemy's cannon in front, and commanded with his clear, strong, firm voice, heard above the roar of the enemy's fire "Steady, men, forward." Over the stiffening forms of the dead skirmishers, lying with pale, upturned faces; on passing wheat-stacks, down one slope and up another without a pause, to where the enemy's lines of battle and the battery stood in the uncut wheat beyond, their guns glistening in the sun....

Colonel Lane and his Confederates did all that they could do to stymie the Federals. Butterfield's regiments overlapped both of Lane's flanks. Lane attempted to refuse his flanks, but the four regiments of Butterfield's brigade were just too much. Lane called for a retreat, but several of his men were cut off by this time. Lane also left an ambulance, an old wagon, and the regiment's knapsacks. They were also unable to bring off the brass howitzer belonging to Latham's battery, due to one

The Hanover County Court House in 2004 (author's collection).

horse being killed and the other three wounded by long-range skirmish fire and artillery. As the Federals formed for their charge, Captain Benson ordered his gunners to concentrate on the Confederate artillery. Just before the Federal soldiers swarmed around the piece, a Confederate cannoner was able to get off a final shot before being killed by a member of Company A, Seventeenth New York. Skirmishers from the Eighty-third Pennsylvania "passed around the right of the" cannon, and returned a short time later with "some 10 prisoners." The Pennsylvanians then ordered the Confederate prisoners to drag the cannon to a large tree." One Confederate officer recalled the retreat:

> While we were passing along the road by Mr. Winston's the minnie balls came thick & fast after us striking the fence on all sides of us with their deathly whistle. Also the shells at this time was following us with their awful death howl, bursting over our heads & striking the ground & throwing dirt all over us ... one struck a smokehouse & exploded in the house shattering everything. One other at the same time cut the top off a large rake in the yard.[26]

Many within the Twenty-eighth North Carolina were completely exhausted. Captain Speer wrote: "By the time I got up to the road I was entirely broke down & thought I could go no further but the idea of having passed safely though the fight & then falling in the hands of the enemy spurred me on." The Twenty-eighth North Carolina continued retreating to the north, through Hanover Court House, the Federal cavalry having cut off any hopes of the regiment's rejoining the rest of Branch's brigade, located to the southwest. Butterfield, upon being "informed by a prisoner that eight regiments of the enemy had gone to our right and rear ... deemed this of sufficient importance to halt from the pursuit and await support on my right or further orders." The Federal regiments halted, threw out skirmishers, and a courier was sent back to General Porter, advising him of the situation. This also gave Butterfield's regiments a chance to reform.[27]

Generals Porter and Morell soon arrived with artillery and cavalry and ordered Butterfield to continue his advance. The Twelfth New York "formed column by division, and moved forward in rear of the artillery through the open fields as far as the railroad; flanked through the woods, and reached the road to Hanover Court House." Their sister regiment, the Seventeenth New York, likewise was ordered to proceed "toward Hanover Court-House on the right of the Eighty-third Pennsylvania Volunteers, but was separated by a deep ravine and compelled to go to the right, and thus lost sight of the Eighty-third, but continued to advance...." The Pennsylvanians were also ordered to advance. Company G was

> ordered to scour the woods to the extreme left of our line of skirmishers beyond the railroad, and to report what was there. This was done. Having take[n] some prisoners and reported the woods clear, [they] were ordered to skirmish to the front. Meantime the regiment and the other skirmishers were advancing. The two companies of skirmishers along the woods on the main road to Hanover Court-House captured some 30 prisoners, a captain among the number, who fired and endeavored to retreat. The main body of the regiment passed along the railroad to an open field on its right through this line ... then advanced to the Hanover Court-House road and up it to the Court-House, and passed then into a field to rest.[28]

Likewise, the Fifth United States Artillery advanced. Captain Griffin believed that his battery "fired 169 rounds of percussion shell and shrapnel ... nearly every projectile bursting...." In an effort to slow the pursuit of the advance, Lieutenant Potts, with his 10-pounder Parrott, would occasionally halt, unlimber, and fire a few rounds. He did so when he neared the courthouse, and the Federal artillery under Benson and Griffin likewise halted, unlimbered, and returned the fire. Having slowed the Federals, Potts limbered up and continued bringing up the rear of the retreating Confederates. Due to the position of the Federals, Colonel Lane was forced to proceed to Taylorsville to make good his retreat. Lane wrote in his official report: "The cavalry pursued us beyond Colonel Wickham's farm, and were only prevented from making a charge by our throwing the regiment into a field and making it march along the fences, while Lieutenant Potts protected our rear with his Parrott gun." The Confederates reached Taylorsville about sunset.[29]

Not all of the North Carolinians were so lucky. Even after the Federal infantry had halted, squadrons of Federal cavalry continued to scour the area. Captain Speer of the Twenty-eighth penned this account of his adventures:

> We pushed on & tried to gain the bridge, but it was impossible to do it as the enemy's cavalry was now just behind us. I filed off to the right in a wheat field.... Our Regt. was then in sight on a high hill over a mill ahead of us on the opposite side of the river. I had no hopes of overtaking our Regt. I, with a small party of 15 men, made for the riverbank. When we got there we found it very deep & much wider than I

expected.... I could have swam the river but my men could not & they begged me to stay with them.... I contented myself to stay and seal my fate with them. We were in hopes we would yet be rescued. But Alas! As the sun was setting & its last bright rays were kissing the tops of the trees, on came the furious cavalry charging upon us, to whom we had to surrender, or to be destroyed.... Here I had the most awful feelings I ever have had in my life.... I almost wished I was back on the field of battle with my comrades in the cold embrace of death.

Another member of the Twenty-eighth North Carolina recalled that he had "run rite into a Reg of Fifteen hundred cavalry and too pieces of artilory there was only twenty of us together and so Capt Stowe Surrendered himself ans us to the enemy...." Capt. Samuel M. Stowe, Jonas Cloninger, and the other 18 members of this small group were taken back "on the battle ground and there we lay all night the cold wet ground was our bed."[30]

Companies D and E of the Thirty-seventh North Carolina, sent out on picket the previous night, found themselves in a tight spot. As Lane and the Twenty-eighth North Carolina battled the Federals, these two companies were cut off from both Lane and the main body of Confederates at Peake's Turnout. Captain John Ashcraft of Company D led 44 of his own company and 15 of Company E on an elusive route, evading the Federal cavalry searching for them. Some of the Federal cavalry assigned to the pursuit belonged to the Fifth United States Cavalry, under the command of Charles J. Whiting. The cavalry was following the artillery when

> we came to an opening giving us a view of the enemy and what I supposed to be a wagon train, which I pointed out to General Emory, who ordered me to try and cut it off. I started across the country to do so, but upon nearing it found that it was not a wagon train. I kept on, however ... [and came] to a road leading to Ashland, which I followed until we came to a dense woods, unfit for cavalry.... Captain Royall, on my right, had halted and sent me word that the enemy was in front of him....

Commanding Company G, Fifth United States Cavalry, Capt. William B. Royall had proceeded "about a mile beyond the Court-House" and captured five Confederates when he was rejoined by the rest of his regiment. They were "deployed on the right of the road as skirmishers, where [they] captured in all 73 men." The remaining members of Companies D and E of the Thirty-seventh North Carolina lost 78 men captured, with one soldier, Andrew J. Hasty of Company D, killed, and Elijah J. Parker of the same company wounded.[31]

The Sixth Pennsylvania Cavalry also arrived to participate in the hunt for Confederate soldiers. The regiment had been sent "out by Squaddrons in different directions" to reconnoiter roads in the area. One of the troopers remembered in a letter:

> Our Squaddron went off first. We went to the Right and Travelled 10 miles, when we came to a Place whare three Road met. There were two Rebbel cavalry pickets but they Galloped off. We came in right toward them and then our Captain came up to us to go on and Reconoiter the woods ahead. We went up to within 300 Yards of the woods when the First Platon of Company C went through while we halted. They had not been gone ten minutes when we heard Firing ahead and I with three

men were sent in to see where they were. We went through at a Gallop and when we came out the other side we met Lieutenant Leves with his Platton comming back. He told us that he came out of the woods there was a party of 30 Rebbel Cavalry drawn up in front of them across the road, They had fired a volley at Leves' party without doing any harm when they skedaddled down the Road with Leves after them.

But the lieutenant was afraid that the retreat of the Confederates was a decoy and called off his chase. Skirmishers were deployed and a request for further orders was sent to Colonel Rush. About midmorning, the cavalrymen could hear the

> firing for miles through the woods to our left and soon heard artillery and vollies of musketry in the Neighborhood of Hanover Court House and knew that a general engagement was going on. Col. Rush sent word ... to make for Hanover, with all Haste. Which we did by taking a Bye Road, over the Fields, and through the Woods. We had 5 miles to travel, and when we reached there, the Enemy had retreated and our Regiment was about starting in pursuit of them. We joined in. The 5th Regiment took one Road and we took another, we chased them across the Pamunkey River taking about 60 Prisoners, and then cut down the Bridge...."[32]

As the cavalry and infantry rounded up the Confederate prisoners, word suddenly arrived from General Martindale that a large body of Confederates was moving upon the rear of the Union column. Porter sent orders out to his commanders to return as rapidly as possible to the turnout at Peake's Station.

5

"Pop! Pop! Bang! Bang! for About an Hour": The Battle of Peake's Turnout

During the late morning hours of May 27, Lt. David A. Timberlake of Company G, Fourth Virginia Cavalry, spotted a column of Federal soldiers moving toward Peake's Turnout. He rode north, toward the camp of the nearest Confederate regiment. Timberlake "galloped" to where the colonel of the regiment was sitting, reined in his horse, and reported his observations: there were Federals within half a mile of the Confederate camp. That camp belonged to the Thirty-seventh North Carolina Troops. Their colonel, Charles C. Lee, quickly sent two companies of the regiment (F and I), under the command of Lt. Col. William M. Barber, to protect the woods to the front of their position at Lebanon Church. He also sent Company A to reinforce the pickets at the intersection of the New Bridge Road and the Ashcake Road. After seeing to the disposition of his companies, Lee mounted his horse and rode toward Slash Church, the headquarters of General Branch.[1]

Born in South Carolina in 1834, Charles Cochrane Lee graduated from West Point in 1856, fourth in his class. After resigning from the United States Army in 1859, Lee taught at the North Carolina Military Institute in Charlotte with James H. Lane and Daniel H. Hill. All three served in the First North Carolina Volunteers and fought at the battle of Big Bethel, Virginia. Upon the promotion of Hill, Lieutenant Colonel Lee was promoted to colonel of the Bethel Regiment, and held the post until the regiment was mustered out of service. Lee became colonel of the Thirty-seventh North Carolina Troops on November 20, 1861. The Thirty-seventh North Carolina was composed of men from the western portions of the state who fought their first battle in March 1862 at New Bern, North Carolina.[2]

Branch approved of Lee's actions and then ordered the colonel to return to his regiment. At the same time, Branch requested his horse saddled and sent orders to his other regimental commanders "to get under arms and prepare for action immediately." The Seventh North Carolina, under Col. Reuben P. Campbell, "was ordered to throw skirmishers through the woods to the railroad...." Campbell was born in 1818 in Iredell County, North Carolina, and graduated from the United States Military Academy in 1840. He was a Mexican War veteran and a captain in the Second United States Dragoons prior to resigning from the United States Army and being elected colonel of the Seventh North Carolina Troops in May 1861. Lt. Col. Robert F. Hoke's Thirty-third North Carolina Troops were ordered to "throw out skirmishers 100 yards from the camp, to check any body of the enemy that might attempt to approach through thick undergrowth." Hoke was born in Lincolnton, North Carolina, in 1837, and had attended local schools and the Kentucky Mili-

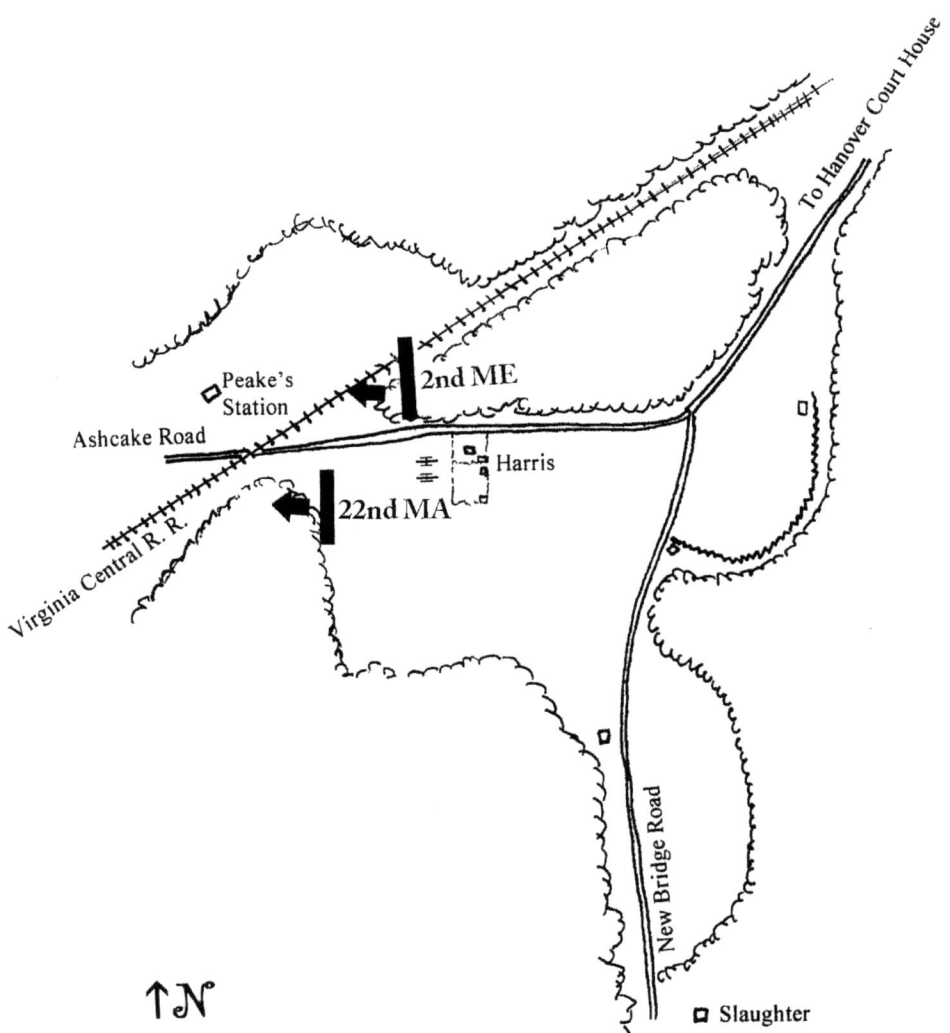

Portions of the Second Maine and Twenty-second Massachusetts advance toward the Virginia Central Railroad, destroying tracks and cutting telegraph lines.

tary Institute. The advent of war found Hoke managing various enterprises owned by his family. Hoke served as a major in the First North Carolina Volunteers, alongside James H. Lane and Charles C. Lee, and was appointed a major in the Thirty-third North Carolina Troops on November 13, 1861. It was Lieutenant Colonel Hoke's 25th birthday. After issuing his orders, Branch mounted his horse and rode toward the opening salvos of the battle.[3]

General Martindale's Federal soldiers had broken camp and started north, toward Hanover Court House, a little after 3:30 a.m. After the Twenty-fifth New York was detached and ordered forward as skirmishers, Martindale was left with only two regiments: the Twenty-second Massachusetts and the Second Maine. The Twenty-second Massachusetts had a strength of "about 800 men" and the Second Maine was "about 350 strong." When Martindale's brigade reached the junction of the New Bridge and Ashcake Roads, Porter ordered him to advance along the left of the New Bridge Road in skirmish order, destroying the railroad and telegraph wires and driving off any enemy troops that might appear. Martindale was allowed to use his discretion in execution of his orders. A section of the Second United States Artillery was assigned to Martindale's command.[4]

Skirmishers were deployed, and the Twenty-second Massachusetts was ordered into a line of battle to the rear. The Twenty-second Massachusetts Infantry was known as "Henry Wilson's Regiment," after the regiment's first colonel, who was also a United States Senator and future vice president under Grant. The regiment was mustered into service in September 1861. Colonel Wilson resigned to resume his seat in the Senate, and was replaced by Col. Jesse A. Gove. Colonel Gove was from New Hampshire and was a veteran of the Mexican War, having served in the Ninth United States Infantry. He was admitted to the bar in 1851, and from 1850 to 1855, was the deputy secretary of the state for New Hampshire. In 1855, Gove was commissioned a captain in Company I, Tenth United States Infantry, and was stationed on the frontier until the outbreak of the war. The Twenty-second Massachusetts was one of the first regiments to enter Yorktown after the retreat of the Confederates up the Peninsula.[5]

After seeing to the deployment of the Twenty-second Massachusetts, Martindale took a survey of the ground over which he had been ordered. He wrote on May 30:

> west of the route by which we had approached from New Bridge was cleared land, the north side of which was bounded by a dense wood for a length of 700 yards. On the edge of this wood was a ditch and bank surmounted by a close wicker fence. At 592 paces or yards on the left or west of the junction of our route from New Bridge with the Richmond and Hanover road was a house with outbuilding, door-yard and garden. West of the garden and yard was a swampy piece of ground, which made a clearing of about 200 paces, when woods again were reached. Passing through these woods about 100 yards cleared ground was again reached about 300 paces from the junction of the highway to Richmond and [the] railroad. From this junction the railroad bore in a straight course northeasterly toward Hanover Court House, passing through a large wheat field until it entered the dense woods north of the highway and door-yard already described.[6]

Company A of the Twenty-second Massachusetts fanned out in skirmish order, with Company D in support, followed by the rest of the regiment. "We loaded our guns, and our regiment was ordered forward," recalled Company F's Cpl. Joseph Simonds. A section of the Second United States Artillery was in the road near the Harris house as the Twenty-second Massachusetts advanced. Company F was deployed as skirmishers and the regiment continued toward the railroad. Company A, under the command of Capt. Walter S. Sampson, "seized the railroad and the telegraph, destroying some sections of the latter, and taking up the rails for some distance." From the railroad, the skirmishers continued to advance, "across a slough, to a belt of woods, beyond which there was a large opening in the timber and two regiments of the enemy drawn up in a line of battle." Colonel Gove ordered the rest of his regiment up, and sent back word to Martindale that the "enemy was moving to our right." The colonel then rode back to find Martindale, and expressed the need to advance artillery and the Second Maine Infantry.[7]

Lieutenant Colonel Barber of the Thirty-seventh North Carolina took his two companies, F and I, and advanced from Lebanon Church toward the main road. As they neared the crossroads, Barber sighted two infantry regiments and a squad of cavalry. His two companies quietly filed into the woods and began to observe the Federals. Barber sent word back to Colonel Lee informing him of the size of the Federal column. When Barber ascertained that the Federals were moving toward Peake's Turnout, Barber withdrew his men back toward camp and reformed the regiment.[8]

Peake's Turnout in 2004. The Second Maine advanced over these tracks a little farther to the right (author's collection).

A section of Confederate artillery under Captain Latham arrived and deployed. The artillery of both sides began a serious debate at 1,500 yards. Fairly early in the duel, the section of the Second United States Artillery assigned to Martindale was withdrawn, and a section of Battery D, Fifth United States Artillery took its place. "One piece," chronicled the battery's captain, Charles Griffin, "was placed on a little rise in the road and the other in a plowed field to the left...."[9]

Colonel Lee of the Thirty-seventh North Carolina returned to his regiment, and correctly judged that the Federals to his front and left were a much larger force than first reported. Lee deployed the rest of his regiment (seven companies) and requested a section of artillery from Latham's battery. The colonel believed the enemy force contained "at least two regiments of infantry, a squadron of cavalry, and a battery of artillery." Lee then sent a request to Lt. Col. Benjamin O. Wade of the Twelfth North Carolina for help. The Twelfth North Carolina State Troops started the war as the Second North Carolina Volunteers. They were mustered in May 1861 with Solomon Williams, a recent graduate of the United States Military Academy, as colonel. Williams was absent from the regiment, and Benjamin Wade was in command. Wade was a prewar druggist and captain of Company F prior to becoming lieutenant colonel on May 1, 1862. Colonel Lee requested the Twelfth North Carolina to "advance in front of the railroad and, changing front towards left, move round on the enemy's flank...." The Twelfth North Carolina's movement relieved the two companies of the Thirty-seventh North Carolina, which Lee had dispatched earlier. Colonel Wade drew his regiment

> in line of battle about one-half mile from Lebanon Church, and immediately on the road; it however, only remained in that position for a short period, when it was removed to a point farther back in the woods and near the Railroad — Two Companies were then detached as skirmishers, and the balance of the Regiment were ordered to [in] "place rest."[10]

The men of the Thirty-seventh North Carolina positioned themselves in support of the battery, with Latham's guns on their right. Barber deployed "skirmishers on each side to a considerable distance." Latham's volunteers were battling regular United States artillerymen, and the skill of the regulars soon began to take its toll. One of Latham's caissons was struck "twice, one shot exploding the ammunition-chest of the limber...." An anonymous member of Latham's battery recalled that "one of their shells struck one of our caissons loaded with shell and canister, causing it to explode with great violence, but, strange to say, without doing us any serious damage, save the loss of the caisson." Maj. Charles N. Hickerson of the Thirty-seventh North Carolina was within a few feet of the caisson when it was struck. Hickerson was knocked off his horse by the explosion and his horse "was burnt by the powder." Captain Griffin was reported to be sighting his pieces personally, and "was patting the side of one of them" exclaiming "A good shot! now another like that" after the destruction of the caisson. The Federal gunners had the range of the Confederate battery, forcing Captain Latham to redeploy his guns.[11]

While the batteries continued in their long-range struggle, an additional Federal regiment joined the line of the Twenty-second Massachusetts, and Battery D, Fifth United States Artillery: the Second Maine Volunteer Infantry. Formed in late May 1861, the regiment's first colonel was Charles D. Jameson. The Second Maine was one of the well-seasoned combat regiments on the field. They had participated in battle along Bull Run the previous July, and Colonel Jameson was promoted to brigadier general for his actions. The regiment's lieutenant colonel, Charles W. Roberts, took command. Roberts, born in 1828 in Old Town, Maine, was a graduate of Bowdoin College, and had been a prewar lumber merchant and banker.[12]

From left to right, the Federal line of battle was the Twenty-second Massachusetts, Battery D, Fifth United States Artillery; and the Second Maine. Orders soon came for Colonel Roberts to advance skirmishers across the Virginia Central Railroad and through the wheatfield to his front "to ascertain, if possible, whether there was any enemy in the woods beyond." Roberts called upon Capt. Daniel F. Sergeant to lead his Company G in the task. "Meanwhile," recalled Roberts, "another portion of my command was very industrious in destroying the railroad, telegraph, &c.," Another member of the regiment, Richard Kelleher, left this recollection:

> Gen. Martindale ordered our regiment to cross the Virginia Central Railroad, a few rods to our right, and cut the telegraph wire and tear up the track. To do this we had to pass down a ravine, which was speedily done and the work accomplished.... At 1 o'clock we got orders to cross the railroad and charge upon and capture the rebel battery. We marched slowly through a very large wheat field, perhaps a quarter of a mile, and could see the rebels advancing on us, and it was plainly visible that their force was much larger than ours.

Captain Sergeant sent word back to Colonel Roberts about the size of the Confederate force. Roberts halted his troops and sent word back to Martindale that the Confederates had "changed the position of their artillery and were in strong force on my right." Martindale ordered Roberts to recall his skirmishers, and to reform his regiment "across the road to my original position," which Roberts did.[13]

Based upon the information that Colonels Gove and Roberts had sent back, Martindale sent word to Porter asking for reinforcements, "two regiments, or at least one...." Porter soon replied with an answer that astonished Martindale. The general was to take his two regiments and artillery, and "to push to the right" and rejoin the main body of Federal soldiers. Porter believed that the main Confederate body was retreating toward Fredericksburg. Martindale quickly fired back: "the enemy [is] on my left–not my right–along a road to my left, and not to my right." Nevertheless, Martindale obeyed his orders, recalled his soldiers, and "placed them in the road to Hanover Court House, leading with the Twenty-second Massachusetts, followed by the battery, and closing with the Second Maine."[14]

The Twenty-second Massachusetts quickly advanced up the road toward Hanover Court House. The Second Maine, however, had to help free "several caissons" that were "slightly imbedded in the mud...." Colonel Roberts estimated that this operation took 20 minutes. As the Twenty-second Massachusetts proceeded up the road, it came upon Captain Mason, who informed Colonel Gove that Mar-

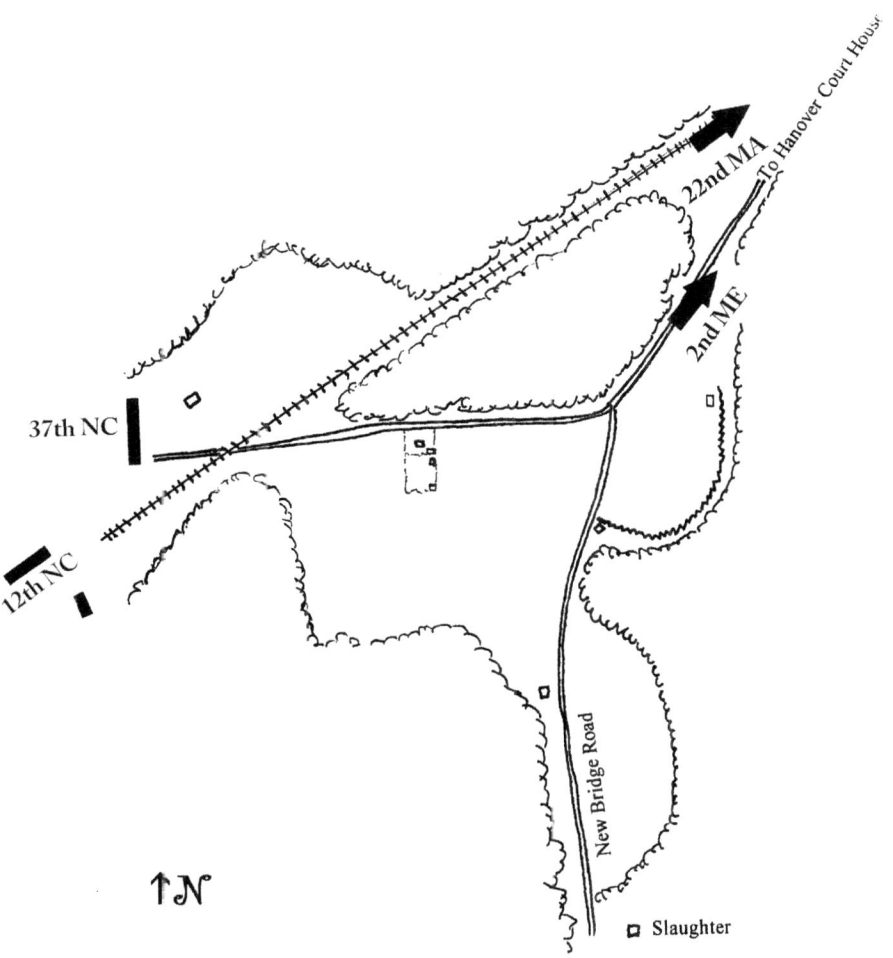

Martindale moves his regiments and artillery toward Hanover Court House. The Confederates advance.

tindale's brigade was ordered "up the railroad to make a junction with his advance forces." Gove tried to impress upon Mason the gravity of the situation to the rear. Mason rode away and Gove countermarched his regiment. When the regiment came upon Martindale, he ordered the men "to file into the woods, and after striking the railroad to follow it to where the road to the station crosses it." One of Gove's men, Corporal Simonds, recalled that the regiment advanced toward Hanover Court House, "tearing up the railroad and burning one small bridge...." Colonel Gove added that his regiment "cut the telegraph wire in several places, destroyed a water tank and culvert, and removed several rails." The order to move up the railroad would effectively remove the Twenty-second Massachusetts from combat.[15]

After being freed from the gelatinous mud, the Fifth United States Artillery continued toward Hanover Court House. As the artillerymen rounded a corner, the tongue on one of the guns broke, and the entire battery halted for repairs. This broken artillery piece removed Battery D from the impending action. Martindale held the Second Maine back to act as a rear guard. Likewise, he left a "small force of cavalry" near the Harris garden and house to maintain surveillance on the Confederates. Two directives arrived from Porter. The first ordered Martindale to advance his command up the railroad "as fast as I could and to halt when I came to the road from Hanover Court House...." The second was a reply to a message that Martindale had sent to Porter earlier. The commanding general informed Martindale that the Confederates were "on my left, and not my right, directing me to let them go, and informing me that Stoneman would strike them...." Martindale was "convinced ... that the commanding general of the corps was acting under some great mistake and misinformation" and the brigade commander started forward to confer with Porter personally. Martindale ran into his division commander, George Morell. Martindale and Morell had been classmates together at West Point, graduating in 1835. Morell served in the Corps of Engineers for two years, then resigned and became engaged in civil engineering, and later became a lawyer, and then commissioner of the United States Circuit Court for the Southern District of New York. Martindale tried to get Morell "to go forward to the commanding general of the corps and inform him in person of the force in rear and the danger to our line." Morell bluntly told Martindale that he could "communicate by an orderly...." Martindale sent another aide to Porter, sent the Twenty-second Massachusetts up the railroad, but gained permission "to assume the responsibility of remaining with the Second Maine Regiment to cover the battery and the column in rear" from General Morell.[16]

General Branch had already gained the field before the Federal artillery ceased firing. A messenger from Colonel Lane and the Twenty-eighth North Carolina arrived, asking General Branch for assistance. Branch quickly sent forward the Eighteenth and Thirty-seventh North Carolina, both under the command of Colonel Lee. Command of the Thirty-seventh North Carolina fell once again upon Lieutenant Colonel Barber. The Eighteenth North Carolina was originally mustered in as the Eighth North Carolina Volunteers in August 1861. Their first colonel, James D. Radcliffe, was defeated for reelection in April 1862 and was replaced by Robert Harper Cowan. Born in Wilmington, North Carolina, in 1824, Cowan was a graduate of the University of North Carolina. He was elected lieutenant colonel of the Third North Carolina State Troops on May 16, 1861, and in April 1862 became colonel of the Eighteenth North Carolina Troops. On May 27, the regiment contained approximately 570 men. Colonel Lee put the Eighteenth North Carolina in the lead, "keeping it well covered in front and on the flanks by skirmishers...." Next came the Thirty-seventh North Carolina, only seven companies strong, with an estimated strength of 500 men.[17]

Company I of the Eighteenth North Carolina was one of those companies posted as skirmishers. One of the members of that company, Thomas F. Wood, recalled that after the orders came to deploy as skirmishers, his company had a run of about a mile. I remember I had on a fancy knapsack which was sent out as a pattern for the Wilmington Light Infantry, a civil military company existing before the war. The knapsack consisted of a slender white pine frame covered with patent leather and made a snug square parcel, with a place on top for a blanket. It was only suited for holiday soldiering but I was too proud of the appearance it made to give it up for the poor rag of a thing the men had. I had a very fine pair of white blankets which Ma had given me when I left home. As we were running into battle, my knapsack got too heavy — I was very thirsty — and confident that we would return the same road when the fight was over, I threw my precious knapsack into a tangle of smilax vines and went on, now and then stopping to scoop water from the cart-ruts which were running with muddy water.

Just as we neared the battlefield, I saw the first wounded man I had ever seen in battle. He was coming along the road we were traveling, between two men. He had been shot in the bowels, and was pale and a horrible sight.[18]

Federal cavalry quickly informed Martindale of the advance of the Confederates. Martindale "immediately sent forward a notice to the commanding general of the division, and asked for the return of the Twenty-second Massachusetts." Then Martindale ordered the Second Maine to halt. The regiment "changed front to the rear on its first company" threw out skirmishers, and moved back toward the intersection of the New Bridge and Ashcake roads. Colonel Roberts deployed Company A, under Capt. Rinaldo B. Wiggin, as skirmishers, who quickly made contact with their Confederate equivalents, "some 400 yards" from the main Federal force. Martindale noticed the Forty-fourth New York, with a section of Martin's Massachusetts battery in tow, coming up the road.[19]

The men of the Forty-fourth New York, in Butterfield's brigade, had named themselves the Ellsworth Avengers. The regiment was formed in August 1861, following the death of Col. E. Elmer Ellsworth, commander of the First New York Zouaves, (later the Eleventh New York Volunteers). Stephen W. Stryker was commissioned colonel. Stryker was born in 1836, and prior to the war had been a merchant and traveled with Elmer Ellsworth's U.S. Zouave Cadets. Earlier that morning, the Forty-fourth New York, along with a section of the Massachusetts Light Artillery, received orders to secure one of the many crossroads on New Bridge Road. Colonel Stryker "posted one company of the Forty-fourth on each side of the road about one-half mile from the crossing, with sufficient videttes in commanding positions to guard against any surprise." The Federal soldiers had been in position about an hour when orders came for Stryker "to move the force under my command to the front as soon as possible." Upon approaching Martindale's position, the sounds of battle became audible. Two companies of the regiment were sent as skirmishers into the woods to protect the left of the column. Soon, the clamor of battle could be heard coming from their right; the two companies were recalled and the regiment hastened its step. General Martindale asked Colonel Stryker for support, and the colonel acquiesced, placing his men under Martindale's command. General Martindale positioned the Second Maine on his right, the section of Martin's battery in the center, and the Forty-fourth New York on the left.[20]

Colonel Lee cautiously moved his Tar Heels forward until discovering "the enemy strongly posted on the top of a hill about one-half mile distant." Lee positioned his men with the Thirty-seventh North Carolina on the left and the Eighteenth North Carolina on the right, and continued to advance to "within 400 yards of the enemy's position." Branch rode forward and conferred with Lee about the size of the Federal force. "My plan was quickly formed and orders were given for its execution," wrote General Branch in his official report. Branch ordered Colonel Lee, with the Thirty-seventh North Carolina, to move through the woods on the Confederate left and flank the Federal artillery. Lieutenant Colonel Hoke, with the Thirty-third North Carolina, along with the Twelfth North Carolina under Colonel Wade, was to move to the Confederate right and attack the battery on its other flank. Colonel Cowan was to lead the Eighteenth North Carolina in a charge across the open field, and lastly, Latham was to bring "all his guns to bear on their front."[21]

Branch's plan fell apart almost from the beginning. Hoke's Thirty-third North Carolina would not return from its mission of sweeping through the woods in time to attack the left flank of the Federals. The regiment was dispatched to "sweep through the woods," and secure the right flank of the Confederates. Just where the bulk of this Confederate regiment went is unclear. Two of the 10 companies were detached to scout for Federals: Companies A and B. Capt. Joseph H. Saunders of Company A was in charge of the operation. He had "two small companies ... with orders to go to a certain road no one knowing where the road was...." Saunders chronicled the events to his mother a few days later:

> After [we] were deployed we advanced about three miles when my guide informed me we were close to the road and that he thought we might find the enemy there. I then sent him to the left to inform Lt. Gatlin so we might draw our companies together so as to make our line stronger. Gatlin had got so far ahead that he could not find him. This delay threw me behind. I then pushed on [and] came to a field about three hundred yards wide the woods so thick the left of my company had gone to the left of the field they were commanded by a Corporal I had explained to him how I wanted him to do his part splendidly he got so close to the Yankees that they ordered him to throw down their arms and surrender but instead of doing that he ordered his men to fall back to a fence and fire which they did with such an effect as to cause them to run in a hurry when the firing commence I deployed my men behind the fence finding they could not get a shoot [sic] it being too far they sprang over the fence and ran across the field firing as we went (if they had been commanded by west point man it would have been called a charge across) the Yankee Ambulances got out of the way faster than anything that I ever saw run on wheels. Gatlin then came to me when we surrounded the Hospital and summoned them to surrender, which was done by a Dr. coming out with a white shirt and surrendering the whole concern. There was about fifty of their wounded one poor fellow lying on the table they had not finished cuting his leg off they were nearly dead for water. Men wounded *every* where. We released two of Col Lanes regiment who was taken prisoner in the morning. Our firing brought the enemy on us in such force that we fell to retreat.

Saunders and Gatlin brought back 11 horses, one lieutenant, a surgeon, and three privates, but were forced to leave the ambulances due to their trek back through

5. "Pop! Pop! Bang! Bang! for About an Hour" 77

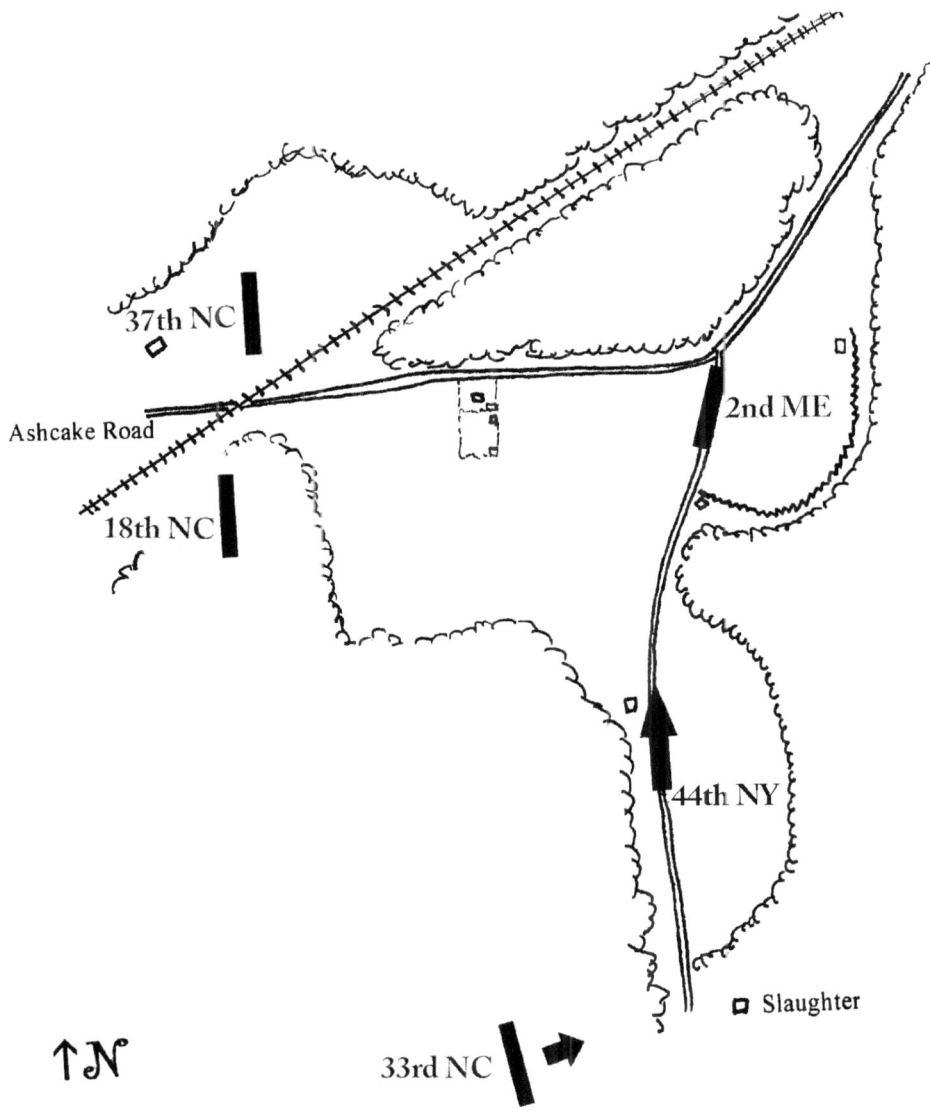

The Second Maine returns to the junction of the road, and the Forty-fourth New York advances up New Bridge Road. The Thirty-third North Carolina captures a Federal hospital, and the Eighteenth and Thirty-seventh North Carolina prepare to advance.

the woods. They also almost acquired the ambulance(s) of the Forty-fourth New York; Dr. Elias L. Bissell, the regiment's assistant surgeon; and a small guard. Bissell and the others "escaped, the bullets whistling around them." Had the Confederates spent just a little more time in the impromptu field hospital, they would have discovered Lt. Col. Henry F. Savage, wounded earlier during the fight with the

Twenty-eighth North Carolina. Savage "had his coat off," and was lying amongst the privates when the Confederates raided the hospital. Had they discovered the colonel, who was wounded in the arm, they would have placed him on one of the horses and taken him prisoner.[22]

The lieutenant whom the Thirty-third North Carolina captured was a Lt. Perkins of Butterfield's staff. Ailing with typhoid fever, Perkins had ridden toward the battle in an ambulance, "thinking he might be strong enough to take part in the battle." Once on the field, Perkins was placed in a field hospital, under the care of Dr. Waters. When the Thirty-third North Carolina captured the hospital, they took Perkins prisoner. Dr. Waters

> tried hard to keep Lieut. Perkins, but the captain would hear of no excuse. "He is too weak to walk," said the Doctor. "Then we will mount him," replied the rebel.
> "He is too ill to ride, and besides, he has no horse," was the rejoinder.
> "Well, here is a horse, and we will take care of him," persisted the rebel, pointing to Dr. Waters' horse, standing in the yard. The Doctor did not relish this peculiar style of politeness, which necessitated the confiscation of his faithful steed. Hoping that our forces would come up the road ... he endeavored to parley with him long enough to bring about their capture. It was in vain. Mounting Lieut. Perkins, and grabbing up all those able to walk, even to the Doctor's ambulance driver, off they marched, leaving the doctor in the doorway, taking a last, long, lingering look at the slowly receding proportions of his beloved Rosinante.[23]

Word of the plight of the wounded Federal soldiers filtered back through stragglers to General Martindale, and he dispatched half of the Forty-fourth New York to the area. "We had gone but a short distance," recorded one of the soldiers, "before a volley was fired from the woods that lined the road, which was promptly returned, although we could see no one to fire at, they being well protected by trees. The Colonel ordered us back on the double-quick...." One member of the regiment, James B. Hitchcock, of Company K, recalled many years after the war, that

> the 44th N. Y. was marching along this road with guns at right-shoulder shift, route step, and was passing a wooded ravine on the left of the road, with no fence between the road and woods. They were fired upon by rebel skirmishers in the ravine. Instantly the regiment dropped in the middle of the road, not waiting for the order to lie down. I remember trying to keep something in my throat from choking me, at the same time lying on my back, hastily loading my Springfield, and safe to say, not going through the regulation nine-time movement in loading.

Stryker, fearing that he had come upon a much larger force than his five companies, ordered his men "as a feint ... to prepare for a charge, and immediately marched the force to the rear and formed a line of battle facing the woods...." The colonel sent for his remaining companies, and "doubled the line of skirmishers, giv[ing] them the proper support...." Next, Stryker sent an orderly to Martindale, seeking permission to clear the woods to his front "of any concealed enemy found there." Before the regiment could move out, the Second Maine and the section of artillery opened on the Confederates, and Stryker returned his regiment toward the sound of the fighting.[24]

5. "Pop! Pop! Bang! Bang! for About an Hour"

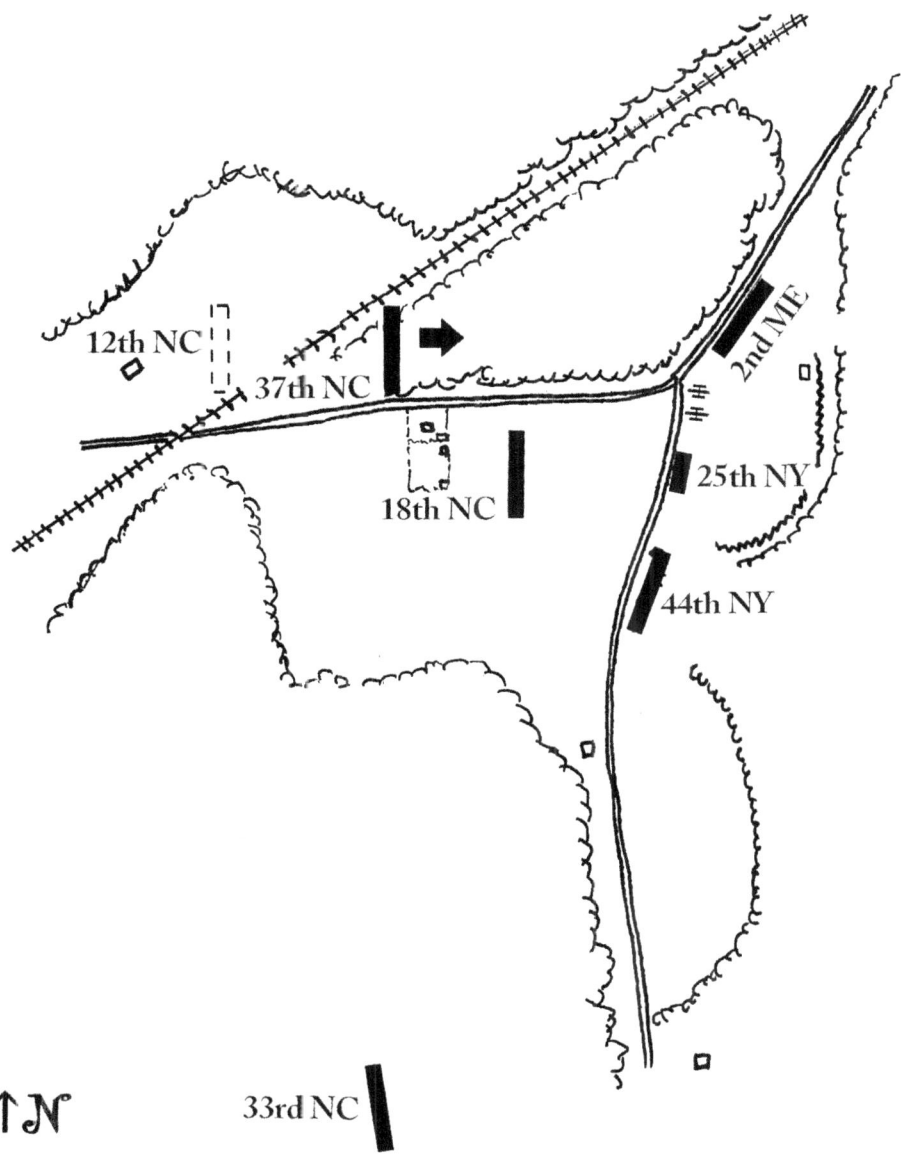

The Second Maine, Twenty-fifth and Forty-fourth New York, along with a section of the Masachusetts Light Artillery, engage first the Eighteenth and later the Thirty-seventh North Carolina. Possible position of the Twelfth North Carolina.

The Twelfth North Carolina, without the support of the Thirty-third North Carolina, made little progress against the Federal line. Colonel Wade

> brought them to attention, and addressed them in a few words very appropriate to the occasion, and highly characteristic of the transcendent good sense of the man.

He then marched the Regiment in line of battle through the dense piece of timber and out to a wheat field directly in front of the woods occupied by the enemy, who fired a considerable number of shells at us, but fortunately doing us no damage.

The regiment then marched across the road, "and took up an advanced position in a wheat field on the right of a battery that the enemy had posted in the woods," only a few hundred yards away. The regiment remained in this position for half an hour, "exposed to a most terrifically galling fire of grape and shell, which did us considerable damage, and the only way I can account for its not decimating the Regiment is, that we were in a horrizontal position.... So exactly did the Yankees have our range, that every shell that missed, came so near our heads as to fan our hair, and invarialbe bursted a few hundred yards behind us." The fire of the Federal artillery, along with the lack of support, neutralized the Twelfth North Carolina.[25]

Helping to direct the fire of the Federal artillery were members of the signal corps, Lt. Frank W. Marston, of Company F, Fortieth Pennsylvania Volunteers. Marston was traveling with General Porter when he was sent to open communications with General Morell. "I rode forward with my men and had just taken my position near a barn in the open field on the right of the main road," reported Marston, "when the enemy opened their fire upon me. A section of Martin's Battery then came dashing upon the field and in a few seconds opened their fire...." Marston was ordered to advance and select a position in front of the battery and observe the effects of their fire. After signal officer Lt. Frederick Horner was positioned at the battery to relay information to the commander, Marston secured "a position for my flag, veiled from the enemy by a curtain of the woods. I crossed the road and watched the effect of our shells. Perceiving that many of the shots fell too far to the right, I reported that fact with the signal flag to the battery and the effect was very apparent, our shells then exploding around the enemy, creating no little discomfiture."[26]

With the Twelfth North Carolina in an inoperable state, the Thirty-third North Carolina out capturing hospitals, the Twenty-eighth North Carolina retreating back through the town of Hanover, and the Forty-fifth Georgia repairing railroad tracks, Branch was left with three infantry regiments: the Seventh, Eighteenth, and Thirty-seventh North Carolina Troops. Branch chose to hold the Seventh North Carolina in reserve, a lesson the former politician learned from the debacle at New Bern two months earlier. It would fall to the Eighteenth and Thirty-seventh North Carolina regiments to attack the Federal lines.

Looking for any forces that he could lay his hands upon, Martindale sent an aide to find the Twenty-fifth New York and to order them to his assistance. But for the present, he was left with the Second Maine, portions of the Forty-fourth New York, and a section of the Massachusetts Light Artillery. The Second Maine was on the right, with the section of artillery next, and the Forty-fourth New York, on the left, "under cover of a ravine, faced southwesterly toward the woods on the left of the open ground in front." Skirmishers from both regiments were deployed. Colonel Stryker of the Forty-fourth New York turned command over to Lt. Col.

James C. Rice, a native of Massachusetts. Rice graduated from Yale in 1854, worked as a teacher in Mississippi and as a journalist and lawyer in New York prior to becoming a soldier. According to a member of the Forty-fourth New York, Cpl. Charles H. Blair, who was wounded in the fight and sought medical aid in the rear, Colonel Stryker was found "dismounted and seated quietly by a tree." In his official report, Stryker stated that he was sent by General Martindale to rally stragglers to shore up the Federal left.[27]

Cowan and Lee, unaware that other elements of the attack had stalled, proceeded to carry out their orders. "Boys, you have stern work before you. It is no child's play — do your duty," were the words of admonition from Colonel Lee. He then placed the Thirty-seventh North Carolina in the woods on the left side of the field. The Eighteenth North Carolina was formed in a strip of woods, and was told the Federals were not more than 200 or 250 yards from their present position. When the regiment emerged from the woods, the distance they needed to cover to reach the Federal lines increased from 250 to more than 600 yards of open ground. Notwithstanding, the Eighteenth continued to advance. Cowan ordered the regiment to "forward at charge bayonets," and the Tar Heels stepped off. Moving forward at the double-quick, the Eighteenth North Carolina found themselves on the receiving end of Federal artillery. "The artillery was playing upon our men the whole while — throwing shrapnel principally," recalled one member of the regiment. "[S]oon the Minnie rifles began to assist the artillery. Still the regiment continued to advance — the line in perfect order — withholding its fire because the range was too great for effective musketry, and thus it continued until within two hundred yards of the battery, its brave men falling at every step." One member of the Forty-fourth New York recalled several days later that he "never saw a more imposing sight," than the Eighteenth North Carolina, "though the ensign of treason floated in the centre." When the Eighteenth North Carolina neared the Federal line, the fire became so great and "deadly ... [that] the regiment faltered and the men lay down...."[28]

Struggling towards Martindale's small line of battle came the remnants of the Twenty-fifth New York, all 175 of them. One member of the regiment recalled that after the fight with the Twenty-eighth North Carolina, the New Yorkers had "lain down exhausted, drenched with rain, and hungry also." General Martindale's aide, his own son, according to a letter writer whose account appeared in the *New York Sunday Mercury,* arrived "and ordered our colonel to send the regiment to support the Second Maine regiment — the enemy trying the flanking movement on them also." Maj. Edwin Gilbert chronicled much the same story in his official report: "Lieutenant Martindale came ... to Colonel Johnson and desired him to have his regiment join the regiments in the rear, as most of the column had passed on and General Martindale expected an attack.... After some further delay we ... marched back to where we first deployed as skirmishers...." As the Twenty-fifth New York arrived and went into position, the Second Maine and the Federal artillery were already in action.[29]

"The enemy," wrote Colonel Roberts of the Second Maine, "appeared boldly in our front, advancing in perfect order, the red colors of the right and left general guides, also the Stars and Bars defiantly flying." Roberts ordered his men to the prone position as the Confederates unleashed their first volley, and "most of their bullets passed harmlessly over us." The colonel ordered his regiment to rise, fix bayonets, and to fire by battalion. The Eighteenth North Carolina, Second Maine, and the two artillery pieces traded lead, producing ghastly wounds. One member of the Maine regiment recalled in the local Bangor newspaper:

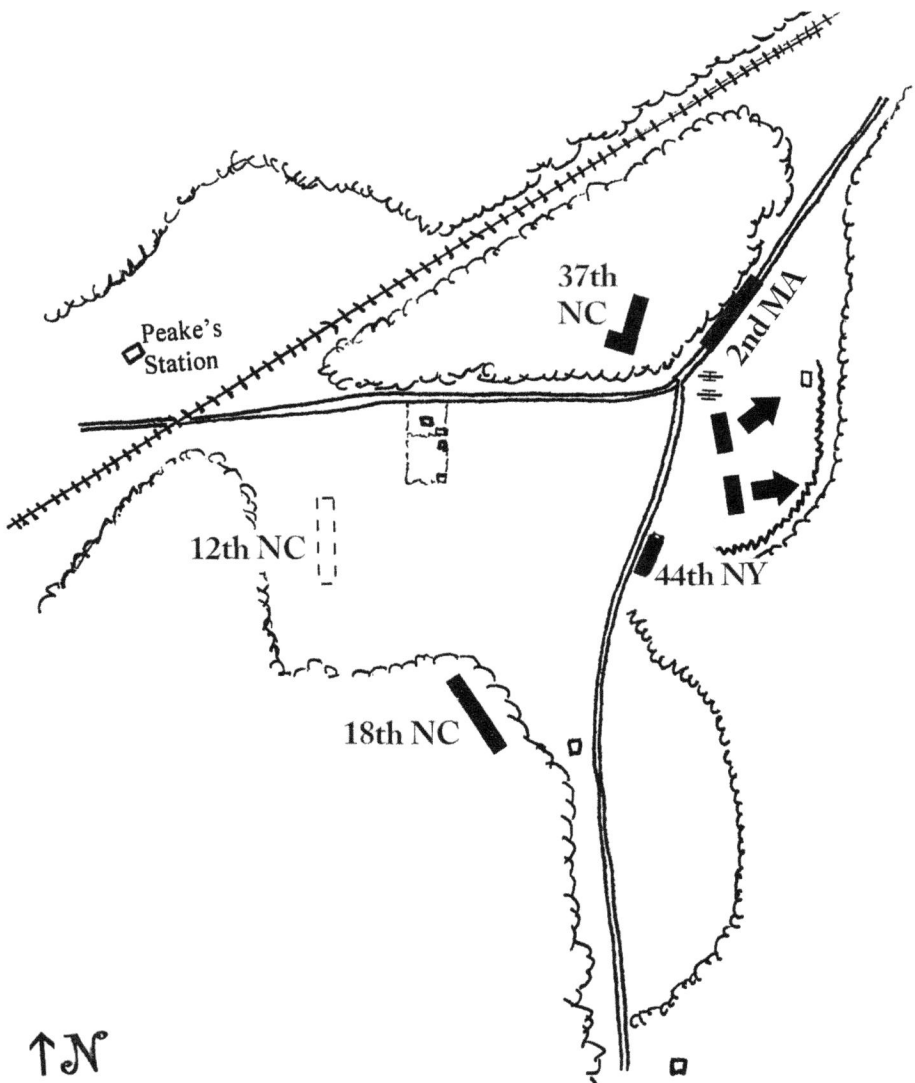

The Eighteenth North Carolina redeploys in the woods to the regiment's right. The combined fire of the Eighteenth and Thirty-seventh North Carolina forces the withdrawal of the Twenty-fifth and portions of the Forty-fourth New York, along with the gunners of Massachusetts Light Artillery. Possible position of the Twelfth North Carolina.

> In the first fight in the road, [Sgt. Benjamin F.] Smart was standing between Currier and myself, loading, firing and cheering on the men, when a ball struck him in the left breast, and he fell back. I asked him where he was shot, and he put his hand to a great hole in his coat. I saw it was all up with him, and ordered some men to take him to the rear, which they did, and he died in a few minutes. Poor, brave Smart! He was as brave a man as I ever saw.... Shortly after he fell, [James H.] Smith, of our company, was shot in the shoulder, the ball coming out of his back. Wentworth was shot in the leg rather badly and little Hammett had a slight wound in the arm, but he kept on fighting.

The Eighteenth North Carolina suffered just as severely as the Second Maine. Capt. Willie J. Sikes of Company B was killed, as was Pvt. Samuel Dyer of Company G. Lt. Neill Townsend was struck in the arm, Pvts. Elias Prevatt and Forney Privett each in the shoulder, Neill Edwards and Clark Barnes each in the leg, and Amos Britt in the foot. All of these men were in Company D.[30]

Unable to withstand the pressure of being caught out in the open and with no support, Cowan ordered the Eighteenth North Carolina to the protection of the woods on the right side of the field. Cowan "poured in four or five destructive volleys; and under the cover of the smoke threw his regiment into the piece of woods." It is likely that Company I of the Eighteenth North Carolina advanced as skirmishers through the woods and that the rest of the regiment dressed on this company. Private Wood recalled that where his company was deployed, "cord wood was stacked about in the piece of woods we occupied, and we could hear the patter of lead from the enemy on the trees, but could see no one before us.... The battle raged hotly...." During the fight, one of the junior company officers ordered Wood to deploy to the right. To accomplish the order, Wood and his comrades needed to "get down a steep bank, pass a road being scoured with artillery, and climb another bank, then divide the company into parts. The Lt. kept repeating the order, but finally the Capt. overhearing it bade me not to mind and silenced our would be 'general.'"[31]

Martindale soon had all three regiments on line. The Twenty-fifth New York went into the position previously occupied by the Second Maine. Roberts "ascertained that the enemy were rapidly advancing on my right through the woods" and informed Martindale, who ordered the Maine men to change front and meet the attack. The Second Maine shifted to their right. Colonel Roberts directed his first company into the position he wished them to take, and ordered the rest of his command to dress on the first company, and his orders were "cooly executed."[32]

One member of the Thirty-seventh North Carolina recalled that they had to move through "a Dence forest in which under growth was so thick that a man could not be seen more than 30 steps." The regiment had moved close to 300 yards, by Colonel Lee's estimate, when it discovered "the enemy behind logs and trees and draw[n] up along a dirt fence just to the right of the 37th and running diagonally to it." The Tar Heels continued to advance through "undergrowth ... so thick, [that] the foe was not seen until within about 15 yards...." Capt. William G. Morris of Company H, recollected in a letter to his wife that

> the 37th Rushed forward with Enthusiasm until it encounted the yankeys who were concelaed behind logs, trees and in the cut of the road way which was boarded by a fence ... heare the enemy had every advantage of position while his force was vastly superior, but Coln Lees men stood like victorious officers & men stood as firm as rocks within 15 or 20 paces of the Yankee line. Volley after volley of grape from their cannon & Minie Balls from there Infantry Mowed Down our men. Still the 37th moved forward Driving the enemy before it...."

Another officer in the regiment, Capt. Moses N. Hart of Company I, left a description equivalent to that of his fellow captain. There was a "strip of woodland separating us—we passed through it and marched up to within thirty yards of the enemy before we discovered them. We then opened on them, which was returned with great vigor, and I suppose, the conflict while it lasted, was as fierce as any during the war."[33]

For men on both sides, Colonel Roberts spoke the truth when he wrote: "muzzle met muzzle, the fight waxing warm." The Federal artillery began to focus its attention on the Thirty-seventh North Carolina. To counter this, "the four right companies of [the Thirty-seventh North Carolina] threw themselves along a cedar fence driving the enemy therefrom, and commenced a crossfire" on the artillerymen. The Eighteenth North Carolina, in the woods on the opposite side, did likewise. This caught the gunners, the Twenty-fifth New York, and portions of the Forty-fourth New York, in a crossfire. Lieutenant Colonel Rice was heard shouting to his command, "Be careful men, be careful men, you are making history." The horse of Colonel Johnston of the Twenty-fifth New York was killed beneath him, felled by four balls. Johnston himself was struck in the thigh, and the regiment's adjutant, Lt. Olivia C. Houghton, was hit in the groin. The crossfire was wreaking havoc on the artillery as well. One infantry soldier observed that one of the two pieces was "silent, the other was working by only two men. One would ram home, and the other fire the piece.... At last, in the act of charging the piece, one fell; the other man took the rammer and sponge, laid it down, and left the gun."[34]

"Pop! pop! Bang! bang! for about an hour," recorded a member of the Forty-fourth New York. Musket fire from the two North Carolina regiments "crossed on the battery, the Twenty-fifth New York and the right of the Forty-fourth New York," recalled General Martindale. The general was posted "65 paces in rear of the left of the Second Maine and right of the Twenty-fifth New York." The Twenty-fifth New York, "seeing that it was impossible to hold such a position," began to fall back. The remnants of the regiment attempted to reform "a few yards to [the] rear, just under the brow of a hill, but having so few men and the fire being so severe," they found the task hopeless. The remainder of the regiment retreated to a "skirt of woods to the right and a little to the rear of the Forty-fourth." Several companies of the Forty-fourth New York also started to falter. One veteran reminisced after the war:

> Lieut. Col. Rice had his horse killed and his sword shot from his side. The colors of the regiment showed the severity of the fight. The Color Sergeant was shot through the head. Corporal James Young of Company F raised the colors twice from

the ground and was twice shot down. Samuel W. Chandler of Company F, who had been wounded in the leg and arm, with wounds bleeding, crept to the flagstaff and with great effort raised it a third time. In a moment he too, was shot in the breast and felled. Frank B. Schutt of Company G then raised it. The flag was pierced by forty bullets.

Maj. E.P. Chapin was struck in the small of the back while bending over one of his wounded soldiers. The regimental adjutant, Edward B. Knox, was struck in the wrist as he was urging on his men. His "arm was extended, when a ball struck him in the wrist, twirling his sword out of his hand and sending it up into the air for several feet." The adjutant retrieved his sword and went to the rear in search of medical aid. After Lieutenant Colonel Rice's favorite mount was killed, he retrieved "his pistols from the holsters of his saddle, and standing on his dead favorite ... emptied his pistols and then dashed down the lines, fearless of the bullets that were whistling about him, cheering on the men...." Another veteran of the regiment recalled that the rifled muskets of the men grew so hot from prolonged firing that water from the men's canteens was used to cool the weapons. Martindale found his line rapidly collapsing. "The smoke was moving toward me," he wrote, "and I could not identify at this time the parties, but there was a rapid and presently a disorderly movement to the rear." Martindale attempted to stop the flow of soldiers, with little success. He found Colonel Stryker falling back, and "concluded that his entire regiment had broken."

> I called to him to rally the men and form them behind the fence on the edge of the woods. For a time my orders were not heeded, but presently the men began to obey my commands, and quite a number came forward from the fence and formed a line on the rising ground in front. Here Captain Gleason, of the Twenty-fifth New York, under my orders, took command of this line. Lieutenant McRoberts, of the Forty-fourth, seeing what I was attempting to do, came to me, saying that he had 10 men with him and awaited my orders. He immediately aided in the formation of the line.

Even as his center collapsed, Martindale's left and right still held: the larger part of the Forty-fourth New York, under their lieutenant colonel, still dueling with the Eighteenth North Carolina, and the Second Maine, in a heated contest with the Thirty-seventh North Carolina. Lieutenant Colonel Rice asked one of his company officers if his command would follow him in a charge. "All of my company will follow you save the dead," was the captain's reply.[35]

Members of the Thirty-seventh North Carolina would fire, drop to the ground, reload, rise, and fire again. The number of the wounded and dead began to mount. Colonel Lee was knocked from his horse by the explosion of a shell. William T. Nicholson, adjutant of the regiment, had his horse killed. Lieutenant Colonel Barber was wounded in the neck, and had his horse struck and killed. Private Andrew Summey, a member of Company H and a Mexican War veteran, was killed. His last child, a daughter, was born six weeks later back in Gaston County, North Carolina. The greatest tragedy fell to the Robnett family of Alexander County. Of the four Robnett brothers in Company G of the Thirty-seventh North Carolina, three, Joel B., John C., and William P., were killed on the field of battle around Peake's Turnout.[36]

The Second Maine was faring little better. "I fire 60 rounds of ammunition," wrote Richard Kelleher of Company G, "and the smoke of battle was so thick and the smell of powder so strong, that it made men almost drunk with excitement." Capt. Frank A. Garnsey believed that "If we had fallen back they would have slaughtered every one of us." Sgt Maj. Charley Ellis had his jaw broken by a musket ball. The hunk of lead took most of his teeth and severed his tongue into three pieces. One member of the regiment recalled a few days after the fight: "Sanborn of our company had part of his hat shot off. He looked up at me with that broad grin on his face, and says—'Lieutenant look at my hat.' Hanson had a bullet pass through the top of his cap.... Johnny Jordan had his gun in front of him, loading it, when a ball struck it just at the muzzle, where it stuck, which saved his life." The supply of ammunition with which the Bangor Regiment had started was beginning to dwindle. According to one anonymous correspondent in the *Bangor Daily Whig and Courier*, "Col. Roberts appealed for a chance to use cold steel if he could not get cold lead." Maj. Daniel Chaplin lost his sword to a Confederate musket ball. In many cases, the living were rummaging among the dead and wounded for extra ammunition. Even General Martindale was wounded, struck in the foot by a spent ball.[37]

General Martindale's plea for reinforcements and the sounds of a pitched battle coming from his rear finally alerted Fitz John Porter to the threat coming from Peake's Turnout. After Butterfield's brigade had driven off Lane's Twenty-eighth North Carolina, Porter ordered Martindale to gather his men and proceed north along the tracks of the Virginia Central Railroad. Porter also ordered Colonel Warren "to push on with his cavalry and destroy the public and private bridges across the Pamunkey east of the railroad." Porter, with his main force, advanced toward Hanover Court House in pursuit of the Twenty-eighth North Carolina and in search of the main body of Confederates. The second brigade, under the command of Col. James McQuade, was within a mile of Hanover Court House when one of Porter's staff officers, Captain Mason, came by and informed the colonel that Martindale was being attacked. Captain Mason went on with the information to Porter, and McQuade halted his regiment and awaited orders. "Shortly afterward I received an order to march back to the assistance of General Martindale," chronicled McQuade in his official report. "The brigade returned left in front, and the regiments formed in column of companies as they successively arrived in the wheat field in rear of Kinney's house." McQuade had led his men through fields, keeping the roads open for artillery. Information then came that two guns of Martin's battery had been captured, and that Martindale's command "was in imminent danger" of collapse.[38]

McQuade "appealed to [his men] to hurry to the support of their comrades, and they obeyed with the utmost alacrity." The first regiment in line was the Fourteenth New York, the regiment that James McQuade had first commanded in May 1861. Lt. Col. Charles H. Skillen, from Rome, New York, succeeded McQuade as regimental commander. McQuade ordered the Fourteenth to disregard excess equipment to speed the regiment's march. The "way overcoats, blankets, ponchos,

&c., were thrown away itself testified to the anxiety of the boys to be on time," recalled a member of the regiment. General Morell arrived and took personal command of the Fourteenth New York. Skillen ordered the regiment to "right-wheel by companies, and then [change] front forward on the sixth company." Colonel Roberts and the Second Maine were overjoyed to see the New Yorkers, and raised a shout in their honor.[39]

Still trudging up the railroad tracks, the Twenty-second Massachusetts also heard "heavy firing" in their rear. The regiment's officers were having trouble with their mounts. Maj. William S. Tilton's horse, General, refused to jump a ditch, and the major was forced to dismount, pass over "the chasm, after which the sagacious animal took the leap." Colonel Gove had problems as well. He had dismounted and turned the reins over to a "boy," when the animal broke away. "The adjutant, being mounted," recalled the regimental historian, "went in pursuit of the runaway. A slave belonging to a neighboring farm caught the horse," before the adjutant arrived. One of the occupants of the farm, a "Miss Kidder engaged" the adjutant "in conversation, asking about our forces, etc., at the same time flirting a handkerchief in a coquettish manner. The adjutant's suspicions being aroused, he cut the interview short ... for in the woods near at hand was a force of the enemy; and no doubt it was Miss Kidder's hope that she might detain him until her friends could come up and capture him." Some of those "friends" alluded to might have been members of the Twenty-eighth North Carolina. Colonel Lane, in his official report, wrote that "We were at one time deceived by the flag of the Twenty-second Massachusetts ... which is nearly white, when our firing ceased, and John A. Abernathy, our regimental hospital steward, volunteered to meet it, and was fired upon by the enemy." But, the regimental historian, Pvt. John L. Parker of Company F, Twenty-second Massachusetts, doubted Lane's remarks, writing in his history that had Abernathy advanced, it would have been with a flag of truce and "no one can be found in the Twenty-second who saw such an attempt." The Twenty-second Massachusetts marched toward their rear and the battlefield they had just come from.[40]

The arrival of fresh Federal soldiers was more than the Thirty-seventh North Carolina could endure. Lee applied to General Branch for instructions, informing the general that his "men had failed to do what they were ordered, that is to take the battery." As Lee conferred with Branch, even more Federal regiments arrived and went into position on the Thirty-seventh North Carolina's left. The Sixty-second Pennsylvania came next, and "entered the woods about 150 yards from the front and [took] the enemy on the flank." Colonel McQuade rode back to find his third regiment, the Ninth Massachusetts, under the command of Col. Thomas Cass. McQuade informed Cass that "the enemy has taken two piece of Martin's battery, and I want the Ninth Massachusetts to retake them, which I know they can and will." Cass deployed his regiment into a line of battle, passed along the instructions of McQuade, and ordered his soldiers forward. J.P. Harley, of Company D, Fourth Michigan, recalled that they started off at the double-quick. He estimated the distance he had to cover was six miles. "I must say," he wrote to *The National*

Tribune, that I was entirely out of breath when we got there, so tired I could hardly stand on my feet." Their sister regiment, the Ninth Massachusetts, gave

> A loud and vigorous cheer ... and a bold dash made into and through the woods by my command. For some time not a shot was fired by them. Every eye seemed distended to catch a glimpse of the retiring foe in some direction. Prisoners of war were captured in fives, tens, and twenties. Onward heroically and determinedly the boys of the Ninth pushed their way, notwithstanding a long and fatiguing march from early in the morning, it then being about 5 o'clock. Our charge was over felled trees, through brush and tangled brambles, swamps such as Virginia produces....

Battery D, Fifth United States Artillery also returned and went into position about 1,000 yards from the Confederates.[41]

More Federal regiments arrived. The Fifth New York, Duryea's Zouaves, also reached the field. The Zouaves had been hampered earlier in the morning by having to stop and replace a bridge. They too were almost at the courthouse when a

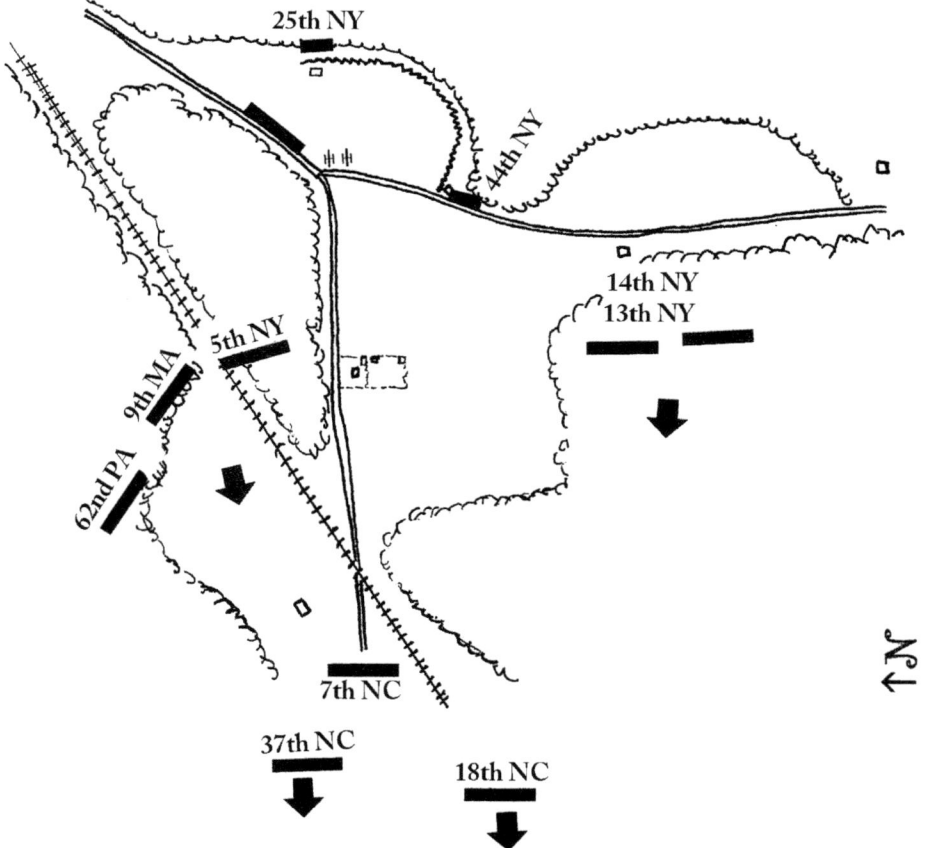

Federal reenforcements arrive, forcing the Eighteenth and Thirty-seventh North Carolina to retreat. The Seventh North Carolina covers their withdrawal.

member of Porter's staff informed Lt. Col. Abram Duryea, a New York-born merchant, of the battle in the rear. The regiment "faced about and hurried back" toward the sounds of battle. Some of the Zouaves were overcome by sunstroke, but the regiment continued ahead at the "double-quick." Likewise, the Thirteenth New York, which had proceeded along past the Cary house, received orders to march back toward the firing in their rear. According to one veteran, the regiment did not even countermarch, but simply about-faced and proceed at the double-quick. "By the time we reached Dr. Kinney's I felt like the broadside of a barn with an ache all over," recalled one veteran many years later. Once they reached the Kinney home, the regiment deployed into a line of battle and continued to advance into a clover field. "The clover, about knee-high, in a large field near Dr. Kinney's," recollected the same veteran, "came near to finishing all of us. It was wet and clung to our feet and legs, tripping many a soldier, and it was only by the utmost exertion that we succeeded in 'double-quicking.' We were hardly able to walk."[42]

"For two hours," General Branch wrote, "cavalry pickets had been coming in from the Ashcake road reporting a heavy force of the enemy passing around right by that road, and Col. B.H. Robertson, of the Virginia cavalry, who was near Hanover Court House, had sent me repeated messages to the effect that a heavy body from that direction was threatening my line of retreat." Brig. Gen. Charles W. Field was close by with two brigades. He sent Branch a note via a courier, asking Branch if he needed reinforcements. Branch replied that he "was engaged with the enemy in two places, did not know his strength, but would like to get all the aid" possible. No reinforcements ever arrived to support Branch and his embattled brigade. A member of the Thirty-eighth North Carolina recalled that he and his comrades were "in hearing of the Hanover Court House fight, but were not ordered to participate, and consequently are entitled to none of the laurels, won or lost, on that bloody field." Dismayed, Branch ordered his wounded men and small wagon train back to Ashland. Bob Turpin, Robert Hardeman, and two other members of the Forty-fifth Georgia were in charge of the wagons for that regiment. At one point, "the going was so rough and the enemy so close [that they] took out the mules and left the wagons stuck in the mud, and went on galloping toward Ashland knee deep in mud, a motley crowd, hungry, cold and tired."[43]

Many of the wounded were carried to various establishments set up as field hospitals, possibly to Lebanon Methodist Church and Slash Christian Church. John Shaffner, surgeon for the Thirty-third North Carolina troops, was ordered by Branch to move all the wounded who could be moved to Ashland. Shaffner rode to the brigade field hospital and informed the brigade surgeon of Branch's instructions. "Surgeon Miller ... most disgracefully mounted his horse, as did two other surgeons, and left the wounded, ambulances, instruments and supplies lying unprotected in the yard." Shaffner got off his horse, loaded the wagons with medical supplies and "whatever was of value," along with 30 of the wounded soldiers, and sent them toward Ashland.[44]

With the Fourteenth New York and Second Maine in the front, and the Ninth Massachusetts and Sixty-second Pennsylvania on the left flank, the Thirty-seventh

North Carolina quickly retired from the field. Major Hickerson gave his horse to Lieutenant Colonel Barber, and Lee had to "give the order [to retreat] separately to each Company...." One member of the regiment recalled that he did "not see a single man move faster than a slow walk. They were exhausted and worn out by the fight.... Not a man flinched from his duty." Two companies of the regiment, A and F, did not hear the orders to retire, and fought on for an additional 10 minutes before being compelled to retire. The Thirteenth New York arrived and went into position to the rear of the Forty-fourth New York, to the left of the abandoned artillery pieces. The Fifth New York and the First Connecticut also arrived. "General Butterfield came dashing up in front the Fifth as they were going on the double-quick in line of battle, battalion front, for the woods," recorded Alfred Davenport of Company G, Fifth New York. "He took off his cap and waved it about his head and said: 'Go in, boys! and I'll see you supported!'" The Zouaves entered the woods "with a Zouave cheer. The sulphurous smoke hung so thick that it was impossible to see any distance." The Fifth New York "advanced through the woods, stepping over the Union and Confederate dead and wounded, who lay thick, and out of the woods to the Ashland road; down the road to the railroad cut, and after some difficulty, climbed up the bank and advanced over an open field." Despite the efforts of the Zouaves, the Confederates "reached the cover of a wood the other side of the field in full retreat, and the men could not get at them."[45]

As the Thirteenth New York passed General Martindale, they gave him "three cheers and a tiger" and proceeded toward the far left of the Federal line. They deployed in a line of battle to the rear of the drained Forty-fourth New York. Colonel Marshall sent skirmishers out, and then the remainder of the regiment advanced, forcing the exhausted Eighteenth North Carolina from their position. The soldiers in the Eighteenth North Carolina held only praise for their officers during the ordeal. Pvt. William J.H. Bellamy, wrote in his diary: "We went in battle knowing that we had a patriot soldier & gallant leader ... to lead us through the Battle. We trusted in him [Colonel Cowan] as a God. Through the whole engagement he displayed great coolness & fortitude, did not stand by idly looking on, but emptied time after time the well put in load from his Navy repeater." The Thirteenth New York crossed "a plowed lot and through a small piece of woods, then into a corn field" in pursuit of their foe.[46]

Also coming toward the sounds of the last engagement of the day were elements of Butterfield's brigade. The Eighty-third Pennsylvania and the Sixteenth Michigan were near town, having stopped near the Railroad depot "in the open field of a country inn," when they heard the firing in their rear. After receiving orders from General Porter, these two regiments moved down the railroad tracks towards the sound of the fighting, the Pennsylvanians in the lead. The men followed the tracks for a mile; then Col. John W. McLane, skirmishers to his front, led his men into the woods which contained a deep ravine that came out of the woods not far from the Federal line. The Pennsylvanians halted to catch their breath and to reform their ranks. The regiment's skirmishers advanced a little farther and came into contact with Confederates in the woods. The Eighty-third Pennsylvania passed through a Federal battery, formed to the right of the Ashcake road, and advanced toward the railroad. After crossing over the tracks, the Confederates fired at the Federals, causing them to drop to the ground. McLane ordered his men to return fire while in the prone position.[47]

General Branch had held the Seventh North Carolina, under Col. Reuben P. Campbell, in reserve to cover the retreat of his other forces. Some would later criticize the general for not using all of his available force to assail the Federal lines, but at this point in the daylong engagement, Branch's decision made perfect sense. As the Thirteenth New York came out of the woods and into the wheat field "that came nearly to our knees,"

> On the opposite side of this field was a ... fence, paralled to our front, and less than 100 yards away; upon our right, with an interval of cleared country between timber, and timber upon our left and left front. Towards our right front ... the country was open; and at a distance of from one half to three-fourths of a mile away stood a house from which floated a yellow flag.... It was the Confederate hospital. As we came into the wheat-field referred to, the sun, which was getting well-down in the west, dazzled our eyes; but we, nevertheless discovered a body of men — we saw the colors of two regiments— marching by the flank across our front from right to left, behind and partly concealed by the fence enclosing the wheat. We could not exactly make out whether they were friends or enemies, owing to the fence and trees and bushes growing along it, and several of us sang out to our own color-bearer: "Shake her out, Jack!" (The flags had been furled on the march), "shake her out, and let's see who they are."

Branch positioned the Seventh North Carolina across the road after the Eighteenth and Thirty-seventh North Carolina had passed, and the two remaining guns of Latham's battery, which failed to get into position for the second attack, had passed. "The flag was given to the slight breeze that prevailed," recorded one of the New Yorkers across the field, "and as its folds gently spread out, aided by the swaying of the hands that held it, the passing column halted, coming to a front by a 'left-face,' and before we had scarcely time to think, delivered a tremendous volley full at us. But as we saw the movement of leveling the muskets every man of us dropped to earth, and the storm of lead passed harmlessly over our heads."[48]

"A cautious attempt was made by the enemy to follow," Branch recorded in his official report, "but a single volley from the rear guard of the Seventh North Carolina arrested it." The official reports of the Federal commanders, particularly that of Colonel Cass of the Ninth Massachusetts and Colonel Marshall of the Thirteenth New York, tell a different story. "They poured at us a scorching and heavy fire, flying over and around us in a perfect torrent.... Having cleared the railroad, a solid front is again presented to the enemy. Another dash at right-shoulder shift arms is made toward him, when he precipitately fled, closely pursued by the two companies deployed as skirmishers," Colonel Cass chronicled. During the pursuit, Company G's Sgt. Daniel J. Regan was mortally wounded. The regiment's Irish banner was "pierced by eight buck-and-ball shots and the lower tie torn away." Colonel Marshall's New Yorkers dealt as much destruction:

Then kneeling, with our caps pulled low to shut out the glare of the sun, we opened by volley, and then kept it up as rapidly as possible, each doing his best. The enemy shot wildly, whereas, judging from the way the splinters flew from the fence and the confusion in their ranks, the heavy 58-caliber of our Remingtons was rapidly making their position too uncomfortable to hold. After perhaps twenty-minutes they began to waver, and we were ordered to charge. Ahead we went but they did not await our coming. Away they flew to the rear, a majority of them seeking the friendly shadows of the woods adjacent.

Darkness and the exhaustion of the combatants, more than the volley of the Seventh North Carolina or the charge of the Ninth Massachusetts or the Thirteenth New York, brought about the close of hostilities.[49]

The vanquished Confederates had a long, cold hike back to Ashland. For the victorious Federals, many simply dropped where they were and went to sleep — the adrenalin that had carried them through the day gone. Many of the Federal surgeons were busy throughout the night, operating on the wounded, Union and Confederate alike. One gravely wounded Federal, as his commanding officer passed close by, called the officer by name. Lieutenant Colonel Rice "paused and stooped over to hear some dying request to a fond mother or sister, but all he said was this: 'Colonel, is the day ours?' "Yes,' I replied. 'Then I am willing to dye.'"[50]

"Night closed in," wrote Pvt. Oliver W. Norton, of the Eighty-third Pennsylvania, to his brother and sister, "and we went back to our blankets and, wrapping up, lay down between the rows of corn to sleep. Generals and privates alike spent the night on the ground."[51]

6

"Every Room a Sickening Contrast to the Splendid Furniture": Hospitals

A member of Battery C, First Rhode Island Light Artillery, chronicled in his diary the "sickening" sight of the battlefield after the contest had concluded. He wrote: "Youth and mature age, dead and wounded, lay thickly mingled, and many a poor fellow breathed out the little remnant of life there, before the hand of humanity could be stretched out to seal his glazed eyes, or the voice of sympathy inquire his last wishes." For many Confederate and Union soldiers, the battle left more than psychological strain and physical exhaustion. Many would carry the visible scars of the engagement forever. The care of wounded soldiers was still in its infancy at this stage of the war, with the larger campaigns still looming on the horizon.[1]

Within the ranks of each Union and Confederate regiment were a surgeon and an assistant surgeon. Many of these surgeons were doctors prior to the war, but the medicine practiced by a country doctor or even his urban counterpart, did nothing to prepare these men for the horrors attendant upon combat surgery. At the commencement of a battle, the regimental surgeon established a hospital behind the lines and prepared for the arrival of the wounded. Sometimes, surgeons from the different regiments in a brigade pooled their resources and established a brigade hospital. The purpose of these hospitals was to stabilize the wounded, dress wounds, and perform surgery in an effort to save the wounded soldiers' lives.

One Federal surgeon, writing many years after the war, provided an adequate summary of the limitations of the knowledge of surgeons in both armies. "We operated in old blood-stained and often pus-stained coats," wrote the old surgeon:

> the veterans of a hundred fights.... We used undisinfected instruments from undisinfected plush-lined cases, and still worse, used marine sponges which had been used in prior pus cases and had been only washed in tap water. If a sponge or an instrument fell on the floor it was washed and squeezed into a basin of tap water and used as if it were clean. Our silk to tie blood vessels was undisinfected.... The silk with which we sewed up all the wounds was undisinfected. If there was any difficulty in threading the needle we moistened it with ... bacteria-laden saliva, and rolled it between bacteria-infected fingers. We dressed the wounds with clean but undisin-

fected sheets, shirts, tablecloths, or other old soft linen rescued from the family ragbag. We had no sterilized gauze dressing, no gauze sponges.... We knew nothing about antiseptics and therefore used none.²

When the onset of combat became imminent, surgeons began to cast about for suitable locations for their field hospitals. Often, local cabins and houses, along with their outbuildings, including barns, became front-line trauma centers. At other times, mere clearings were used. Dr. Robert Gibbon, surgeon for the Twenty-eighth North Carolina, established his field hospital near a branch, about 200 yards from Dr. Kinney's home. During the hostilities at Hanover Court House and Peake's Turnout, many structures were appropriated to treat the wounded.

After the battle was over, the home of Dr. Thomas H. Kinney was pressed into medical service, and the medical officers of the Twenty-eighth were ordered to move their wounded into the structure. The Kinney house was witness to the first phase of the battle as the Twenty-eighth North Carolina struggled with both the Twenty-fifth New York and later the regiments of Butterfield's brigade. Other local structures, such as the unfortunately named Slaughter House and the Harris House, were also used.³

Once the surgeon established his "headquarters," he sometimes raised a flag to denote the purpose of the structure. Pvt. David H. Grows of the Fifth Massachusetts Light Artillery confided in his journal of seeing such a flag. As his battery "pushed ahead ... in a short time [we] came in sight of a house with a red flag. It was a hospital for the sick and wounded. In passing it I saw some wounded being carried in." Another Federal soldier, a member of the Thirteenth New York, recalled seeing a yellow flag floating above a Confederate hospital.⁴

After selecting a site for the hospital and marking it as such, the surgeon and his staff set to work. Tables for surgery were erected. While some portable tables were available, often any level surface would suffice, and dinner tables or doors placed on sawhorses were frequently employed. Scalpels, tourniquets, probes, forceps, and surgical kits containing amputation saws were readied for use. Most surgeons also carried chests, or medical panniers, full of bottles of medicine to help with the treatment of the wounded, as well as bandages, ichthyocolla plaster, and pins. Fires were built and pots were hung, to either boil sponges or prepare coffee or soup. If straw was available, it was strewn about the floor to soak up the blood. Food was also prepared for the incoming wounded. After the collapse of the Confederate line late in the day on May 27, Federal soldiers found, near the Confederate field hospital site, that their enemies "had evidently been preparing dinner. Fires were burning, cups of water steaming, hard-tack, meal, and bacon lay scattered about, and in one instance a dish of batter...."⁵

Even properly marked field hospitals sometimes came under fire. General Branch, in his report of the battle, was dismayed that his field hospital was the subject of artillery fire. One Federal soldier recalled that late in the day of the battle, while the Seventh North Carolina was protecting the retreat of fellow Confederates, that Griffin's battery "was giving the rebels shell as fast as two pieces could be worked...." The Confederate hospital would have been close to the position of the covering Confederate force. "My senior surgeon established his hospital in a house on which the hospital flag was conspicuously displayed," Branch wrote. "It was not in nor near the line of fire. I saw many shells thrown by the enemy explode immediately over and around the house. It could not have been undesigned."[6]

At the commencement of a battle, the assistant surgeons and members of the infirmary corps, or stretcher-bearers, generally went to the front lines and established a location for a front-line trauma station. At times, the assistant surgeon circulated among the front-line troops. The assistant surgeon usually carried "a pocket case of instruments, ligatures, needles, pins, chloroform, morphine, alcoholic stimulants, tourniquets, bandages, lint, and splints." Assistant surgeons preformed triage: they evaluated the condition of wounded men, applied bandages, plasters, splints, and stimulants; oversaw the transportation of the severely wounded; and in critical cases performed surgical procedures. Once the battle began, those with wounds who were still able to walk or hobble, made their way to these triage stations, while the seriously wounded were brought by either the infirmary corps or their friends, even though regulations forbade the latter. At times it might take one to four men to carry a wounded comrade to the rear, thus depriving the regiment of effectives on the firing line. The slightly wounded were treated, and sometimes sent back to their regiments. The more serious cases were loaded onto ambulances or placed into wagons and transported back to the recently established hospitals. On arrival, the wounded were examined, with the most serious taken to the operating tables, while others were placed on the ground to await their turns.[7]

Surgeons performed a variety of tasks: ligatures of arteries, resections of bone, adjustments to and permanent repairs of fractures, and amputations. The surgeons, often with their sleeves rolled up and besmeared with blood, then probed the wounds, looking for the projectile or cleaning out bits of debris: dirt, leaves, or pieces of uniforms and shirts. Given that the muskets and rifled muskets of the time period fired a large, soft lead slug at a low velocity, the arm or leg bones that were struck were easily shattered or splintered. If the ball or bullet continued through the body, the deformed piece of lead created massive tissue devastation, and the size of the exit wound was out of proportion to the original diameter of the projectile. There was little hope for these mangled limbs, and common practice of the day held that the amputation of these limbs must be performed within 24 hours. If chloroform, ether, morphine, whiskey, or opium pills were available, they were given to the stricken soldier before the operation. Often times surgeons ran out of these staples or were unable to acquire adequate supplies, and the surgery was performed with attendants holding the patient down. After finishing the operation, the surgeon would wipe off his instruments and call for the next patient. Dr. Gibbon of the Twenty-eighth recalled amputating a couple of legs and setting four or five broken bones in his position beside the creek.[8]

Homes, cabins, barns, and tents quickly became spectacles of near-incomprehensible gore. At the Kinney house and outbuildings, a war correspondent painted this picture: "The floors were littered with cornshucks and fodder, and the maimed, gashed, and dying lay confusedly together ... these poor fellows were frightfully convulsed, breaking into shrieks and shouts, some of them iterated a single word, as 'Doctor!' or 'Help!' or 'Oh!' Commencing with a loud spasmodic cry, and continuing the same word till it died away in sighs." The Eighty-third Pennsylvania's Capt. Henry Austin, of Company K, wrote home on June 12, "The hospital is a dreadful sight. The one we are using is stained with blood; through every room a sickening contrast to the splendid furniture.... Out on the piazza in front the surgeons are very busy at work taking off limbs of our poor fellows." Fellow Company K member Egbert Hulbert was one of those amputees. He was shot in the ankle which necessitated the removal of his leg below the knee. Federal surgeons not only used the bone saw on their own men, but on the wounded Confederates as well. Pvt. Jacob M. Pigford of Company E, Eighteenth North Carolina Troops, was wounded multiple times, including a "compound, comminuted fracture of right leg," a leg that was removed below the knee. The same happened to fellow Eighteenth members Bunyan Stansel and Samuel King.[9]

Many of those wounded Confederate and Federal soldiers were brought to the field hospitals by ambulance. These came in both two-wheeled and four-wheeled models, and often, simple wagons were used when other types of ambulances were not available. A member of the Thirteenth New York, encamped near one of the field hospitals, recalled in a letter to his hometown newspaper: "Our ambulances were at work all night bringing in the wounded...." Maj. Charles S. Tripler, medical director for the Army of the Potomac, upon hearing of the battle, dispatched ambulances to bring the wounded Union soldiers and Confederate prisoners back to the main army. Tripler recorded that 123 wounded prisoners were under his care. For these prisoners, Tripler prepared the "William Gaines and Hogan houses and outhouses." The buildings on the Hogan property soon came under fire and Tripler ordered the Confederate wounded transferred to the Gaines property.[10]

When it came time for Porter to move his command back toward the main Federal forces, the wounded were loaded back upon the ambulances and driven to the rear. The wounded men were then placed in hospitals in the rear of the Federal lines, or were loaded upon transports and taken by sea north. A surgeon in the Nineteenth Massachusetts Volunteers, of the II Corps, chronicled in his diary on May 30, "Near Beaver Dam Creek.... A train of ambulances has just passed containing wounded from the fight day before yesterday at Hanover. Several hundred prisoners passed yesterday." One Federal soldier, belonging to the Twenty-fifth New York, was tormented with the treatment of the his wounded comrades. "Most of our wounded men have been sent to White House, the rest, that is, those too heavily wounded, are left here; but in what condition[?]" he wrote to the *New York Sunday Mercury*. "The arrangements are awful. The idea of a hard biscuit being offered to a wounded man with pallid cheek, looks rather wanting...."[11]

One of the biggest concerns for the wounded was the contraction of diseases. In the 1860s microorganisms, or bacteria, were not associated with infections. The unsterilized silk, linen, or cotton used to stitch up wounds carried infections, along with the unsterilized surgical instruments that were used upon an uninterrupted series of patients. Numerous diseases were contracted, including gangrene, which was almost always fatal. Some soldiers lingered in hospital wards for months before dying of the wounds they received during the battles of Hanover Court House and Peake's Turnout.

Clear cases of post-traumatic stress disorder during the Civil War rarely find their way into medical reports and letters home. The disorder would not be officially recognized for decades to come. Nevertheless, it was definitely present during the war. Following the battle of Hanover Court House, Maj. Edwin S. Gilbert of the Twenty-fifth New York, now in command of his regiment, provides such a glimpse. His letter home, most likely written on the morning of May 31, was printed in the *Rochester* (New York) *Democrat and American*. Gilbert's missive gives details of the role the Twenty-fifth New York played in the battle and outlines the deaths and wounds of higher-ranking members of the field and staff. Toward the end of his letter, Gilbert writes: "No man can describe his feelings as he walks over a fresh battlefield. It is terrible and the sight haunts one for many days— The Lord deliver me from another such sight." Another soldier, a member of the Eighty-third Pennsylvania, confided in a letter home: "I have seen many hard sights within the last 24 hours, to see the horrors of war you must see a battle field.... I have felt the uncertainty of life to-day, looking upon the mangled dead as they lay in rows upon the field."[12]

For all of the pain and anguish the wounded had to endure, it was often those still living who had a great burden of grief to bear. It would fall upon the captains, colonels, and chaplains to inform the loved ones at home of the deaths of their sons and husbands. Chaplain John F. Mines, of the Second Maine, had to write one such letter on May 31, 1862.

> Mrs. Abigal L. Pollard—
>
> Dear Madame—The telegraph report of the battle near Hanover, on the 27th, has probably made known to you the fact that your dear husband was severely wounded during the battle; and it becomes now my sad duty to inform you of his [death] on the night of the 28th. A brave soldier—a good man—a kind comrade—he has fallen asleep in the Lord. He rests on the field of battle and of victory—but his memory remains with us who knew him well, and saddens the joy of this hour of victory.
>
> From my heart, my dear madame, I sympathize with you in your bereavement. I well know how much he thought of his home—of his wife and child—for during his long imprisonment in Richmond, he had anxiety for them than for himself. The blow will fall very, very heavily on you—and what can I say except, "Lift up your hearts unto the Lord!" He is the Father of the fatherless, and comforteth the widow, and with an everlasting comfort he healeth the sufferings of those who are afflicted. Look unto him—look to that heavenly place where He had called your husband—and then, when the earth seems desolate, you can and yes you *will* find refuge from your sorrows.
>
> Your husband died nobly, for he fell with his face to the enemy; and he counted his life nothing, for his country's sake. It was a great deal for him to do so, when

he had been wounded, and had experienced the horrors of a long imprisonment, to enter the field for a second time. His comrades all appreciated it; and his officers, every one of them, speak of him as a courageous soldier, and one who did his duty *everywhere*, in camp and in field, like a man and a Christian. Quiet and unassuming among his companions, he was held as a man before the enemy. "Death loves a shining mark," is the old saying, and this time the Destroyer has taken away some of the very best of our soldiers.

The little testament that was your husband's constant companion, I will send you by mail — It bears the mark of constant use, and will no doubt be prized by you beyond measure.

Your husband is buried on the field of battle, near the hospital in which he died. The grave has been marked with his name, regiment, &c. I was with him, and ministered to him until near his last moments.

Praying that God will mercifully heal your sorrows, and comfort yourself and your little one in this dark hour,

I am, Faithfully,

Your servant for Christ's sake,

John F. Mines.[13]

7

"Morning Came, and Stiff and Sore We Rose": The Day After

"On the morning of the 28th," recorded a soldier of the Fifth New York, "when the men awoke, some of them found that they were lying among the dead; it was after dark when they laid down the previous night, and what they supposed were soldiers sleeping with blankets over them, were dead men." For the Federals encamped in and around Hanover Court House and Peake's Turnout, May 28 was spent in the retrieval of the wounded, the burial of the dead, the pursuit of the Confederates, and the transfer of Confederate prisoners of war.[1]

Daylight brought the resumption of the search and recovery of wounded soldiers. The Eighteenth Massachusetts, a regiment belonging to Martindale's brigade, had been on picket duty the morning that the Federal forces advanced toward Hanover Court House. After a few hours' rest, the regiment followed the rest of the V Corps, picking their way along the decimated roads, only to catch up with their comrades as darkness brought a close to the day's hostilities. While some Federal regiments were sent to pursue the Confederates, the Eighteenth Massachusetts was ordered to comb the battlefield for discarded weapons and war materials, "bring in the wounded," and "to bury the dead of both armies," work that no soldier enjoyed. Thomas H. Mann of the Eighteenth, recalled in a letter home on May 31, that "two or three wagon loads of muskets, equipment, etc.," were forwarded to the Federal lines.[2]

Confederate and Union soldiers lay in heaps and by themselves all over the fields and woods where the two opposing forces had been engaged. Lewis Bramer, Jr., a member of the regimental band of the Twelfth New York, did not arrive on the field until dark on May 27. The following morning, he "got up ... before day light and went to the fire and got warm." Bramer then "went down to the spring to get some water and near the spring lay a rebel with the top of his head taken off by a rifled cannon shot. Close to where I lay last night was another with a piece of a shell through his breast and they [soldiers] were scattered all over the ground." Oliver Norton also provided a glimpse of the day's grisly task. "Morning came, and stiff and sore we rose," he wrote to his brother and sister on June 2:

> The work of collecting and burying the dead soon commenced. The woods were full of dead rebels who lay, as they fell, in all shapes. They were all carried out and laid in a ghastly row on the grass. One fine looking young man was shot through the heart as he was loading his gun. His hands had not changed their position, one extended above his head drawing his rammer and the other grasping his gun by his side. His eyes were open and the expression of his countenance as calm as though he was sleeping, but the fearful wound in his breast told that he would never wake on earth again. We buried over one hundred of them.

The dead of the Twenty-fifth and Forty-fourth New York were buried together, their names marked "on pieces of rude boards." David H. Grows of the Fifth Massachusetts Battery likewise described the dead Confederates, most likely seeing some of the same soldiers that Norton described. "The dead rebels were lying in every position and posture," confided Grows in his journal, "some with hand extended as though they were using a gun, others drawn up as though they died in great distress, among them a boy not more than 14 years old."[3]

Details of the Fifth and Fourteenth New York Regiments were also given the lurid task of burying the Confederate dead. David M. Perry of the Fourteenth recalled in a letter home that May 28 was "devoted to burying our own and the rebel dead. A large ditch was dug, and in it they were placed and covered up, with nothing to mark their last resting place...." After the war, one member of the Fifth regiment recalled that "Trenches were dug large enough to hold twenty-five." The 25 Confederates that the New Yorkers buried were interred "as decently as their circumstances would allow. They were all placed in a single trench with an orderly sergeant at their head, the post he occupied when alive; at each corner of the plot they placed stakes, and at one end of it, cut on the trunk of a tree, '25 N.C. X killed.'" A Confederate prisoner, observing the Zouaves, confided in a letter home that he had seen the large trench the Federal soldiers had dug. This North Carolina officer wrote that "the N.Y. Zouaves were busy pillaging [the dead Confederates'] pockets after money, pocket knives and other little tricks. I felt sorry for these poor men far from home and friends."[4]

Those regiments not detailed to follow the retreating Confederates pitched camp. "Here we made ourselves as comfortable as possible by building bough shades," recalled a member of the Thirteenth New York, who pitched camp across from a hospital and General Porter's headquarters. The Eighty-third Pennsylvania moved into "a clover field," and began to search for food. "The men ... were permitted to go out foraging, and they came back loaded with pigs, turkeys and fowls, together with several demijohns of good liquor captured from the cellars of the fleeing inhabitants." Another member of the regiment recalled that General Porter "gave permission to slay and eat, and, if an army ever made havoc with an enemy's provisions, we did. We killed all the beef, pork, veal, mutton and poultry we could eat and carry away." Still yet another member of the Pennsylvania Regiment, whose letter eventually found its way into print in the *Erie Weekly Gazette,* painted this picture: "I will give you a bill of supplies our Regiment are having today: beef, pork, mutton, potatoes, flour, meal, sugar, salt, onions, honey, chickens, turkeys, guinea-hens, tobacco, bagging,

7. *"Morning Came, and Stiff and Sore We Rose"* 101

Brig. Gen. Fitz John Porter and staff in camp (courtesy the Library of Congress).

whisky, wine, pickled cherries, strawberries, boquets, &c., a little of everything in the cooking utensil department." A soldier of the Eighteenth Massachusetts "went into a house owned by an old woman, for the purpose of buying sweet potatoes, for which she asked me the modest sum of $3 per bushel. I purchased a half bushel and paid $1 in money and gave her a pound of coffee for the balance."[5]

Many of the Federals were able to freely loot a locomotive that was captured the day before. Luther C. Furst, a member of the signal corps, chronicled in his diary, we "captured one train of cars loaded with tobacco, meal, sugar, etc."[6]

Having won the battle, Federal soldiers were able to freely look for prizes. Lt. Charles A. Phillips wrote home on the evening of May 28, recounting the battle of the day before and his activities of the 28th. He wrote that he and his comrades had "been skylarking round doing nothing in particular." A fellow member of the Fifth Massachusetts Battery scribbled in his diary: "Picked up several trophies, such as cartridge boxes, belts, &c." One member of the Eighty-third Pennsylvania wrote that "*Secesh* knapsacks were scattered everywhere, and our boys, if they could have carried away the things, would have got a good many comforts, but we could not. We got a good many love letters, etc., bowie knives and pistols ... I send you a letter that I got in a knapsack and a *secesh* stamp." Another member of the same regiment, Alexander May, wished that his relatives back in Pennsylvania could "read some of the letters that was taken from the rebs out to Hanover that their sweethearts have written them ... such loving talk you never heard or read of." Signal corps member Furst recalled finding "nothing of value" in the Confederate knapsacks, "except some tobacco, old letters, etc. Some of our men who were opening the knapsacks, when coming across a clean shirt, would throw off theirs & put it on." Writing after the war, a veteran of the Eighty-third Pennsylvania, "J.S.S.," recalled that his regiment came upon the "well-filled knapsacks" of two North Carolina regiments, the Eighteenth and the Thirty-seventh. This soldier and his comrades, had "fine pickings ... I secured a full and elegant dress suit, with 'biled' shirts, collars and cuffs, two pair of silk stockings—what a dandy he must have been— besides a villainous-looking bowie-knife with a blade about eleven inches in length...." Still yet another Federal soldier, this one an anonymous member of the Twenty-second Massachusetts, wrote to the *North Bridgewater Gazette* about the captured Confederate correspondence:

> Mr. L found in the abandoned rebel camp two letters from a wife of a North Carolina soldier. In one, dated April 28, the writer thanks her husband for ten dollars received from him, and adds—"I had rather see you than the money, but I know I cannot, and if you were home you could not stay, for they are going to carry off all men under thirty-five." In another, on May 2, she says she is in great trouble on account of her neighbors children having been brought home dead, and not knowing how soon a like event may happen to herself. She wants to know how it is that her husband's officers were allowed to have a discharge at the close of twelve months for which they enlisted. While the privates could not even get a furlough home or a few days. She says she has done the planting, and the times are hard.

Confederate letters seemed to hold a certain fascination for the Union soldiers picking up souvenirs of battle. A member of the Twenty-fifth New York wrote to his mother: "This is rebel ink that I am writing with. I will enclose you a letter that was written by one of the North Carolina rebels to his father the day before the battle, but he did not have time to send it away. I found it in his knapsack." Members of the Thirteenth New York apparently went even further than their comrades. One soldier recalled that after the Confederates were forced to abandon their knapsacks, "our boys had the pleasure of putting on airs in complete suits of rebel underclothes, shawls and blankets, and in some cases sported watches and other jewelry left by the flying fugitives."[7]

While rummaging through the abandoned Confederate camps, several Federal soldiers were able to pick up the most prized battlefield finds: Confederate flags. Pvt. Michael Kane, of Company E, Ninth Massachusetts came away with the flag of Company E, Twelfth North Carolina. The flag was of white silk, with a white stripe that bore the words "Cleveland Guards." Colonel Cass sent the flag to Boston, where it was received on June 3 at City Hall. On their return from the pursuit of the Confederate soldiers on the evening of May 28, a member of the Second Massachusetts Sharpshooters "picked up a tent that was rolled up, with a view to have a shelter that night." Much to the dismay of the soldier, his commanding officer ordered him to leave it behind. Two members of the regimental band came along, and picked up the canvas. That evening, when they unrolled it, they discovered "a rebel regimental flag, on the white bar of which was wrought 'McCowan Guards.'" This flag belonged to Company D, Forty-fifth Georgia. Lt. Robert Dillingham, of the Fifth Massachusetts Artillery, also captured a "Secesh" tent, "almost new," but he and his comrades did not find a flag rolled up in theirs.[8]

Scores of Confederates woke up on the morning of May 28, 1862, as prisoners of war. Many of these prisoners were members of the Twenty-eighth North Carolina. After his capture, Capt. William H.A. Speer was marched back toward the Kinney farm. "It was now dark," Captain Speer wrote,

> but, O! how the place was changed. The enemy was camped in every direction with all the implements of war and [I] wonder how it was that we had escaped as long as we did or how it was that any of the Regt. was not all taken or killed.... The privates were marched to the stables where they had other prisoners & put under strong guards. I was taken with some other officers to Genl. Butterfield where I was asked several questions as to the fight. [I was asked] about the Union sentiment in N.C., all of which I had some fun in answering. I was paroled & sent over to Col. Lancing's quarters.

When Speer reached the headquarters of the Seventeenth New York, he found other officers of the Twenty-eighth North Carolina who had been captured, including Maj. Samuel D. Lowe and Lt. Neal Bohannon of Company I. Speer recalled:

> I passed a retched night upon the cold wet ground. A little oil cloth under me was all I had to keep me off the wet ground & mud. I had nothing to cover with. I was very cold that night, having sweated myself nearly to death ... I was so tired my limbs ached, so I could not sleep. I longed to see day come. I went to the sentinel fire in the night to warm. The moon was then in full blaze & the whole field was covered with the sleeping soldiers, horses, cannon, & ambulances.

Another of Speer's comrades in the Twenty-eighth North Carolina, Jonas Cloninger, made the same observations. He was taken back to the battleground where he "lay all night [and] the cold wet ground was our bed an the Cloudy heavens our cover...."[9]

Not all of the Confederates were captured. Robert Gibbon, the surgeon of the Twenty-eighth North Carolina, after stabilizing the wounded of his regiment, looked for further wounded. He was soon informed by an assistant that the Federals were sending an ambulance to move his wounded from their field hospital beside the branch to the Kinney home. Gibbon had talked to no Federal officer, but returned to his hospital and

> began to consider he had done all he could for the wounded ... so he ... sat down for a few moments to cool off; when picking up his coat, without consultation, quietly walked up the branch to the neighboring woods, where he concealed himself until night, listening in the meanwhile to the fight between the balance of Gen. Branch's brigade and the Federals, which continued till sundown, our force falling back gradually to Ashland, some six miles. The next day the Doctor joined his regiment after walking all night through swamps and woods to avoid the enemy's camps and pickets. He then recovered his horse and servant who had joined the cavalry with the prisoners.[10]

General Porter promptly sent out Federal troops in all directions on the morning of May 28. At 10:00 a.m., Colonel Gove and his Twenty-second Massachusetts, along with a company of the Sixth Pennsylvania Cavalry under the command of Henry P. Muirhead, moved toward Richmond. As Gove advanced, he came across a company of the Fifth United States Cavalry. The lieutenant in command informed the colonel that he had observed Confederate pickets about a mile from their present position. Gove asked the cavalry lieutenant to "advance his company to the forks" of the Richmond and Ashland roads, and "to throw out [pickets] along the Ashland road and in the trails and woods leaving out" and watch for any sign of the enemy. Gove was concerned that the Confederates might pass his flank unobserved in the dense foliage and attack the rear of his column. The colonel then sent out skirmishers and flankers to guard his front and sides, and began to advance. "My progress was necessarily slow," the colonel wrote, "owing to the thick undergrowth in the heavy timber to the left of the road, rendering it almost impossible to get through." Portions of the Pennsylvania cavalry company that accompanied Gove were also sent out in advance.[11]

As the head of the column reached a bend in the road, three mounted Confederates were spotted, and quickly retired before the Federals. From there on out, "at every turn in the road these horsemen on our approach would fire and retire." An opening in the timber was discovered about three miles from the Richmond and Ashland roads. Several shots rang out, and, according to Colonel Gove, a large force was "advancing at a charge." Gove ordered the infantry to countermarch as his cavalry hastened back to the main column. Company F of the Twenty-second Massachusetts, which was the company in the lead, wheeled across the road and "prepared to receive the enemy" troops that the Federals thought were chasing their cavalry. But the Confederates declined to come close enough to the boys in blue. Company F rejoined its comrades along the edge of the woods, out of sight, and Gove sent out his cavalry again, trying to entice the Confederates toward his trap, but they once again declined to pursue the Federal troopers. Seeing what he believed to be a large numbers of Confederate soldiers passing to his right and toward his rear, Gove determined that it was a prudent time to retire toward the main Federal force. The company of the Fifth Cavalry, which was posted along the Ashland road, also confirmed the presence of a large body of Confederate soldiers. "There is no point along the road, as far as I went, where cavalry or artillery could be used outside of the road.... The character of the whole country is low and swampy," Gove concluded in his report to Porter.[12]

At the same time, Colonel Lansing was ordered to take his regiment and commandeer the depot and any provisions he found at Hanover Court House. Portions of the Federal cavalry, along with Benson's Battery of the Second United States Artillery, were also deployed to Hanover. Once at Hanover, orders arrived for the cavalry, part of the infantry, and a section of artillery to move toward the South Anna River and destroy the bridges that they came upon. Five companies of the Seventeenth New York, under Lt. Col. Thomas F. Morris, along with four squadrons of the Sixth United States Cavalry under Maj. Lawrence Williams and a section of Benson's Battery, were assigned the task. This expedition of combined arms proceeded cautiously toward the river until it reached the farm of Colonel Wickham. Major Williams judged the ground around the bridge over the South Anna near Wickham's to be "such as to preclude a large cavalry force acting with safety or advantage...." Accordingly, he sent Lieutenant Kerin with a platoon, supported by infantry, to destroy the railroad trestle, a task that took three hours to complete.[13]

Emory then directed Capt. Charles Whiting to take a portion of his regiment, the Fifth United States Cavalry, and reinforce the Sixth United States Cavalry. Portions of the Fifth Cavalry had already been sent out to round up a group of prisoners reportedly trying to cross the Pamunkey River. Whiting arrived with his portion of the regiment, and when he observed the bridge burning returned back toward the main Federal body. Emory then sent Whiting toward Ashland, both to "ascertain if the enemy was in force," and to "hold in check and threaten the [Confederate] forces in Ashland...." Captain Whiting advanced to within three miles of Ashland before his advance party ran into Confederate pickets. Those pickets were driven in and one was captured. From the testimony of the unlucky Confederates and the report of his own officer in charge of his advance party, Whiting determined that the Confederates in the area were a "large force, and that the only course was for me to return...." This portion of the Fifth Cavalry reached camp about dusk.[14]

Yet another detachment of the Fifth United States Cavalry, this one under the command of Capt. J.E. Harrison, met with a group of Confederate soldiers. Reports came in about a group of Confederates trying to elude the Federals by escaping over the Pamunkey. Harrison took two companies, B and E, and rode four and a half miles "over very bad roads and heavy plowed fields...." The Confederates were "in a thick woods near the bank of the river...." Harrison's men, with drawn pistols, approached cautiously. The North Carolinians, obviously portions of the Thirty-seventh North Carolina, "sprang up in a body and called me not to shoot, [and] that they were willing to surrender. The captain commanding them came forward and handed me his sword and surrendered to me 96 prisoners...." Harrison ordered the Confederate captain to form his men, had them remove their bayonets and uncap their rifled muskets, and marched them back to General Emory, who ordered that the Confederates be turned over to the provost marshal and sent to the rear.[15]

The Sixth Pennsylvania Cavalry also went out in an effort to help round up even more prisoners and to destroy their own bridge. Portions of the regiment were sent out at 5:00 a.m. and drove in Confederate pickets. Company I was further deployed, "to scout the woods, and cut down a Bridge on the Pamunkey," recorded Thomas W. Smith.

> We reached the Brigade, and learnt from some Niggers that a party of Rebbles had crossed about a half hour before we got thare. Our Company drew up on this side of the Bridge and I was sent with three men to Reconoiter on the other side. I stationed one man about 100 yards from the Bridge where the Road took a sharp turn to the left and another man 100 yards further on where it took a turn to the Right. On both sides of the Road thare was a deep Ravine with thick woods, and a heavy groath of under brush. Sam Boyer and I, went on up the Road, which ran straight for a good distanse. And after going about 500 yards we came to a Farm [most likely the Wickham Farm] on the Right (There was a heavy Thunder Shower at this time and the rain was almost Blinding)— was a large wheat field and on looking across

it I seen a Head making for the Barn, which was on the Road about 200 yards ahead. We kept on up the Road behind the Hedge Fence and when within 20 yards of the barn another Rebel came in sight, close on us, making for the Barn. I raised my Pistole, spirred my Gallant Nag forward and cried out drop that Gun or die. He Dropped his Gun through up his hands and cried I surrender. The other one on seeing us disappeared after into the Barn. We were going after him, when Furnace came up and would not let me go as the man I caught told us that the Woods were full of them, on the other side of the Field.

Smith retraced his steps back across the Pamunkey, destroyed the bridge, and returned to camp. Company I was barely back in camp before orders came to move out again. The regiment chased the Confederates "across a Stream" then burned the bridge across that stream, along with a railroad bridge, and also cut the telegraph wires. Some of the skirmishing was in close quarters. Smith recorded that one of the Confederates "fired 3 shotts at Lieutenant Morrow of Company B at a distance of 5 yards, but no harm done." For all of their work, they could account for "32 Prisoners including 7 Cavelrymen." The regiment would not return to camp until 6:00 p.m., having spent an estimated 14 hours in the saddle.[16]

Even the regiments not sent out to pursue the Confederates were able to capture a fair number of prisoners. One member of the Thirteenth New York reported that his regiment went out in squads and brought back 92 Confederate prisoners.[17]

More than one Federal soldier confided in his letter home that the captured Confederates were "dressed mean and miserable enough." An anonymous member of the Eighteenth Massachusetts found that the "North Carolina prisoners are a hard looking set." A correspondent to the *Philadelphia Press* thought that the Confederate prisoners "were a sorry-looking set of men, and most of them were clothed in gray homespun. The majority of them seemed rather glad to have been captured. One German, from the manner of his walk and the grin on his face, was evidently going North to search for the heart he could not find in the Southern country." One Federal soldier shouted to the German-Confederate, most likely a member of the Eighteenth North Carolina: "There goes a Union man." The prisoner was quick to answer, according to the correspondent, "Yes, me a Union Man!"[18]

Confederate prisoners were lined up in front of the Kinney House and told that they were to be taken to McClellan's headquarters. One officer in the group estimated the size of the party at 300 prisoners of war. "As we marched along the road," wrote Captain Speer of the Twenty-eighth North Carolina, "we were continually meeting troops, Regts., Brigades. Artillery after artillery was hurrying on with numerous cavalry & every now and then we would pass long lines of baggage wagons, sections of them drawn by the best horses and mules I ever seen." The party traveled until noon when the order to halt was given for a short period of rest, then they were on the road again. "In some places we had to wade in mud and water up to our boot tops," concluded Speer. Many of the soldiers either gave out due to fatigue, or were on the verge of collapse. Speer was one of those. As they approached a "fine residence," one of the Federal cavalrymen charged with transporting the prisoners took Speer's "canteen and rode out to a well and got me a canteen of water. When he came back he offered me a drink of good whiskey...." A little later, the cavalryman dismounted and allowed Speer to ride the rest of the way into camp, a distance that the captain estimated to be five miles. "We were soon in a mile of camp," wrote Speer.

> The Yankee soldiers were now on all sides of the road to get a good look at the dirty rebels. We were gazed and stared at as if we had been live Devils and they were nearly as fearful of us.... We were marched under heavy guard into camp where we were halted and our names, rank, and Regt. taken by the Federal officers. The heavy guard could hardly keep the outsiders off. They seemed to be amazed to see that we were human beings.... Many odd remarks were made as to our looks and dress.... After our names were taken, we were put then into a bull pen and a double guard put over us, who was very ill to us.
>
> We were now almost starved to death, not having had anything to eat in 36 hours.... We soon had plenty of crackers and fresh beef issued to us and all hands went to cooking. Some of the men were so hungry they eat the beef raw as though it was the best diet in the world. We were all soon done cooking and eating and down upon the cold ground to sleep, as though it was the best bed in the world.[19]

Surgeon Shaffner, of the Thirty-third North Carolina, along with many of the wounded under his care, was moved "2 miles McClellanward" on the morning after the battle, to a "private residence, converted into hospital...." The next day, they were again moved, "this time to the left bank of Chickahominy, distant 15 miles from battlefield...." Shaffner was given a barn for the patients under his care.[20]

However, McClellan was not at his headquarters when Speer and the other prisoners arrived. When news arrived on the day of the battle, McClellan fired off a telegram to Secretary Stanton, stating that he had just heard from Porter, and that he had taken Hanover Court House and defeated a force of 13,000 Confederates under General Branch. At 12:30 a.m., McClellan sent his second communiqué to the secretary of war regarding the previous day's victory. McClellan informed Stanton that he was sending reinforcements to Porter "to secure the complete destruction of the rebels" in and around Hanover Court House. He also advised Stanton that the Confederates were "in greater force than I supposed." He asked for every available soldier, and the ability to choose his own commanders. He summed up his telegram with, "It is absolutely necessary to destroy the rebels near Hanover Court-House before I can advance."[21]

The next day, McClellan rode out to view the battlefield. According to a soldier in the Thirteenth New York, McClellan arrived at Porter's headquarters around 3:00 pm., taking the time to offer his congratulations to the survivors of the battle. "Col. my compliments to the 2d Maine. You had a noble fight," he declared, shaking hands with Colonel Roberts as he praised the regiment. The members of the Thirteenth New York "turnout in *en mass* and gave him three cheers." Another Federal soldier commented that when McClellan arrived, "such cheering I never heard." Once on the field, he dispatched another telegram to Stanton, declaring Porter's battle "a glorious victory.... The route of the rebels was complete — not a defeat but a complete route." McClellan believed that the Confederates were concentrating their troops at Richmond, and promised to "do my best to cut off Jackson," but still doubted his ability to do so. Once again, McClellan prodded the secretary for reinforcements. "It is the ... duty," wrote the general, "to send me by water all the well drilled troops available. I am confident that Washington is in no danger." McClellan then slipped in the fact that his forces had destroyed all of the railroad bridges but that of the Richmond, Fredericksburg, and Potomac Railroad. After spending part of the evening at Ford's Theater where Mrs. Lincoln and others were attending a performance by opera star Clara Louise Kellogg, President Lincoln went to the War Department, undoubtedly to read incoming telegrams. The telegraph office was located within the War Department, under Stanton's control. Lincoln visited the office almost daily, and had unlimited access to the incoming information. "I am very glad of F.J. Porter's victory," Lincoln responded to McClellan's missive. The rest of the president's telegram was quite blunt. "Still," he wrote, "if it was a total rout of the enemy, I am puzzled to know why the Richmond and Fredericksburg Railroad was not seized.... The scrap of the Virginia Central from Richmond to Hanover Junction without more is simply nothing." Lincoln further quipped, "That the whole force of the enemy is concentrating in Richmond, I think can not be certainly known to you or me.... I am painfully impressed with the importance of the struggle before you; and I shall aid you all I can consistently with my view of due regard to all points."[22]

McClellan apparently got the message, and a spate of new orders went out during the evening hours of May 28. Major Williams of the Sixth United States Cavalry was reinforced by four companies of the Seventeenth New York and a section of artillery. Williams's assignment was to destroy the Virginia Central bridge over the South Anna River. As the Federal soldiers approached the bridge, Williams ordered reconnoitering parties out in three directions to cover the advance. Captain Abert's command found the bridge and destroyed it. The party then turned back toward camp. Lieutenant Kerin of the Sixth United Sates Cavalry took 20 men and destroyed a bridge 200 yards above the railroad bridge eliminated earlier the previous day. Likewise, Captain Cram's command destroyed another bridge, one that the Sixth Pennsylvania Cavalry had attempted to destroy earlier.[23]

Capt. William P. Chambliss took four companies of the Fifth United States Cavalry out toward Ashland in an attempt to capture the town and further destroy the railroads and communications. If Chambliss was not able to take the town, he was ordered to "induce the belief on the part of the enemy that an attack was intended, and continue thus to amuse him until" the cavalry force under Williams could complete its destruction of the bridge north of the town. Chambliss's men scoured "the woods on each side" of the road "to a point about three-fourths of a mile from the station...." He then halted his troopers, and sent two of his lieutenants and a few men forward to reconnoiter the roads ahead. One of these detachments drove in Confederate pickets, capturing two. After questioning their new prisoners, and based upon reports from his scouts, Chambliss determined to captured the town "by a dash...." The captain recalled his troopers, and once in position, ordered his bugler to sound the charge. "At full speed" the Federals entered the town, sending the Confederates toward the woods "without firing a shot." The troopers "captured 10 prisoners, a quantity of commissary stores and forage, some camp and garrison equipage, ammunition, and arms." Furthermore, Chambliss "destroyed the telegraph wires" and "took possession of a hospital of the enemy full of his sick...." The Confederate hospital was overseen by "hospital-Steward Minor, of the Forty-third Virginia Regiment...." Minor was paroled and allowed to remain with his charges. Having been told that a large body of the enemy had left town just over an hour ago, Chambliss sent Lieutenant Arnold, with two companies, down the road to Richmond to "gain what information he could as to the retreat of the enemy." Arnold had gone only about a mile when he made contact with the Confederates and exchanged shots before being recalled. Chambliss expected the town to be occupied by more of Porter's force (or possibly McDowell's), and did not destroy the depot nor the stores within, believing also that to have fired the depot would have also destroyed most of the town.[24]

Gouverneur K. Warren's brigade, which had missed the fighting on May 27, went out in support of the cavalry expeditions. Warren led a large part of his command, proceeded by two companies of the Sixth Pennsylvania Cavalry, toward Ashland, and occupied the intersection of the Richmond and Ashland roads. Colonel Rush, in his report, described capturing eight men of the Fourth Virginia Cavalry, along with their mounts. While in this position, they removed portions of the rails from the railroad.[25]

During the evening hours of May 29, McClellan dispatched two telegrams to the War Department. One of these informed Stanton about the size of the Confederate force that was withdrawn from Fredericksburg and had passed on to Richmond via Ashland. The other telegram was written by McClellan's chief of staff and father-in-law, Brig. Gen. Randolph B. Marcy, who informed the War Department, "A detachment from General F.J. Porter's command, under Major Williams, Sixth Cavalry, destroyed the South Anna Railroad Bridge at about 9 a.m. to-day. A Large quantity of Confederate public property was also destroyed at Ashland this morning." Lincoln, ever vigilant in perusing the telegrams coming into the War Department, replied: "Your dispatch as to the South Anna River being seized by our forces ... is received. Understanding these points to be on the Richmond and Fredericksburg Railroad, I heartily congratulate the country, and thank General McClellan and his army for their seize."[26]

With the removal of the threat to his right and the destruction of the railroad bridges, McClellan deemed it time to recall Porter and the V Corps back to the main army. Porter's infantry regiments had been given time to rest after their trying ordeal in battle, but his cavalry regiments had been in the saddle continuously for several days. Nevertheless, every Union soldier found the return trip fatiguing. "About 10 this forenoon" recorded a member of the Fifth Massachusetts Battery, "we were told to strike tents and hold ourselves in readiness to march at a minutes notice." The soldiers then "lay around in the hot sun" until orders came at 3:00 p.m. for the men to return to their original camps. The soldiers of the Forty-fourth New York were not on the road until 4:00 p.m. They found the trip "wearisome and trying. The artillery and baggage trains frequently got stuck in the mud, increasing the fatigue and impatience of the troops." Fellow New Yorkers in the Thirteenth Regiment did not begin the march until 6:00 p.m. Other regiments, such as the Ninth Massachusetts, remained on the field until the 30th, performing picket duty and covering the rear of the army. As the Twenty-fifth New York passed the Ninth Massachusetts, the Massachusetts men raised a cheer for what the Twenty-fifth New York had accomplished. Martindale requested that every surviving member of the Twenty-fifth New York who marched away from the battlefield "wear a small twig of pine from the field in our caps in memory of the place...." Martindale did likewise. According to the Federal soldiers who undertook the return trip, it took 11 hours to cover 18 miles. A member of the Eighty-third Pennsylvania, writing after the war and a score of battles, thought that the trip from Hanover back to their old camps was "one of the most trying that we have ever undergone. The artillery and wagon trains got frequently stuck in the mire, often occasioning an hour's delay; and profiting by these delays, the weary soldiers, exhausted as much in patience as in body, sat down to rest and fell asleep in the woods.... many of them did not come up till the next day." At least one soldier noted in his postwar reminisces the large numbers of "contraband" that followed the regiment back to camp.[27]

Those able to make it back en masse arrived in camp between midnight and 3:00 a.m. Lewis Bramer, Jr., of the Twelfth New York wrote in his diary that he "went to bed as soon as possible and did not get up until noon." Bramer then ate, and "laid down again and took another nap [and] went to bed early this evening." The Thirteenth New York got no such privileges. After arriving in camp at 2:00 a.m., they were rousted out of their slumber at 8:00 a.m. and given orders to prepare to march. "But it was a false alarm" concluded an anonymous member of the regiment. A member of the Twenty-fifth New York was much more poetic about their plight when he wrote his hometown newspaper on June 10: "When we arrived in camp, all were weary and very much fatigued. It was an empty looking encampment, not one of the tents being occupied...." On June 9, the regiment's orders came for 175 members of the Twenty-fifth New York to go out on picket. An additional order came for 100 men for fatigue duty. "They could not be got. We had but forty men in camp. We think that we are entitled to a little rest somewhere until we can appear as a regiment, or some duty assigned in that our members are capable of performing."[28]

Fitz John Porter and his V Corps were now a veteran fighting force. While some of his regiment had seen combat prior to the battles of Hanover Court House and Peake's Turnout, their experiences since the beginning of the Peninsula campaign and up until this point had all worked together to bring about a certain cohesion to the brigades and divisions. Porter placed his casualties for the campaign at a total of 355. He reported four officers and 58 enlisted men killed, 12 officers and 211 enlisted men wounded, and two officers and 68 enlisted men captured or missing. The majority of those casualties occurred in the Second Maine, Twenty-fifth New York, and Forty-fourth New York.[29]

8

"Our Boys Are Yet Cheerful, and Feel Confident of Success": Richmond

Gen. Lawrence O'B. Branch and his battered force hobbled back toward Ashland on the night of May 27. Once in town, medical treatment was administered to the wounded soldiers the Confederates had been able to transport from the field. A member of the Eighteenth North Carolina recalled being one of the first of his regiment to enter Ashland. He "set about looking after the wounded. But I found that there was great confusion and little to do, and slept very soundly on the hospital floor." Likewise, members of the Forty-fifth Georgia struggled into Ashland around dawn on the 28th. They were "cold, wet, tired and hungry." Members of the medical corps already in Ashland from the Georgia regiment built fires and cooked what food was available. Later that morning, some members of the regiment went back toward the battlefield to try to reclaim some of the camp equipment and clothing that was left behind, but were sorely "disappointed" at the loss of "clothing and bedding," recalled a member of the regiment many years after the war.[1]

No doubt Branch was upset over the lack of reinforcements. He hoped that the sound of the battle would "attract" reinforcements. General Field, according to a letter Branch wrote to North Carolina governor Henry C. Clark, was within four miles of the battlefield. Field sent a note via a courier to Branch, asking if he needed reinforcements. Branch "replied that I was engaged with the enemy in two places, did not know his strength, but would like to get all the aid I could." A member of the Sixth North Carolina Troops, at Ashland, recorded in his diary: "about 3 oclock in the evening the fight comenced down about Hanover corthouse we surposed but we was not cauld out." No reinforcements were ever sent to Branch.[2]

All of the Confederate infantry and artillery began leaving Ashland on May 28. Branch led his brigade to Brook Church, just a few miles north of Richmond. Members of the Twenty-eighth and Thirty-seventh North Carolina regiments continued to make their way into camp for the next few days. Portions of Company D of the Thirty-seventh North Carolina arrived at the camp near Brook Church on the morning of May 31. Many members of the regiment were so fatigued that wagons had to be sent out to bring them in. "On their retreat," recorded Private Daniel W. Chambers, "they had to construct a raft made of fence-rails to pass over the river." Despite the hardships they had endured, Chambers was able to report that "our boys are yet cheerful, and feel confident of success." Writing at about the same period of time, Private Bellamy of the Eighteenth North Carolina was not so cheerful when he lamented: "It is sad, sad indeed to see the night after the Battle, when the orderly Sergeant at Roll Call that many a gallant young lad who so oft has replied — "Here" — to his name when called, has gone to his Long, Long Home, to lead either an eternal life of happiness or of ruin & torment, according to his acts below on Earth."[3]

All of the wounded whom the Confederates had been able to bring off the field, and who could be moved, were transported to train cars on the Richmond, Fredericksburg, and Potomac Railroad, and transferred to hospitals when they reached Richmond. Many wounded members of Branch's brigade found themselves in Ligon's Factory Hospital, also known as General Hospital #23. The building was a former tobacco warehouse that belonged to John L. Ligon and was opened on May 31, 1862. Among the members of the brigade there were Alexander Simmons and Sampson B. Tolar of the Eighteenth North Carolina; David K. Evans, William J. Davis, J.P. Gordon, William Gerley, and George W. Williamson of the Thirty-seventh North Carolina; and N. Peacock of the Seventh North Carolina. General Hospital #23, and other hospitals in Richmond in which members of the brigade found themselves, were soon taxed beyond endurance with the wounded from other battles.[4]

Richmond was all ablaze with excitement. Many within the city expected it to be captured any day. The Confederate Congress had adjourned on April 22, much to the dismay of local citizens. "To leave Richmond at the very moment of hazard is not the way to encourage the army or help a cause in peril," quipped one local newspaper. On May 10, Jefferson Davis had sent his family to Raleigh, North Carolina, for protection. That very day, Secretary of War George W. Randolph sent a memorandum to his bureau chiefs:

> Have such of your records and papers as ought to be preserved, and are not required for constant reference, packed in boxes, for removal and marked, so as to designate the bureau to which they belong. Books and papers necessary for constant reference may be kept in the presses, but boxes must be prepared for them. This is only intended as a prudent step, and is not caused by any bad news from the army. There is no need, therefore, for any panic in the city, and it should be prevented by the assurance that we have every reason to think that the city can be successfully defended.[5]

On May 15, Governor John Letcher asked the citizens of Richmond to meet at City Hall to organize militia companies to help with the protection of the city. As the month passed, more money was appropriated for more river obstructions, and locals contributed to a fund for the removal of women, children, and the infirm, should the city come under Federal siege artillery. In the event that the city was captured, the city council determined to burn all tobacco and cotton, even if it meant destroying the city. They even went as far as to allow a temporary seat of government to be established if necessity dictated.[6]

8. "Our Boys Are Yet Cheerful, and Feel Confident of Success"

The Confederacy's worst fears seemed to be realized on the day that Branch battled Porter in Hanover County. Confederate cavalry reported Federal forces crossing over the Rappahannock and heading south. On May 25, General McDowell, acting on his own, sent portions of McCall's and King's divisions to "make a strong demonstration ... to mislead the enemy as to our movements and intentions." By late on May 25, McDowell's advance was eight miles south of Fredericksburg. By May 27, the 20,000 men that McDowell sent across the river were just a hard day's march from Porter's V Corps at Hanover. President Lincoln telegraphed McDowell at 1:00 p.m. on May 28, stating that he had received communication from McClellan about the action at Hanover Court House. Lincoln wanted to know that if Porter "effects a lodgment on both Railroads near Hanover Court House, consider whether your forces in front of Fredericksburg should not push through and join him." McDowell wired back: "I do not think, in the present state of affairs, it would be well to attempt to push through a part of that force, or to leave Fredericksburg otherwise than strongly held, which could not be done as the troops are now posted. I trust in a few days to be able to affect the object you have in view, and which no one desires more than I do." McDowell was partially correct. To leave Fredericksburg undefended would have invited the Confederates to reoccupy the city and interpose themselves between McDowell and Washington, not to mention being in McDowell's rear.[7]

All of this was unknown to the Confederate high command, who continued to prepare for the worst. On May 28, Secretary of War Randolph ordered the boxes of records from the War Department to the railroad depot. Other bureau officers were told that "wagons will be ready tonight at 9 o'clock to commence the removal, which should be conducted quietly and from the rear of the building to avoid panic or excitement in the city."[8]

While Branch was fighting Porter's Corps south of Hanover, the Confederate high command was in the process of creating a new division from some of the reinforcements that had arrived in the recent months. This new command was placed under Ambrose Powell Hill, the youngest major general in Confederate service at that time. Hill was a Virginian and a graduate of West Point. Besides Branch's command, the new division was composed of Joseph R. Anderson's Georgia brigade; Maxcy Gregg's South Carolina brigade; Field's Virginia brigade; Dorsey Pender's North Carolina brigade; and James J. Archer's mixed brigade, with men from Alabama, Georgia, and Tennessee. In command of Hill's artillery was Virginia Major Reuben L. Walker. Powell Hill established his headquarters at "Mrs. Jones' home" near Stony Run, and announced his new orders in a letter to General Branch. On June 1, Hill wrote to Branch, and coined the moniker "Light Division"; the men under Branch's command proudly counted themselves part of this organization for the entire war. One soldier in Field's brigade thought that "The name was applicable, for we often marched without coats, blankets, knapsacks, or any other burdens except our arms and haversacks, which were never heavy and sometimes empty."[9]

At Brook Church, on May 29, Branch penned his official report of the battle, a common practice for the commanders of both Confederate and Union regiments, brigades, and divisions, as well as army commanders themselves. Colonel Lee of the Thirty-seventh North Carolina had already submitted his report. In his record, Branch explained his orders from Johnston, the position of his troops, his orders during the battle, and the necessity of retreat. Branch would conclude his report with: "The officers and men of my command conducted themselves in a very handsome manner both in the engagement and on the march."[10]

For the campaign, Confederate casualties are estimated at 798. There was a total of 609 captured, 105 of which were wounded, with 45 of them dying of their wounds in Federal hospitals. Besides the 105 captured wounded, another 105 men were wounded and brought off by the Confederates, placing the wounded at 210 men. Fifty-nine North Carolinians were killed, and an additional 14 died of their wounds. Six additional men were declared "deserters," meaning that they were captured and upon their release never returned to their respective commands, and another five, all from the Thirty-seventh, were declared missing.[11]

9

"I Take Exception": The Battle in the Press

"As the rude hand of war has not silenced my lips up to this present moment," wrote a New Yorker on June 15, 1862, to the *New York Sunday Mercury*, "I wish to let you know some of the scenes that the Twenty-fifth has passed through." This anonymous soldier was only one of the many voices who contributed to newspaper accounts of the battle. Written by participants, witnesses, and those whose information was less experiential, these accounts were the first public documentation of the events that transpired at Hanover Court House and Peake's Turnout May 27, 1862.[1]

Nineteenth-century Americans, both North and South, received most of their information from newspapers. There were approximately 2,500 newspapers in the United States in 1860, with twice as many in the North as in the South. Of these, 373 were published daily, with 17 dailies in New York and five in Richmond alone. Eighty percent of these newspapers classified themselves as being "political in their character." While modern newspapers do have political biases, editors in the 1800s took no pains to even affect journalistic objectivity and had no qualms about publicly vilifying or canonizing candidates and causes with a zeal often alarming to modern readers.[2]

The telegraph, which during the Mexican War was little more than an experiment, cris-crossed the eastern half of the county, with a transcontinental line completed in 1861. An estimated 50,000 miles of line connected the major cities. These lines allowed Abraham Lincoln, and to a lesser degree Jefferson Davis, to keep in almost constant contact with their commanders in the field, both giving orders and receiving battlefield reports. In October 1861, the Federal government established the U. S. Military Telegraph Service, and placed Anson Stager in charge. The following month, the office of Military Superintendent of Telegraph Lines was established and reported directly to Secretary of War Stanton after he replaced Cameron in early 1862. Stanton imposed a set of rigid guidelines on the information sent by the telegraph units that accompanied all of the army and corps headquarters.

Never before had an event in history been so well reported. Each of the major newspapers sent reporters and artists to cover the conflict. Since photographic technology was in its infancy, newspapers were not illustrated with photographs but with sketches that often incorporated the artist's imagination as well as the events he witnessed. While some of these images are highly dramatized interpretations, others are fairly accurate renderings of places and events. The one sketch of the Hanover Court House battlefield, drawn by Alfred Waud, is quite realistic and offers a glimpse of the site as it appeared after the battle occurred.

There were more than 340 reporters for such newspapers as New York's *Herald, Tribune,* and *Times.* While these reporters traveled with the army, they usually stayed away from the front lines, getting their information secondhand, or possibly through informants. This information was then telegraphed through proper channels to their respective papers. Very few reporters wrote under their own names. They often wrote anonymously or used pen names to protect their identities.

The *New York Times* was one of the first to mention the battles fought in Hanover County. On May 29, the paper reported "Further Particulars of the Battle of Hanover Court-house." The type read:

> Washington, Wednesday, May 28
>
> Gen. McClellan telegraphs to the Secretary of War that the battle of Hanover Court-house resulted in a complete rout of the enemy.
>
> It is stated that we have taken 500 prisoners, and more are coming.
>
> The loss of the enemy is set down at 1,000. Our men buried *one hundred* of their dead.
>
> Our loss is 379 killed, wounded, and missing, of which 63 were killed.
>
> The forces opposed to us were principally from North Carolina and Georgia.[3]

Two days later the *Brooklyn Eagle* ran a lengthy column describing the battle. The *Eagle* was one of the newspapers that had been suppressed by the Federal government the previous August. Along with the *Journal of Commerce,* the *Daily News,* and the *Freemen's Journal,* the *Eagle* and its editors were charged as aiders and abettors of treason, and with being pro-Confederate. Many censured newspapers lost their right to use the telegraph or have reporters embedded with the armies. A few presses were even destroyed by lawless pro-Union mobs. But that did not stop the *Eagle* from gaining information regarding the battle. Their anonymous correspondent (or even the editor) wrote on the bottom of page 2:

> We have on a former occasion pointed out the great importance of the movement in the direction of Hanover Court House. The anticipation of Gen. McClellan seems to have been fully realized by the events which have just transpired in that locality. The force selected for that important work, so successfully accomplished, was Gen. G.W. Morell's division of General Fitz John Porter's Fifth Provisional corps, an admirably disciplined body of men. On Tuesday morning, under a heavy rain, they marched to the designated point. A halt took place at the intersection of the Virginia Central and Fredericksburg Railroads, when it was found that the troops were thirteen miles north of Richmond and five from Hanover Court House. The 22nd Massachusetts, Col. Gove, were ordered to disable the road, which was speedily effected. It may be said here in advance that the rebel force in Hanover on Sunday

last was composed of six North Carolina Regiments, a thousand strong each, and it is not probable that their strength was less on Tuesday. The Federal force in round numbers about three thousand. When the division reached a point two miles north of the intersection of the roads, the advanced guard discovered the enemy's pickets. Fire was opened by the skirmishers and the rebels slowly withdrew for a mile or so, being pursued by the 25th N.Y., Col. Johnson, who thus got ahead of the main column, and even the protecting section of Benson's Light battery which was in front. The rebels drew up in line of battle in an open field near the forks of the main road leading to Richmond and Mechanicsville. They took position behind a house and in support of two of their field pieces. Col. Johnson pressed forward and charged them at close range. Hot work continued on both sides for some fifteen minutes, before our supports came up. Suddenly a large force of the enemy issued from the woods on the right flank of the 25th N.Y., and captured a part of Co. G. The Massachusetts's battery and a couple of pieces from Griffin's regular battery came up and engaged the earnest attention of the rebels who were firing the grape and shell with much energy. The rebels no doubt imagined that the force in sight was our entire strength, and that it would be easy work to repulse or capture it — hence their determined stand. Gen. Butterfield, however, being apprized of the state of affairs immediately ordered the 17th N.Y., Col. Lansing, and the 83rd Penn., Col. McLane, supported by the 12th N.Y., Col. Weeks, and the 16th Mich., Col. Stockton, who made short work of them. So completely did their sudden appearance and well directed volleys disconcert the rebels that they "skedaddled" in all directions. One volley picked off most of their men at the guns. The 17th New York charged with a wild shout, the other regiments joined in, the enemy abandoned their guns without spiking them, and the retreating rebels were pursued for some two and a half miles to Hanover Court House. The rout of the enemy was complete: the pursuit was continued by the cavalry along the by roads leading from the Court House, resulting in quite a harvest of prisoners....

The guns captured from the enemy were 12 pound smooth bore brass howitzers, belonging to Latham's celebrated New Orleans battery, and they were left in good order. The timber boxes were almost full of ammunition. One of them was blown up by a shell from Griffin's battery at an early stage of the engagement. The enemy fought with great determination, but they could not withstand the impetuous onslaught of our troops, which, besides the regiments already mentioned as being engaged, also embraced the 62d Pennsylvania, Col. S. Black; 9th Massachusetts, Col. Chase; 14th N.Y; 2d Maine, Berdan's Sharp shooters, 12th N.Y., 5th U.S. Artillery battery, 6th U.S. Cavalry and Martin's Mass. battery. But it would appear as though the brunt of this fierce encounter was borne by the regiments first named....

While the *Brooklyn Eagle* was one of the first newspapers to run an article about the battle, many of the "facts" were askew, and the anonymous author left out the entire second half of the battle.[4]

The special correspondent of the *Philadelphia Press* was one of the next newsmen to a have an account of the battle published in his newspaper on June 2. This correspondent, who signed his dispatch "W.M.," started filing his story at 2 p.m. on May 27, reporting that "cannon can be heard on the distant right at this moment" from his position "Seven Miles from Richmond." A half hour later "W.M." reported that "Banks or McDowell have engaged the enemy near Hanover Court House, and that firing heard is from their guns. Part of General Keys' force passed by here this morning, to support McDowell, it is said." This newsman, whatever his source, was able to get better information than the *Brooklyn Eagle,* reporting that the Confederate forces were composed of a "North Carolina brigade and a Georgia regiment." He went on to describe Confederate prisoners and the importance of Ashland.[5]

On Wednesday, June 4, the *New York Times* ran front-page coverage of the battle. "The Late Victory Near Hanover Court-House, Virginia" was the headline, and the article was illustrated by a fairly accurate map of the battlefield, complete with numbers and a corresponding table to describe the key sites of the engagement. "The gallant fight of Gen. Fitz John Porter on last Tuesday, called by some the battle of Hanover Court-House, and by others that of Peake's Station, was one of the most brilliant fights," read the lead used by the correspondent of the *Times*. With vivid detail the author painted the picture of the Federal victory. This was followed by another report of the battle, from a different correspondent. Both writers spoke highly of the Federal regiments involved in the fray. The coverage by the *Times* included a large casualty list from the different regiments involved, and incorporated a partial list of wounded Confederates in Federal hospitals.[6]

Many newspapers were not able to afford telegraph service nor the placement of correspondents in the field. These newspapers usually waited until the arrival of the daily papers from large cities and culled their information for their own articles. The *Indiana Messenger*, from Indiana, Pennsylvania, was one such paper. After providing a brief summary of the "important and hotly contested battle ... resulting in the complete route of the enemy," the paper published a "condense[d article] from the *N.Y. Herald*" on June 4.

Three days later, the *New York Times* ran an additional story about the battle, once again from its own special correspondent attached to the headquarters of the Army of the Potomac. Overall, the article was correct in its assumptions regarding the battle, and even included an additional casualty list and a list of Confederates captured by the Thirteenth New York. But, the correspondent added a story to help "show the people of the North under what delusions" the southern populace "are actually laboring in reference to the character and purpose of the North."

> As Capt. Martin was riding toward the railroad-crossing he observed a boy advancing out of the woods, followed by some women and children, all waving white flags. The boy advanced timidly, crying all the while, and exclaiming "Please, Sir, don't drown me — don't drown me!" "Why, my son, nobody will hurt you. Why do you cry?" "Oh, Sir!" exclaimed the women, "they told us you would cut our throats or drown us," and, grasping his hand, she kissed it.

As the woods on either side of the railroad tracks had been witness to the battle for the better part of the afternoon, it is highly unlikely that there were any civilians hiding therein, and the story is at best suspicious.[7]

Descriptions of the actual battle, places where most correspondents were not allowed or did not care to venture, were the most important contributions that soldiers made. These men were called soldier-correspondents. Large newspapers rarely printed correspondence from soldiers, but small newspapers thrived on such information. "The following letter is from a Rochester boy in the 25th [New York] to his mother" read one title. Another proclaimed that "the following is an extract of a letter from an officer in the Second Maine, giving more of the personal incidents in the fight than have been given by any other letter yet published." The difficulty with the soldier-correspondents was the narrowness of their views. They were aware of what happened among their company, or their end of the line or battalion, and on occasion, with the entire regiment, but often little else. "Capt. Love, Lieut. Fox, and all our Erie County officers conducted themselves creditably; but my position being so far on left, I was unable to see personally what everybody agrees [to] that were witnesses of their management during the fight," recorded one member of the Forty-fourth New York to a friend in an article that appeared in the *Erie Weekly Gazette*.[8]

Starting on June 4, the *Bangor [Maine] Daily Whig and Courier* began running copy about the battle. Its first article was transplanted from the columns of the *New York World,* providing the readers in the Bangor area with "some idea of the part enacted by the 2d Maine."

> The Second Maine regiment, Col. Roberts, being in the rear, was immediately faced about and stationed by Gen. Martindale at the junction of the road by which the divisions had advanced with the main turnpike to Richmond, running parallel with the railroad. Between these two roads it was supposed the enemy would advance. They extended their flank, however, so as to cover both sides of the road by which we had come, advancing under shelter of the timber.
>
> The fight had now become hot. Six regiments of rebel infantry were now in plain sight. Their special attention seemed to be the right flank, where Col. Roberts, having taken a good position in the edge of the woods, was pouring into them volley after volley of the most terrible musketry. Col. Johnson was ordered to relieve Col. Roberts, and the Second Maine filed off to the right, changing front to the right slightly but keeping up its fire with telling effect. This movement, through some unavoidable [occurrence,] exposed both the Twenty-fifth and Forty fourth to an enfilading fire, from which they suffered severely. But the Second Maine, though low on ammunition, still kept the enemy in check. In vain the enemy pressed: these three heroic columns, though losing largely at every discharge, stood their ground most nobly, never yielding an inch. The Second Maine finally got out of ammunition, *when Col. Roberts appealed for a chance to use cold steel if he could not get cold lead.*
>
> While the fight was going on, the brigades which were in the advance were returning on the double quick. They formed in line in the wheatfield near where the first engagement took place, then pressed through the woods vigorously, and were soon face to face with the enemy, who were evidently startled by the appearance of a strong reinforcement... The 14th New York having relieved the 2d Maine, was joined by the 13th New York, from Col. Warren's brigade, on our left supported by Berdan's Sharpshooters, half of whom went in with their Sharps rifles.... Griffin's battery now came thundering in, unlimbered and took position in a twinkling, and commenced throwing shell and shrapnel with excellent effect. The fresh regiments now pressed forward, the 83rd Pennsylvania advancing under several volleys, but reserving its fire for close quarters, losing but slightly. The enemy found the pressure of the 62d [Pennsylvania] on his left, and the other regiments in front, altogether too great,

and, with several well-directed volleys, our advancing columns soon threw him into ... confusion, and he at once beat a precipitated retreat, under the cover of the dense forest in the rear.

The victory was ours! All honor to the three noble bands who so long held the enemy in check without abating an iota of their foothold.

Either this writer failed to witness the collapse of the Federal artillery, the Twenty-fifth New York, and portions of the Forty-fourth North York, or chose not to report those facts. Chances are the writer was not present during the battle at all.[9]

By the following day, the *Daily Whig and Courier* had a first-hand account, written by Richard Kelleher of the Second Maine, and addressed to his brother, Daniel Kelleher. Written on May 28, the day after the battle, Richard told his brother of the early wake-up call, the march through the mud, encounters with Confederate pickets, and the orders to cross over the tracks of the Virginia Central Railroad and "cut the telegraph wire and tear up the track." Later on that same afternoon, Kelleher, along with many in the Second Maine, most likely thought that they would be expected to fight alone against the entire Confederate army. Soon, the "44th N.Y. and 25th ... came to our assistance, and we fired a volley from our trusty rifles making many bite the dust. At the same moment they gave us a volley which thinned our ranks somewhat." Kelleher was much more honest in his appraisal of events than were "professional" war correspondents. After the Federal gunners were driven from their pieces, "the battle was then altogether infantry fighting. The rebels were gradually surrounding us, and our men were cut down fast." Kelleher then went on to write about the casualties in his company, and praised other regiments, mostly the Ninth Massachusetts, and concluded his missive with "Gen. Martindale thanked us warmly and said we saved the whole Brigade from being cut up."[10]

Other letters followed, not only to the *Bangor Daily Whig and Courier,* but also to such newspapers as the *Buffalo* [New York] *Morning Express;* the *Rochester* [New York] *Union and Advertiser,* and *Democrat and American;* the *Erie* [Pennsylvania] *Weekly Gazette;* and the *New York Sunday Mercury.* However, large events, such the battle of Seven Pines or the Seven Days' campaign, quickly replaced news concerning the battles at Hanover Court House and Peake's Turnout.

Even after the war had ended and the veterans returned home, they occasionally refought old battles within the pages of local and national newspapers. Articles pertaining to the May 27 battle appeared in the *National Tribune,* the *Coshocton,* [Ohio] *Semi-weekly Age;* the *Wellsboro* [Pennsylvania] *Gazette,* and the *Steubenville* [Ohio] *Herald.* At times these articles were solely about the battle and at other times about the regiments that participated. Fitz John Porter wrote one of the most complete accounts of the battle for the *Century Magazine,* which was later reprinted in the four-volume *Battles and Leaders.*

Often, old soldiers took to debating the merits of their regiments in the pages of national newspapers and magazines. One such discussion took place in 1901 in the pages of the *National Tribune,* published in Washington, D.C. In response to an earlier article, Jonathan P. Harley, of Company D, Fourth Michigan Infantry, responded with his own article:

9. "I Take Exception"

> I noticed an article entitled "Two Years vs. Two Hours," by W. J. Adams, Co. C, 44th N.Y., Manson, Mich. I take exception to quite a number of his statements regarding the battle of Hanover Court House.
>
> About the latter part of May, 1862, we left camp, near Gaines's Mill, and proceeded south toward Hanover Court House. We heard cannon firing in that direction. We started off at a double-quick, and went about six miles without stopping. I must say that I was entirely out of breath when we got there, so tired I could hardly stand on my feet.
>
> Our brigade was composed of the 62d Pa., 14th N.Y., 4th Mich., and the 9th Mass., all Irish boys, and as good soldiers as ever lived so far as courage is concerned, and in the use of the bayonet unrivaled; in the use of the rifle we had better men, but that was not our Irish boys' fault.
>
> Now the crow I have to "pick" with Comrade Adams is as to who captured the 320 rebels in the timber. He says the 44th N.Y. I say, and I think there are enough men living to prove it, that it was the 9th Mass. I don't know why we had no skirmishers out, unless our going double-quick prevented it. We passed on the road running south; to the left was a stone fence about two feet high, with rail stakes on the top of it. Now, back of this stone fence lay a regiment of rebels, and their colors low, for once, as we could observe nothing of them until the rear of our brigade came up — the 9th Mass. Then the rebels rose and fired a volley into the 9th Mass. But the Irish boys fired into the woods. It sounded like shelling corn, only a little louder: after which they, the 9th Mass., jumped the fence and charged through that piece of timber, and when they came back they had 320 rebel prisoners.
>
> Now, mind you, it is not the 44th N.Y., but the 9th Mass., who are entitled to the honor of the capture of those prisoners. I know we belonged to Morell's Division and the Fifth Corps. I shall be surprised if the 9th boys don't come to the front now, since the ball is opened. The 9th Mass. had the finest set of baseball players I ever saw.[11]

A retort was not long in coming, this time by a member of Company K, Forty-fourth New York: James B. Hitchcock. The former soldier was "amused at the earnestness with which Comrade Harley takes exceptions" to what other composers contributed to the disputation. "Hanover Courthouse," believed Hitchcock, "will continue to have more interest to [former soldiers] than any other battle of the war." The reason, judged the former soldier, was that Hanover was the place were "they first experienced the blighting, withering curse of the impact of war — here received their baptism of fire, burned into them by rebel bullets." Hitchcock then set out to give a long, poetic discourse on the activities of the Forty-fourth New York.

> Well do I remember that May morning in 1862, with what alacrity the boys of the old regiment fell into line as the bugle sounded the familiar "Dan–Dan–Butterfield;" every one of them eager, earnest, buoyant, filled with irrepressible enthusiasm, never doubting their ability to accomplish whatever might be required of them....
>
> Morell's column found the enemy in small force at Hanover, who, however offered little opposition, retreating and being followed by Morell. These tactics of the rebels seem to have been preconcerted and a part of the program to capture our supply train.
>
> Before reaching Hanover Courthouse the 44th was detailed as extra guard to assist in protecting the wagon-train, as it was feared that the enemy might attempt its capture. The sequel proved the wisdom of this action.

After leaving the crossroads they were guarding, Hitchcock's regiment proceeded toward the intersection of the Ashcake and Richmond roads where they met the Confederates. After "stubbornly" holding "their ground" and repelling the attack of the Eighteenth North Carolina, Hitchcock and his comrades were

> cheering ... in the direction of the opening of the woods through which Branch's forces had first appeared. With anxious hearts we directed our gaze in that direction, expecting that reinforcements for the Confederates had arrived. To our glad surprise we recognized the Stars and Stripes proudly floating above our twin regiment, the 83rd Pa.
>
> Wildly cheering, they came dashing toward us. We were immediately ordered to fix bayonets and charge, and the prisoners caught in the triangle formed by these two lines of battle were among those referred to by Comrade Adams as being captured by the Third Brigade.
>
> The jig was up, the circus over, the band had ceased to play. The orchestra had fired its last note. The audience dismissed to seek their homes, the broken regiments of Branch's Brigade were heartily seeking the protection of their fortifications around Richmond and the battle of Hanover Courthouse had passed into history.

Hitchcock finished his missive by posing a question: "I wonder how the old gentleman [General Butterfield] will feel, if he is alive today, and sees the article of Comrade Harley. I bet you it will open his eyes to have his claim thus unceremoniously 'jumped,' and that, too, by regiments of his own division. Trot out your record, comrade, to substantiate your claim."[12]

While Northern newspapers frequently continued to carry war news, even long after the war had ended, Southern newspapers and news correspondents were in a slightly different position. Newspapers were equally important to the South, but there were fewer papers in the Southern states, and as the war grew longer, the supplies for the presses, usually obtained from the North, dwindled. Many papers even ceased to exist. The censorship of military information in Southern newspapers began on July 1, 1861, when then-Secretary of War Leroy Walker asked editors not to print sensitive intelligence. Almost all Southern papers agreed to abide by this request.

Fewer than 100 reporters covered the war for Southern newspapers. The papers in Richmond were the first to report the matter. "The affair at Hanover Court House," wrote the *Richmond Whig*, on May 29, "was of a more serious character than we supposed." The *Whig* had reported previously that the "affair" was between one North Carolina regiment, the Twenty-eighth, and one New York regiment, the Twenty-fifth. "Later intelligence advises us that after this, quite a large Yankee force came upon the ground, and was met by three regiments from our side, who fought them until the overpowering weight of numbers caused us to fall back. Accounts differs as to the casualties sustained, but we fear they were quite considerable."[13]

Reports concerning the battle were also found in the *Richmond Enquirer* and the *Richmond Examiner*. "The skirmish ... near Hanover Court House," chronicled the *Enquirer*, "commenced between a regiment of North Carolina Troops, attached to Gen. Branch's brigade, and an advance party of the enemy." The *Enquirer* was correct when reporting that the Tar Heel regiment "gallantly repulsed the foe," taking "sixty-three prisoners...." But the correspondent informed his readers that the same North Carolina regiment then "found itself fighting a whole Division ... and consequently ... our men fell back upon their own brigade.... The loss in killed and wounded is not believed to have been considerable on either side, though that of the enemy is supposed to have been greater." While the report from the *Examiner* contained much more information than other accounts, many of the "facts" regarding the battle were erroneous.

> From all we can learn of the conduct of the engagement it appears that, Tuesday afternoon, our pickets discovered the enemy advancing, and reported that a body of cavalry, supposed to be from five hundred to one thousand strong, was approaching our lines. On this information the 33d North Carolina and 45th Georgia were ordered to make a movement with the design of cutting off the cavalry force from the main body. The 18th and 28th Carolina were ordered to the front, and bore the brunt of the engagement, as the terrible suffering of these two regiments testify. We had but one field battery in the action — Latham's Battery. The enemy had several batteries on the field — certainly two. It is reported that the 18th and 28th North Carolina were ordered to take two different batteries, and, on dividing, were raked by the enemy's fire in a most terrible manner. Nearly two-thirds of the 28th North Carolina regiment were reported to have been killed and wounded, or captured....
>
> There are said to have been but three regiments actually engaged — the 18th, 28th, and 33d North Carolina
>
> On retiring, our forces fell back in the direction of Ashland, and destroyed the bridge just beyond it.[14]

Not to be outdone, Richmond's fourth newspaper, the *Dispatch*, informed its readers likewise of the battle, of Branch's small brigade battling a superior force, of the success of the first engagement, and the loss of the second. The *Dispatch* then went on to say that it was not a portion of McClellan's army that Branch was battling, but "15,000 men under McDowell.... The train last evening [May 29] brought down thirty of our wounded, and some dozen disabled Yankees. When the train left Ashland, McDowell was within a mile of the place." This could not do anything but add to the anxiety of the already panic-ridden Confederate capital.[15]

All of the Richmond accounts, along with other accounts from the *Wilmington Journal* and the *Petersburg Express,* were found in the June 2 edition of the *Fayetteville Observer*. Once again, most of the descriptions from the battlefield came from the soldier-correspondents. *The State Journal,* published in Raleigh, contained a letter from a member of the Twenty-eighth North Carolina on June 4. The letter, written on May 30, was well written and accurately depicted the Tar Heel regiment's struggles south of Hanover Court House. The *Western Carolinian,* on June 6, blithely reported that the battle had been "Another Victory," and that the Confederates had only suffered losses of "6 or 8" men.[16]

Many company commanders used the North Carolina press to inform loved ones at home about the casualties and captures their respective companies had sustained. Capt. William D. Barringer of Company E, Twenty-eighth North Carolina wrote on June 4, "for the benefit of our relatives and friends, at home who are doubtless anxious," providing the names of those who were "supposed to be prisoners." His missive appeared in the *Fayetteville Observer,* and contained the names of 12 men. A list of wounded from the Eighteenth North Carolina appeared in the *Wilmington Journal* and was reprinted on June 9 in the *Fayetteville Observer.*[17]

Pvt. Daniel W. Chambers, of Company D, Thirty-seventh North Carolina Troops, penned a letter on May 31, which appeared in the *Biblical Reporter,* the Southern Baptist newspaper for the state of North Carolina. Chambers wrote:

> Since we received a copy of the Recorder, we have had a battle with the enemy and have fallen back to within four or five miles of Richmond.... Our regiment was very much cut up–about 275 killed, wounded and missing. I wrote to many of my correspondents yesterday and to day, in which I wrote that Capt. Ashcraft's and Farthing's companies were taken prisoner, or had not yet returned to camp. This morning Capt. A[shcraft] come in, leaving his men behind five miles, too much fatigued to come farther without resting. Wagons have been sent for them, with a part of several other companies. On their retreat, they had to construct a raft made of fence-rails to pass the river. The Yankees were so close upon them, that only 44 of his men got over, the remainder being left with Lieutenant Bost and Capt. Farthing to shift for themselves. Capt. Ashcraft thinks they are taken prisoners. We hope they will come up yet. Some of the Capt's men were captured on their way from fatigue.
>
> Though retreating the second time, our boys are yet cheerful, and feel confident of success. Till the last fight, we have been kept away from any reinforcements, suffering the enemy to come upon us with a force 4 or 5 times larger than ours.... The great decisive battle will be fought near this place, if the wise judge correctly. May Jesus smile upon our cause, and cause our enemies to see the error of their way and return to their helpless families.[18]

Letters continued to pour into the writers' respective publications. "Mack," a member of the Thirty-seventh, reported on May 29, and his letter appeared in the June 4 issue and again on June 11 in the *Raleigh Weekly Register.* Edward F. Lovill of Company F, Twenty-eighth North Carolina Troops, wrote on June 10 to the *Spirit of the Age,* recording the killed, wounded, and dead of his company. "My men fought gallantly until ordered to retreat, which they did in good order," the captain concluded. By mid-June, copies of the official reports of the regimental commanders under General Branch started to appear in the state newspapers. Colonel Lane's report appeared in *The State Journal* on June 18. It was not until early September that the official reports for the Thirty-seventh North Carolina appeared in print. The discourse written by Colonel Lee was penned on May 29, just two days after the battle. Lee was in command of a demi-brigade: both his own regiment and the Eighteenth North Carolina. Accompanying Lee's report was a report written by Lieutenant Colonel Barber, who had actual command of the Thirty-seventh during the engagement.[19]

A day or so after the battle, a letter, signed only "Hanover," appeared in the *Richmond Examiner* and was later reprinted in newspapers in North Carolina. This anonymous writer brought against General Branch charges of incompetence, stating that Branch was not on the field of battle and that he had let a battery of artillery and four infantry regiments lie idle while other regiments fought for their lives.

"The above is a true statement of the facts," "Hanover" concluded, "which make the battle of Lebanon Church a sad, but as far as the men, company, and regimental officers are concerned, a brilliant affair for North Carolinians. Of the rest the public must judge."[20]

In the politically charged atmosphere of nineteenth-century newspapers, such accusations as those leveled against Branch could prove devastating to an officer's career. In the same issue of *Spirit of the Age* that ran the "Hanover" letter, this item appeared a few columns away:

> As one of the State papers remarks concerning this battle and its management by Gen. Branch, we can truly say that we are not one of those who seize every opportunity to underrate the qualifications, or assail the courage of superior officers. In fact we do not like to rear such assaults, but if the reports— one half of them — that reach us touching the conduct of General Branch, as a Military Commander, are true, he is very incompetent and so obtuse or excessively vain that he does not discover his lack of military science.
>
> The correspondent of the Examiner clearly fixes the loss of the battle upon the head of Gen. Branch. His neglect to send reinforcements to support Cols. Lee and Lane is unpardonable, and he ought to be immediately cashiered.
>
> There had been too many precious lives and valuable as well as brave men already sacrificed by incompetent men attempting to fill the place of General Officers. A change is absolutely necessary and we hope that it will soon be made.[21]

Branch was understandably livid, and since both his current military career and any chance of a resumption of his political career after the war were at stake, he set out to find the responsible parties and to refute the charges that had been made against him. After making several inquiries, Branch found two of the officers who coauthored the "Hanover" article: one from the Thirty- seventh and another from the Thirty-third. Lt. William T. Nicholson, adjutant of the Thirty-seventh, was one of those officers. General Branch sent for both men, and

> Received them in that open manner of which he was the master, and entertained them with such courtesy as [to] put them at ease. Handing each his communication he asked "Is that your signature for the purpose therein expressed," with the deliberation of a clerk in chancery probating a paper.
>
> They recognized that a condition, not a theory, confronted them, sweated the great sweat of confusion and acknowledged their deeds.[22]

Not long thereafter, another letter from "Hanover" appeared in the *Richmond Examiner,* and was reprinted by some newspapers in North Carolina, though not as many as had printed the first letter from the two officers. The first article they wrote on June 1, but when it did not appear, they wrote again. "In your paper of May 31st" wrote "Hanover" on June 6,

> appeared an article on the battle in Hanover, by "Hanover." The author afterwards found that some facts had been unintentionally misstated, and that certain expressions had been used which might, if unexplained, be constructed to reflect upon the personal bravery or generalship of General L.O'B. Branch; [therefore] "Hanover," requested you, on June 1st, to insert an article explanatory of this first

article, and was told by your clerk that the article would appear if possible. Will you, sir, please publish said article, if possible; and if not, please publish enough to assure the public that "Hanover" is now satisfied that General Branch was on the field before a gun had been fired, and that he ordered all of his forces into position, and did not keep a battery and four regiments idle at his side while the enemy was mowing down the Eighteenth and Thirty-seventh, as was first stated.

General R.E. Lee had thanked General Branch for his management on that occasion and for the conduct of his troops; and as the first article, if unexplained, might do injustice to a brave officer, it is hoped that you will at least allow an explanation.[23]

In an attempt to salvage his postwar political advancement, Branch wrote his own newspaper article on June 9, and mailed it to respective newspapers that were friendly with Branch. The *Raleigh Register* published the piece on June 14, *The State Journal* on June 18, and a paraphrased version appeared on June 20. "I have been informed by several friends in North Carolina, that an anonymous letter ... published in the Richmond *Examiner* has been republished in the State, and that on it a public opinion has been formed, very unfavorable to me, and which it will be almost impossible to change" Branch wrote.

A public opinion that would consign me to disgrace on such evidence, I cannot be expected to have either the hope or desire to change. Not for the satisfaction of those who feel an interest in my reputation, and still more to quiet the apprehensions of those whose sons are entrusted to my command, I wish it known that General Lee, the veteran commander of all Confederate armies, not knowing me personally, nor having reason to favor me personally, nor having the least reason to favor me above any other officer under his command, (but I fear before he read Hanover's letter) has written me a letter in which he says, "I have great pleasure in expressing my approval of the manner in which you have discharged the duties of the position in which you were placed."

Not in the nature of an appeal from this emphatic judgement of my distinguished commander, to whom all the facts were known, but to spread upon the records of the War Department other evidence of those facts that my own report, I have asked for a *court of inquiry*, before which Col. Lee and his Adjutant will be called to testify. As many of the best known officers of my brigade as the court shall have time and patience to examine will be before it. The court will be requested to call them indiscriminately, without suggestion from myself.

The doors of the court will be wide open to critics, whether they are mere calumniators or honest fools who think themselves robbed of their desserts because they have not been appointed to command armies.

I shall prove before the court, by as many witnesses as the court will allow to be examined–

1st. That my Headquarters, instead of being more than a mile distant, were less than 300 yards from the centre of my Brigade, where I had slept on a bench in my clothes the night before.

2nd. That Latham's battery and all the Infantry regiments, except Col. Lee's were ordered under arms, and Latham sent to reply to the enemy's artillery, by myself. That I reached Col. Lee's camp, which was my extreme left and nearest to the enemy, within five minutes after he did himself, and before his Regiment had got out of camp.

That I was twice at Latham's battery whilst the artillery firing was going on — no infantry being on either side — and was all along my line giving directions to commanding officers, and making necessary dispositions to meet the attack; what these dispositions were will be shown by the statement of the officers who were directed to execute them.

All this and much more will be shown, notwithstanding "Hanover" says I reached the field after Latham's battery had been withdrawn.

3rd. I will show that every Regiment that I had, except Campbell's 7th N. C., which I held in reserve, was engaged in services of the most important character, the withdrawal from which could have exposed my Brigade to instant rout and capture, and that as soon as I could withdraw it from the service it was on, the 33d Regiment was sent to Col. Lee. I will show that for three hours couriers were arriving with scarcely intervals of ten minutes from Col. Robertson of the 4th Va. Cavalry, a brave and experienced officer, informing me that a heavy column of the enemy, having driven his Regiment, were advancing rapidly on my rear from Hanover C. H., and from the Cavalry pickets on the Ashcake road, to the effect that a column was approaching my rear from that direction, and was driving them in. Confiding in Col. Hardemans, of the 45th Georgia Regiment, whom I had ordered to hold the mouth of the Ashcake road at whatever cost, and in the tried courage and discipline of the 7th N. C. to cover the retirement of my command from the field, I maintained my position until near sunset, [with] the hope that reinforcements would arrive and enable me to cut my way through to Col. Lane. When I ordered the withdrawal, the steadiness of the 7th enabled me to effect it in perfect order.

I saw the eagerness of the 7th to participate, and I knew Col. Lee's desire that they should, but I appreciated too much my responsibility as a commander to gratify either. Col. Lee had already reported to me that his own Regiment had dispersed and could not be collected.

Having been forced to the mortifying extremity of bringing my individual [sic] *action* to the attention of my peers and associates in arms, now that the thoughts of all are engrossed by the great transactions in which we are participating.

I shall rest my reputation upon their verdict.— Whilst I shall not attempt to forestall the judgement of the public, I ask no suspension of it. The North Carolina public will form its opinion on such material as it thinks fit, or, when it thinks fit — on no material at all. Those who are too cowardly to take the field themselves, and too mean to do justice to those who are in the field, will continue to slander me as they have done heretofore. If there is not honor and justice enough left in the State to protect me, whilst absent in the discharge of duties to the country, from such base and foul attacks, I will remain without defense until time and circumstances permit me to return.[24]

10

"We Have a Hard Road to Travel": The Battle in Perspective

Morale among the soldiers in the regiments of Branch's brigade was understandably low. One company-grade officer wrote that "we was Defeated through General Branchs bad management. He was told by a Citizen that the enemys force was small & he believed it but No person else did." They had lost their first battle two and half months before at New Bern, and now they had been defeated once again by a numerically superior force. Rations had been poor since they left North Carolina, the state they had enlisted to defend, and now the roads they had to travel over were worse due to unseasonable amounts of rain. "Annie we have had a hard road to travel ever since we came to V[irginia].... Sometimes I get so tired that I can scarcely drag myself along," concluded one member of the Thirty-seventh to his wife back in Mecklenburg County.[1]

General Branch's position near Peake's Turnout was the result of orders from his commander, Joseph E. Johnston. The Confederate commander planned to attack a portion of the Federal army that straddled the Chickahominy River. To consolidate the Confederate forces, both Branch and Anderson were ordered to move their men closer to Richmond and the main Confederate army. It appears that Branch was to follow Anderson, acting as a rear guard, or at least to work in conjunction with Anderson's command. Branch also was charged with guarding the railroads in the surrounding area, railroads that were used as a line of supply not only for his and Anderson's commands, but likewise for Jackson in the valley. Save for a line of retreat back to Ashland where Anderson's forces were due, Branch's selection of the area around Peake's Turnout held little tactical value. The site was approachable from two or three different positions, held few natural barriers in which to anchor a flank, and provided no good artillery positions for the few guns that he had. It is clear that Branch did not expect to remain around Peake's Turnout for any long period of time.[2]

To Branch's credit, he did reinforce his cavalry pickets with infantry. Two companies were sent to Taliaferro's Mill, and it is likely that Branch thought any attack would originate from the Pamunkey River area, or from Old Church, along the river, and through Hanovertown. The command under Colonel Warren did advance along this route, and it is possible that the Confederate cavalry pickets spotted the lead elements of the Sixth Pennsylvania Cavalry. Branch, not knowing the size of the advancing force, reinforced his picket with the Twenty-eighth North Carolina and a section of artillery.

When Lane arrived at Taliaferro's Mill, he could not find the pickets from the Thirty-seventh North Carolina. As he was "examining the ground for a suitable position" for his men, word arrived that there were Federals in his rear, attempting to cut him off from the main body of Confederate troops. Lane positioned his skirmishers and marched back toward Branch's command. Before he could reach Branch, he came upon Federal infantry, the Twenty-fifth New York, in skirmish order. Lane ordered his men to charge and wrecked the Twenty-fifth New York. Lane then reformed his men, and in due order was forced to fall back when attacked by Butterfield's brigade. Lane did not have a good line of retreat, but succeeded in bringing off the majority of his command. This was the first battle the men of the Twenty-eighth North Carolina fought, and given their green condition, they performed remarkably well. After Lane trounced the Twenty-fifth, he should have conducted an orderly withdrawal toward Hanover; but, not knowing what opposition he faced, he chose to stay and fight.

Branch seemed to suffer from a lack of credible or timely information from his cavalry pickets. Col. Charles C. Lee, in his report, wrote that around 11:30 a.m., "Lieutenant Timberlake of the Virginia Cavalry galloped to where I was sitting and stated that a party of the enemy were advancing up the road, which intersected the stage road at Peake's Station, and were then within a half mile of our camp." If the timetable of Colonel Lee's report is to be trusted, the majority of Fitz John Porter's command had already passed when the presence of the Federals was reported by Branch's cavalry pickets. Lee, acting with a level of confidence provided by his training at West Point, sent one of his companies to reinforce his pickets, and two others into the woods and toward the road to both observe and, if opportunity presented itself, attack the body of Federal troops advancing up the road. Had disciplined cavalry been available, this latter task should have fallen upon them. Lee then rode back for orders from his general.[3]

A question arises over Branch's choice of headquarters. Slash Church was well to the rear and required several minutes to reach on horseback. Lebanon Church would have been a better choice, closer to the roads he was ordered to guard and to his own troops. However, Branch approved of Lee's actions, and Lee was sent back to "watch the results." As soon as Lee left, Branch heard the sounds of artillery, and only then (near noon), did he order his horse to be saddled.[4]

When Lee arrived back at his camp, he quickly ascertained that he was up against at least even odds, if not a superior force. He quickly took charge, recalling and reforming his own regiment, calling up artillery support, and asking the Twelfth North Carolina "to advance in front of the railroad and, changing front to the left, move round on the enemy's flank...." Branch was soon on the scene and developed his own battle plan. The general's plan was for two regiments to assault the front of the Federal line, while two other regiments swung around the flank. A fifth regiment was held in reserve. Not a bad plan overall, except that one of the key flanking regiments, the Thirty-third North Carolina, had not returned from an earlier sweep through the woods. Instead of waiting for this regiment, Branch ordered his other regiments to advance. The men of the Twelfth North Carolina never got into a position to be a threat, and once under fire simply lost their nerve, dropping to the ground and hiding in the weeds and bushes instead of pressing the attack. Instead of waiting for the Thirty-seventh North Carolina to get into position, allowing time for the regiment to advance through a dense woods, the Eighteenth North Carolina surged ahead across the open field. The majority of the Federals in line were able to concentrate their fire upon this lone regiment. The Eighteenth was soon forced into the woods to the right. The dense foliage and a resolute foe slowed the Thirty-seventh considerably. By the time the Thirty-seventh was in position, the Eighteenth had already been forced into the woods.[5]

The Eighteenth North Carolina, and six of the seven companies of the Thirty-seventh engaged, were armed with smoothbore muskets. While the smoothbore had an advantage in dense undergrowth — it was easier to load than rifled muskets and fired a buck-and-ball round, one .64-caliber buck and three .30-caliber ball — it only had an effective range of 80 to 100 yards. This greatly limited the long-range attack capabilities of the Confederates. The Eighteenth was unable to overcome the Federals to its front. Colonel Cowan halted his regiment, fired several volleys to create a smokescreen, and ordered his men into the woods to their right, where they continued to press forward. By the time the Eighteenth had advanced close enough to be in range, the Thirty-seventh had likewise advanced through the woods, pushing back the Second Maine. Several of the companies on the Thirty-seventh's right bent back their line, a maneuver called refusing the flank, and opened a crossfire on the Federal artillery. The combined fire of the Eighteenth and Thirty-seventh on the exposed Federal artillery, along with the already rattled remnants of the Twenty-fifth New York, forced both, along with elements of the Forty-fourth New York, from their positions. Had the Twelfth or Thirty-third regiments been in positions to attack at this time, they could have overwhelmed the Federal line, capturing prisoners and artillery.[6]

Both Confederate and Union regiments used the woods to their advantage. Once the Eighteenth North Carolina entered the woods, the Federal artillery was not as effective as it had been when confronting the regiment in the open field. Also, the Eighteenth was able to continue its advance once sheltered by the woods. The Thirty-seventh was also somewhat sheltered by the woods, and the Federals the regiment faced did not know the size of their foe.

Toward the end of the day, Branch, fearing that he would be surrounded, "hearing of no re-enforcements," and believing that Lane and the Twenty-eighth had been able to retreat toward Hanover, called for a retreat. Branch called upon the Seventh North Carolina, his reserve, to cover the withdrawal of his forces. His battered command stumbled into Ashland throughout the night, and the next day the men moved toward Richmond. Branch did a remarkable job considering the lack of credible information. His men fought a detailed engagement at times against a numerically superior force. On the other hand, had Branch kept his force together and waited for the V Corps to pass by, he easily could have sent five or six regiments onto Porter's rear and created massive amounts of damage. Or, had Branch simply withdrawn his pickets and retired up the road to Ashland, he could have found a better defensive position, with reinforcements within a stone's throw. In either case, McClellan likely would have had no good news to telegram Stanton, save the destruction of portions of the railroad.[7]

If Branch had problems with credible information throughout the day, Fitz John Porter's entire campaign was based upon even worse intelligence. Porter, on the morning of May 27, "had reason to believe [that the Confederates] were camped in strong force near Hanover Court-House." The general based his plan of battle upon this knowledge: Morell's division was to advance and take the Confederates from the front, while Warren's command fell "upon him in flank and rear." The trouble was that the Confederates were not encamped "near Hanover Court-House."[8]

Porter started out by placing two regiments of cavalry, with a battery of artillery, as his advance guard, a good arrangement to spearhead his attack. The problems arose when this cavalry was piecemealed away at every crossroads and

A captured Confederate cannon, the 6-pound brass piece that belonged to Latham's battery in the camp of the Seventeenth New York Infantry. The officer standing next to the flagpole is believed to be Colonel Lansing (courtesy the Library of Congress).

intersection that the Federal column came upon. This was a good role for the Federal cavalry to play, chasing away Confederate cavalry pickets, screening the main Federal body, and performing reconnaissance to the right and left of the road. But as the Federal column neared what would become the battlefield, the cavalry force was so small that Porter was forced to call upon an infantry regiment to deploy as skirmishers and scout the advance. This might explain why the Twenty-fifth New York, the regiment chosen for this assignment, was caught unaware by the Twenty-eighth North Carolina. Had an appropriate cavalry screen been in place, possibly scouting along the road to Taliaferro's Mill, the New Yorkers might have been able to better prepare a reception for Lane's Tar Heels.

But this gradual diminishing of Porter's Corps was not limited to his cavalry. Porter furthermore detached whole infantry regiments, with artillery support, to watch side roads. In some cases, as with Martindale's observation of the Ashcake road, this was a valid opportunity. In other cases, as with the Forty-fourth New York, such action was not necessary. A strong cavalry guard at the rear of his column could have performed the task even better.

If there was one brigade that performed as designed, it was the brigade of Dan Butterfield. On reaching the field, near the Kinney home, Butterfield deployed his men into two lines, and then observed the enemy's position, adjusted his own lines, positioned his skirmishers, and sounded the advance. While there was some dis-

Another view of the captured Confederate cannon in the camp of the Seventeenth New York (courtesy the Library of Congress).

organization within Butterfield's command during the advance due to the nature of the ground, his regiments were able to overlap the Confederates and force them to retreat.

Porter seemed to be everywhere on the battlefield. The Twenty-fifth New York deployed under his supervision. He was at the junction of the New Bridge and Ashcake roads when Martindale arrived, ordering his general down the Ashcake road toward the railroad. Similarly, Porter was on hand to show Butterfield's brigade where to deploy. When he discovered the battle going on in his rear, he rode hard and arrived to personally take command and show each regiment where he wanted it placed. This micromanagement left division commander George W. Morell out of a job. Granted, the division had, up until just a few day prior, been under Porter's command, but he should have trusted Morell and sent orders to him on the disposition of his brigades.

When Porter detailed Martindale to go down the Ashcake Road and cut the telegraph line and the Virginia Central Railroad, he provided Martindale with sufficient forces. These men under Martindale, two of his five infantry regiments, a section of artillery, and a small cavalry contingent, were able to accomplish the wrecking of the railroad. They were not able to contend with the six Confederate infantry regiments that lay in the woods not far from the railroad. If an award could be bestowed upon a soldier for contributing the most during a battle, it would fall upon Martindale. When Martindale was informed of the presence of Confederate infantry to his left, he quickly reformed his men in a line. While under Confederate artillery fire, he received an order from Porter, stating that the Confederates were retreating toward Fredericksburg, and Martindale was to follow the main column. Martindale sent back a note to the corps commander, stating that the Confederates were on his left, in force, and not retreating. Porter, not even for a minute supposing that his subordinate was correct in his assessment of the situation and in asking for reinforcements, simply disregarded the intelligence and ordered Martindale to follow the main Confederate column. Martindale disengaged (a victory in Confederate eyes), sent the Twenty-second Massachusetts on ahead, and, with the Second Maine and his cavalry contingent, slowly advanced toward Hanover Court House, all the while watching his rear. He again received a note from Porter, basically informing him that he (Martindale) was wrong about the position of the Confederates, that General Stoneman would pursue any groups of stragglers, and that he was to catch up to the main column as quickly as possible. Martindale then set out to find Porter in person and impress him with the seriousness of the situation. On the way, Martindale ran into Morell, who ordered him to communicate by orderly with Porter, and return to his command, now just one regiment. It was then that Martindale's cavalry reported a large group of Confederates advancing over the railroad and toward the rear of the Federal column. Martindale redeployed the Second Maine and snatched the Forty-fourth New York and some artillery coming down the road. He then sent another missive to Porter, asking for reinforcements. Also, Martindale sent another aide, his son, to find the Twenty-fifth New York. When Martindale got his forces collected — the artillery,

10. "We Have a Hard Road to Travel"

Twenty-fifth and Forty-forth New York, and the Second Maine—he slightly outnumbered his Confederate foe. Credit should be given to these commands for saving Porter's entire force. Porter, in his report, never made mention of the orderlies sent by Martindale. He simply wrote that as his column reached Hanover Court House, "I received information from a signal officer that the enemy were appearing in our rear."[9]

Porter recalled the portions of his command that had been sent out in pursuit of the Twenty-eighth North Carolina, and sent them back toward Kinney Farm and Peake's Turnout. The arrival of a half dozen regiments that had yet to see battle that day was more than Branch's fought-out command could handle, and he retreated. Once again Porter misused his cavalry. They were sent to round up prisoners, but if they sent intelligence back about the absence of the large numbers of Confederates that Porter expected to find, he simply disregarded the information and blindly allowed his infantry to continue the advance.

The defeat of Branch led to fear among the Confederate high command. If McClellan and McDowell joined their forces, which now seemed inevitable, Richmond would be in grave danger. As Branch and Porter dueled around Hanover, General Johnston "thought it absolutely necessary under such circumstances to attack McClellan before the junction [of the two Federal armies]." Johnston sent orders to his division commanders to prepare their men. The general's plan was to attack the Federals on the north side of the Chickahominy by moving to the left of the Federal position and attacking the Federals along Beaver Dam Creek, rolling up their flank. The battle was set to begin on May 29.[10]

May 29 came and went with no attack. Considerable confusion existed among Johnston's subordinates. The attack, which Johnston thought to be a "great day in our history," took place two days later. The Confederate assaults were not well managed, but did succeed in pushing back portions of the Federal army and inflicting heavy casualties. The Federals were able to obtain reinforcements and stabilize their line. After ordering his men to sleep where they "might be standing when the contest ceased for the night, to be ready to renew it at dawn next morning," Johnston was wounded. A spent musket ball struck him on the shoulder, while at the same time a fragment of an artillery shell slammed into his chest, knocking him off his horse. On June 1, 1862, President Jefferson Davis gave his chief military adviser, Robert E. Lee, command of Johnston's army, which Lee renamed the Army of Northern Virginia.[11]

11

"It Still Should Not Be Forgotten": The Battlefield Today

The battles that whirled around the Kinney Farm and Peake's Turnout were just the beginning of military action in Hanover County. J.E.B. Stuart's vaunted ride around McClellan's army started in Hanover County on June 12–13, 1862. At the start of the Seven Days' battles, Branch's brigade skirmished with the Federals at Half Sink and Meadow Bridges, along the Chickahominy River. The first of the Seven Days' battles, Beaver Dam Creek, also known as Mechanicsville, was fought on June 26, 1862. In 1863, the county was the site of several small skirmishes and raids along the South Anna River.

War came in earnest to Hanover County in 1864. Countless skirmishes paled in comparison to some of the most fearsome struggles of the war. Included in this number are portions of the battle of North Anna River, May 23–26; two battles at Haw's Shop, May 28 and June 3; Totopotomoy Creek, May 28 — June 1; Bethesda Church, May 30, June 2, and June 3; Old Cold Harbor, May 31–June 1; and Cold Harbor, June 2–12. The last year of the war brought a raid conducted by Federal cavalry commander Philip H. Sheridan, sweeping through the northern sections of the county and destroying bridges, railroads, and anything left that might benefit the embattled Confederates. Southern soldiers returning after their surrender at Appomattox would find little left in Hanover County except destroyed houses, ruined farms, and fallow fields.[1]

In the years following the war, many battlefields were set aside as state or national parks to honor the history of the sites and the sacrifices of those who fought there. While Cold Harbor became a national military park and North Anna River became a state park, Hanover Court House and Peake's Turnout were not set aside as dedicated lands. None of the ground that was contested between Branch's enlarged brigade and Porter's V Corps has been preserved as a county park, state historic site, or national military park. Fortunately, several of the sites important to the battles and to earlier American history have been preserved. Dr. Kinney's home, also known as The Elms, still stands as a private residence, and the lands surrounding the home are still in cultivation. U.S. 301 lies in front of the house, much as the original road did in 1862. The Twenty-eighth North Carolina, after being overwhelmed by Butterfield's brigade, followed this route back to Hanover Court House. The courthouse itself was erected in 1735 and is on the National Register of Historic Places. It was in this courthouse "that Patrick Henry lighted the torch of liberty in the Parson's Cause — one of the earliest and bravest defiances against the rule of George III in the American colonies." Across the highway from the courthouse complex and a part of the Hanover Court House Historic District is Hanover Tavern, the original section dating to 1732. It was here that Patrick Henry lived when he delivered the Parson's Cause. Near the Tavern is the only Virginia Civil War Trails Marker that makes mention of the battles fought to the south in May 1862. A small map of the battlefield, along with a photograph of a flag of the Twenty-eighth North Carolina (a flag that the regiment had actually not yet been issued in May 1862), shares space with information on Stuart's ride around McClellan's army and operations connected with the Overland Campaign. A Confederate monument bearing the names of many of the men from Hanover County who fought in the Civil War is featured on the courthouse lawn.[2]

Running to one side of the Kenney House is Peaks Road. A traveler heading west along this road crosses over the second portion of the day's fight. The intersection of Hillcrest Road — the modern name of New Bridge Road — and Peaks Road is the site of the Federal position, which the Eighteenth and Thirty-seventh North Carolina Regiments assaulted in the last phase of the battle. A little further down (west) Peaks Road lie the tracks of the Virginia Central Railroad, now owned by CSX. The rails today still follow the original bed. Peake's Turnout is located where

Confederate monument to the soldiers from Hanover County on the grounds of the Hanover Court House (author's collection).

11. "It Still Should Not Be Forgotten" 139

Lebanon Methodist Church in 2004. Peake's Turnout is beyond the trees to the right (author's collection).

Peaks Road crosses the tracks of the CSX. This is also referred to as Peake's Station. Lebanon Methodist Church lies a little farther away on the right. On some period maps, the church is identified as Merry Oaks Church. The building that stood during the war was destroyed and replaced by the current structures. Lebanon Church was the camp of the Eighteenth North Carolina on the night before the battle and was possibly used as a field hospital during the battle. Past Lebanon Church, on Mount Hermon Road, is Slash Church, the structure that General Branch used as his headquarters on the night of May 26, 1862. The congregation and community celebrated the structure's 275th anniversary in 2004. A historical marker on the road in front of the church proclaims that "during the Civil War, Slash Church was used as a hospital and gave a nearby cavalry battle its name. This white weatherboard structure survives as the oldest and best-preserved frame colonial church in Virginia...." Other structures used as hospitals and denoted on maps, such as the Harris House and the Slaughter House, have not survived.

Many of the Federal dead were disinterred and removed to Cold Harbor National Cemetery. This cemetery was established in 1866, when a program was established to concentrate the scattered graves found on battlefields. A handful of the graves of Federal soldiers buried at Hanover were identified, and these graves can be found among the 2,110 burials in the cemetery. In 1877, the Tomb of the Unknown soldier was constructed and commemorates the 800-plus unknown soldiers who lie in a nearby trench. It is believed that the remains of Confederate soldiers were removed and reinterred in Richmond's Hollywood Cemetery. In 1866, the Hollywood Memorial Association began seeking out the graves of Confederate soldiers buried on surrounding farms and reinterred those soldiers within the

Confederate section of the cemetery. Other Confederate soldiers, those who were wounded and captured, and died before they could be sent to military prisons and hospitals in the North, have been reburied in the Yorktown National Cemetery.

The battles of Peake's Turnout and Hanover Court House were neither the largest nor the most important military engagements of the American Civil War. However, the soldiers who struggled there, both blue and gray, gave no less of themselves and their fortunes than those who fought and died on more famous fields, which today boast elaborate visitors' centers and professionally recorded driving tours. While their legacy is a modest one, it still should not be forgotten.

Appendix A

Order of Battle

Confederate

Brig. Gen. Lawrence O'Bryan Branch

BRANCH'S BRIGADE
    Seventh North Carolina
    Eighteenth North Carolina
    Twenty-eighth North Carolina
    Thirty-third North Carolina
    Thirty-seventh North Carolina

ATTACHED TO BRANCH'S COMMAND
    Forty-fifth Georgia
    Twelfth North Carolina
    Latham's (NC) Battery
    Fourth Virginia Cavalry (part)

Federal V Corps

Brig. Gen. Fitz John Porter

FIRST DIVISION
Brig. Gen. George W. Morell

FIRST BRIGADE
Brig. Gen. John H. Martindale
    Second Maine
    Eighteenth Massachusetts
    Twenty-second Massachusetts
    Thirteenth New York
    Twenty-fifth New York
    Second Company Massachusetts Sharpshooters, attached

Second Brigade
Col. James McQuade
  Fourteenth New York
  Fourth Michigan
  Ninth Massachusetts
  Sixty-second Pennsylvania

Third Brigade
Brig. Gen. Daniel Butterfield
  Sixteenth Michigan
  Twelfth New York
  Seventeenth New York
  Forty-fourth New York
  Eighty-third Pennsylvania
  Brady's Company Michigan Sharpshooters, attached

Artillery
Capt. Charles Griffin
  Massachusetts Light, Battery C
  Massachusetts Light, Battery E
  First Rhode Island Light, Battery C
  Fifth United States, Battery D

Sharpshooters
Col. Hiram Berdan
  First United States Sharpshooters

Second Division
Brig. Gen. George Sykes

First Brigade
Col. Robert C. Buchanan
  Third United States
  Fourth United States
  Twelfth United States
  Fourteenth United States

Second Brigade
Lt. Col. William Chapman
  Second United States
  Sixth United States
  Tenth United States
  Eleventh United States
  Seventeenth United States

Third Brigade
Col. Gouverneur K. Warren
  Fifth New York
  First Connecticut Heavy Artillery (Infantry)

Artillery
  Capt. Stephen H. Weed
    Third United States, Batteries L-M
    Fifth United States, Battery I

Attached to Porter's Command

Cavalry
  Brig. Gen. William H. Emory
    Sixth Pennsylvania
    Fifth United States
    Sixth United States

Appendix B

Fitz John Porter's Official Report

Headquarters Fifth Provisional Army Corps,
Camp near Harrison's Landing, Va., July 9, 1862.

General: The various and almost incessant occupations in connection with the repeated movements of this corps have prevented the completion by the proper officers of the reports which should have been received at these headquarters of their respective shares in the services it has rendered, and have thus relayed my report to you detailing those services.

The death of many officers in the late engagements makes it impossible that full reports of the services of their commands should be ever be completed. Now, at the first leisure moment, I have the honor to present in a narrative form a succinct record of some of the earlier operations of this corps.

Under the direction of the major-general commanding certain measures for the protection of the right flank of the army in its advance towards Richmond were put in my hands, beginning simultaneously with the march of the army from the Pamunkey. Among these were the clearing of the enemy from the upper peninsula as far as Hanover Court-House or beyond, and the destruction of railroad and other bridges over the South Anna and Pamunkey Rivers, in order to prevent the enemy in large force from getting into our rear from that direction, and in order, further, to cut one great line of the enemy's communications—*i.e.*, that connecting Richmond directly with Northern Virginia.

In pursuance of these plans I left at the time of our first advance a regiment at Mount Airey (White House road) to operate in connection with the Sixth Pennsylvania Cavalry, for the destruction of bridges, boats, &c., on the Pamunkey above White House. These forces, afterward consolidated into a brigade, consisting of the Fifth New York and First Connecticut Volunteers, Sixth Pennsylvania Cavalry and Weeden's Rhode Island battery, were placed in command of Colonel Warren, Fifth New York Volunteers, and posted at Old Church, from which point their efforts were successful in destroying all means of communication over the Pamunkey as far toward Hanover Court-House as was deemed prudent without the co-operation of an additional force.

In further pursuance of the same plans, and in accordance with verbal instructions of the major-general commanding, at 4 a.m. on the 27th May I marched from New Bridge with the division of General Morell, preceded by an advance guard of two regiments of cavalry and a light battery, under the command of Brigadier-General Emory. At the same hour I put in motion from Old Church the brigade under Colonel Warren. These two commands were to fall upon the enemy, whom I had reason to believe were camped in strong force near Hanover Court-House. The first command, under my immediate direction, was to take the enemy in front, while Colonel Warren, taking the road along the Pamunkey, was to fall upon him in flank and rear. Amidst a pelting storm of rain, through deep mud and water, the command struggled and pushed its way to Peake's Station, on the Virginia Central Railroad, 2 miles from Hanover Court-House, where we came in presence of the enemy.

Here preparations were at once made for battle by sending forward as skirmishers on the direct road to Hanover Court-House the Twenty-fifth New York Volunteers, Colonel Johnson, and Berdan's Sharpshooters, to engage the enemy's skirmishers and to hold him in check while Morell's division, slowly pushing through the swampy roads, could be brought up and deployed under the protection of a portion of Benson's battery, which was thrown into position so as to sweep the road.

In the mean time a squadron of cavalry and a section of artillery, supported by other cavalry, was sent to the left on the Ashland road to guard our flank and to destroy the railroad and telegraph at the crossing. This force soon became engaged with a portion of the enemy apparently attempting to outflank us. On the arrival of Martindale's brigade I dispatched it to support the last-mentioned force, confident that we could with Johnson, Berdan, and Benson hold the enemy in front until another brigade could be formed. Butterfield, soon coming up, formed his regiments and moved them in two lines, under the protection of wood and wheat fields immediately in front of the enemy, where he placed them until he could ascertain the position of the enemy. This done, he moved rapidly to the front, covered by skirmishers, driving the enemy before him, and capturing one piece of artillery and many prisoners. The enemy here having been put to flight, and one body of them seen moving in the direction of Hanover Court-House, the cavalry, with the light artillery, was sent in pursuit. In the mean time the infantry was formed in readiness to move to a point where I knew the enemy had been camped. At this time Colonel Warren's command joined, having been delayed in repairing bridges destroyed by the enemy.

Learning that the retreating force had been seen moving toward our right, I directed Martindale to collect his brigade and move up the railroad, by which route he would fall in rear of the place before mentioned as the former location of the enemy's camp. At the same time I directed Colonel Warren to push on with his cavalry and destroy the public and private bridges across the Pamunkey east of the railroad. I immediately put the rest of the command in motion for Hanover Court-House, but had scarcely reached that point with the head of the column when

I received information from a signal officer that the enemy were appearing in our rear.

The command was immediately faced about and marched back (left in front) to the former battle-field, where I found a portion of Martindale's brigade contending against great odds. Morell's brigade (Colonel McQuade commanding), which was not up in the first action, was thrown upon the enemy in front and flank. A portion of Butterfield's brigade, under his immediate direction, hearing the sound of musketry, had taken the shortest route from the advanced point it had reached, and also moved toward the rear of the enemy. These supports pushing rapidly upon him drove him from his position on the road toward Ashland, and we followed in pursuit till darkness put a stop to the operations for that day.

The succeeding day was occupied in gathering in the results of our victory. Of the enemy's dead we buried about 200. Our prisoners, wounded and unwounded, were forwarded to your headquarters—about 730. The gun already mentioned as having been captured was a 12-pounder howitzer. In addition we took one caisson, a large number of small-arms, some of them of new and valuable description. Two important military railroad trains were captured and destroyed by General Stoneman's and General Emory's commands respectively.

Still more important, however, were the indirect results of our victory, obtained by rapid movements on Ashland and the Richmond and Fredericksburg and Virginia Central Railroads. The reconnaissances on that day were pushed toward Ashland, one under the direction of Colonel Gove, Twenty-second Massachusetts, on the road from Hanover to Richmond. This passed through the abandoned camp of General Branch, from which the enemy in their rapid flight the previous night had carried off but a small part of their baggage and supplies. At the point where the road to Ashland branches to the right the enemy's pickets were discovered, and on being pressed and driven in to their supports, divulged the presence of a large force of all arms south of Ashland, between the turnpike and the Fredericksburg Railroad. The advance guard of another reconnaissance on the direct road from Hanover to Ashland pushed into Ashland, there discovering a brigade of Anderson's division on its way to Fredericksburg to Richmond. Another command, under Major Williams, Sixth Cavalry, was engaged in the destruction of the road bridges over the Pamunkey and the Virginia Central Railroad bridge over the South Anna. These, in connection with the Sixth Pennsylvania Cavalry, were also engaged in pursing the enemy, large numbers of whom were captured. Captain Harrison, of the Fifth Cavalry, took two armed companies of the Twenty-eighth North Carolina Regiment and Rush's cavalry one company. The following day I arranged for the destruction of the turnpike bridge and the Fredericksburg Railroad bridge over the South Anna, which duty I instructed to Major Williams, Sixth Cavalry. It was successfully accomplished.

I beg to refer to the reports of Major Williams and General Emory, and to commend for the consideration of the commanding general the officer and non-commissioned officers therein mentioned with special credit.

In order to hold in check any force which might be detached to cut off Major

Williams I sent one column (cavalry) under the direction of General Emory to threaten Ashland and push in there if possible; also another command (of all arms) under Colonel Warren to push into Ashland in the direct road. General Stoneman's command, which had been on the previous night placed under my orders, I pushed from Leech's Station toward Ashland as a support to Warren.

Syke's division of regulars, which had arrived within 3 miles of my headquarters on the previous night, was held in reserve and directed to support General Stoneman. With these forces I designed to clear Ashland. The advance of General Emory, under Captain Chambliss, entered Ashland and drove from it a small portion of the enemy, destroyed the bridge over Stony Creek, and broke up the railroad and telegraph. About half an hour after he had retired the advance of Colonel Warren entered Ashland and captured 12 of the enemy, who had immediately reoccupied the place on the retirement of Captain Chambliss.

Appendix C

Lawrence O'Bryan Branch's Official Report*

Headquarters in the Field
May 29, 1862

I have the honor to report, for the information of the general commanding the division, that, in order to cover the railroad against small parties of the enemy, and at the same time to carry out the other views and wishes of General Johnston, which he had communicated to me, I moved my camp on Monday last from Hanover Court-House to Slash Church. The position was selected because, while fulfilling other requirements, it was at the mouth of the road leading to Ashland, which assured me a means of retreat if assailed by the large forces of the enemy in close proximity to my front. I took up the position with a knowledge of its dangers, and all of my arrangements were made accordingly. No baggage train encumbered me, and my command bivouacked Monday night, infantry supports being thrown out for the cavalry pickets.

Tuesday morning the enemy were reported to be advancing on the road to Taliaferro's Mill, and I sent Colonel [James H.] Lane, with his own regiment (Twenty-eighth North Carolina) and a section of [A. C.] Latham's battery, to support the pickets and repel any small party. At the same time Colonel [Thomas] Hardeman's regiment (Forty-fifth Georgia) was sent to repair the railroad at Ashcake, where it had been obstructed by the enemy the day before, and watch any approach of the enemy on that road.

About the middle of the day the enemy opened fire from a battery near Peake's Crossing. Latham's battery soon got into position to reply, and, after a sharp action, silenced it. In the mean time a severe cannonade had been going on in the direction of Lane, showing that he too had been attacked. As soon as the battery in the road had been driven off I sent Colonel [Charles C.] Lee, with his own (the Thirty-seventh) and the Eighteenth (Col. Robert H. Cowan's) regiments to re-enforce

---

*Sent to Maj. Richard C. Morgan, assistant adjutant general to Maj. Gen. Ambrose Powell Hill.

him. When these two regiments had proceeded about 1½ miles the enemy was found strongly posted across the road. On learning this I galloped forward (leaving orders for Latham to follow as quickly as possible,) and was informed by Colonel Lee that the force of the enemy consisted of two regiments of infantry and some artillery. My plan was quickly formed and orders were given for its execution. Lee, with the Thirty-seventh, was to push through the woods and get close on the right flank of the battery. Hoke, as soon as he should return from a sweep through the woods on which I had sent him, and Colonel [Benjamin O.] Wade's (Twelfth North Carolina) regiment was to make a similar movement to the left flank of the battery, and Cowan was to charge across open ground in front. Hoke, supported by Colonel Wade, had a sharp skirmish in the woods, taking six prisoners and 11 horses, but came out too late to make the movement assigned to him, and Lee having sent for re-enforcements, I so far changed my plan as to abandon the attack on the enemy's left, and I sent Lieutenant Colonel Hoke to re-enforce Colonel Lee, relying on the front and right flank of the attack. Colonel Cowan, with the Eighteenth, made the charge most gallantly; but the enemy's force was much larger than had been supposed and strongly posted, and the gallant Eighteenth was compelled to seek shelter. It continued to pour heavy volleys from the edge of the woods, and must have done great execution. The steadiness with which this desperate charge was made reflects the highest credit on officers and men. The Thirty-seventh found the undergrowth so dense as to retard its progress; but when it reached its position poured a heavy and destructive fire upon the enemy. This combined attack of the Eighteenth and Thirty-seventh compelled the enemy to leave his battery for a time and take shelter behind a ditch bank.

For two hours the cavalry pickets had been coming in from the Ashcake road reporting a heavy force passing around my right by that road, and Col. B. H. Robertson, of the Virginia Cavalry, who was near Hanover Court-House, had sent me repeated messages to the effect that a heavy body from that direction was threatening my line of retreat. I had already learned that my brigade was engaged with an entire division in its front, but continued to contest in the hope that the cannonade would attract to me some re-enforcements, taking the precaution, however, to keep R. P. Campbell's (Seventh North Carolina) and Hardeman's (Forty-fifth Georgia) regiments in hand to cover the retreat in case my expectations should not be realized. Finding that I could remain no longer without being surrounded, and hearing of no re-enforcements, and feeling assured from the firing that Lane had made good his retreat to Hanover Court-House, I determined to draw off. This, always difficult in the presence of a superior enemy, was rendered comparatively easy by the precaution I had taken not to engage my whole force.

Campbell was ordered to place the Seventh across the road, so as to receive the enemy if they should attempt to follow. Orders were then sent to Lee and Cowan to withdraw in order. They were hotly engaged when the order was received, but promptly withdrew. Colonel Cowan, in an especial manner, attracted my attention by the perfect order in which he brought out his regiment, notwithstanding the severe and long-continued fire he had sustained from both infantry and artillery.

Appendix C: Lawrence O'Bryan Branch's Official Report

The regiments marched to the rear without haste or confusion, and went up the Ashland road. A cautious attempt was made by the enemy to follow, but a single volley from the rear guard of the Seventh arrested it. The march was continued without interruption to Ashland, where I was ordered by General Johnston to report to Major-General Hill. All my subsequent movements having been under orders received from him in person, they need not be detailed.

Having but one wagon and one ambulance, I was under the necessity of leaving a portion of my wounded. The enemy left a portion of their killed on the ground we subsequently occupied.

My senior surgeon established his hospital in a house on which the hospital flag was conspicuously displayed. It was not in nor near the line of fire. I saw many shells thrown by the enemy explode immediately over and around the house. It could not have been undesigned.

Colonel Lane, with the Twenty-eighth Regiment, has rejoined the brigade, but I have not received his report of the engagement he had with the enemy. As soon as received will be forwarded to you.

My loss (excluding Colonel Lane's command) was 66 killed and 177 wounded.

An entire division was engaged against me, and, as you are aware, a large part of General McClellan's army was in supporting distance.

The officers and men of my command conducted themselves in a very handsome manner both in the engagement and on the march. The enemy may have captured stragglers enough to offset the prisoners we took from them in the open field, but they took no body of my troops. Twice during the day the enemy were driven back, the last time taking shelter behind a ditch bank at the edge of the woods. From this position I did not succeed in driving them.

> I have the honor to be, yours, very respectfully,
> L. O'B. Branch,
> *Brigadier General, Commanding*

Appendix D

Casualties

Key

Pvt.— Private
Cpl.— Corporal
Sgt.— Sergeant
1st Sgt.— First Sergeant
Sgt. Maj.— Sergeant Major
Mus.— Musician
Adj.— Adjutant
Comm. Sgt.— Commissary Sergeant
3rd Lt.— Third Lieutenant

2nd Lt.— Second Lieutenant
1st Lt.— First Lieutenant
Capt.— Captain
Maj.— Major
Lt. Col.— Lieutenant Colonel
Misc.— Miscellaneous
As. Surg.— Assistant Surgeon
Surg.— Surgeon
F & S — Field and Staff

Confederate Casualties
(listed by name, rank, company, and fate)

Seventh North Carolina State Troops[1]

Bischerer, Godfrey, Pvt.	F	Captured
Brannon, Patrick, Pvt.	D	Captured
Burns, Michael C., Pvt.	C	Captured
Cambridge, W. R., Pvt.	Misc.	Captured
Campbell, W. R., Pvt.	Misc.	Captured
Castle, Joseph, Pvt.	B	Deserted
Doesinger, Francis, Pvt.	D	Captured
Gallagher, James, Pvt.	D	Deserted
Garman, William R., Pvt.	B	Captured
Gaultney, Josiah P., Pvt.	A	Captured
Haire, Perry, Cpl.	F	Captured
Hartshell, James E., Pvt.	B	Deserted and captured
Hegler, Charles W., Pvt.	F	Captured
Herlocker, David, Pvt.	B	Captured
Johnston, Thomas, Pvt.	D	Deserted
Kanapaux, Alexander E., Pvt.	D	Captured
Keogh, John, Pvt.	C	Wounded, neck or groin or both
Matthews, John, Pvt.	C	Captured

Maxwell, William, Pvt.	B	Captured
McClellan, William A., Pvt.	B	Captured
Messer, Martin, Pvt.	B	Wounded, left thigh, and captured[2]
Morris, James, Pvt.	F	Wounded in the head and captured
O'Bryant, Robert, Pvt.	C	Wounded, right hip
Register, Benjamin T., Pvt.	C	Wounded, back, and captured
Robinson, William G., Pvt.	K	Captured
Sills, Leonard T., Pvt.	F	Wounded
Templeton, Joseph N., Pvt.	I	Wounded

Twelfth North Carolina Troops[1]

Armstrong, H. S., Cpl.	K	Deserted or captured
Bartholimew, Samuel, Pvt.	K	Captured
Bass, David, Pvt.	K	Wounded and captured
Blanton, William C., Pvt.	E	Killed
Brown, James, Pvt.	A	Wounded, thigh, and died of wounds on June 6, 1862, in hospital in Richmond, VA
Bugg, William P.	C	Wounded, left elbow[2]
Bunn, Elias, Adj.	F&S	Mortally wounded
Collins, S. A., Pvt.	I	Captured
Conner, W. W., Pvt.	C	Captured
Conte, Francis, Pvt.	G	Captured
Denton, Henry, Pvt.	K	Wounded and captured
Hawkins, William, Pvt.	I	Captured
Hedgpeth, Lewis W., Pvt.	H	Wounded, right thigh, and captured[3]
Hughes, Andrew J., Pvt.	E	Captured
Hundley, John A., Pvt.	F	Captured
McCroden, Robert, Pvt.	K	Captured
Paschall, Robert H. M., Sgt.	B	Wounded
Pullen, W. P., Pvt.	I	Wounded, back or abdomen or both, and captured
Robertson, Benjamin P., Pvt.	C	Wounded, head, and captured
Robertson, Thomas, Pvt.	C	Wounded, abdomen, and died of wounds[4]
Robeson, Thomas T., Pvt.	E	Wounded, left side, and captured[5]
Settlemyre, Daniel S., Pvt.	A	Captured
Shearin, James O., Pvt.	C	Killed
Sherrill, John A. L., 1st Sgt.	A	Wounded
Thomas, James O'K., Pvt.	K	Wounded, thigh, captured, and died of wounds on May 28, 1862
Todd, Henry A., Pvt.	H	Captured[6]
Warren, Thomas A., Pvt.	G	Wounded, thigh, and captured
Wilkerson, Bentley, Pvt.	B	Wounded, lungs, and captured[7]
Wilson, Andrew, Pvt.	H	Captured[8]
Wood, Ellin, Pvt.	I	Captured
Wood, William R., Pvt.	G	Wounded, pelvis, captured, and died of wounds on May 31, 1862, at Gaines's Mill, VA

Eighteenth North Carolina Troops[1]

Andres, J. A., Cpl.	K	Wounded, throat, captured, and died of wounds on June 16, 1862, at Yorktown, VA
Atkins, William E., Pvt.	K	Wounded
Barefoot, Henry, Pvt.	H	Wounded, right shoulder

Appendix D: Casualties 155

Barnes, Clark, Pvt.	D	Wounded, leg[2]
Barns, John, Pvt.	D	Captured
Bellamy, Isaac E., Pvt.	C	Killed
Bennett, James N., Cpl.	C	Wounded, died of wounds June 13, 1862
Best, William R., Pvt.	C	Captured
Blackwell, John W., Pvt.	B	Wounded[3]
Bonsold, John, Pvt.	A	Captured
Bright, Eli S., Pvt.	G	Captured
Britt, Amos, Pvt.	D	Wounded, "in foot"[4]
Britt, E. J., Pvt.	D	Wounded, leg, captured, and died of wounds
Britt, Isham, Pvt.	D	Captured
Brown, Neill, Pvt.	F	Wounded, "in left fore finger"[5]
Brown, Thomas W. Jr., Capt.	A	Deserted and captured
Brown, William F., Pvt.	E	Wounded, back, and captured
Bryan, Charles W., Pvt.	K	Killed
Buchanan, William Jr., Pvt.	F	Wounded, "in left arm"[6]
Calhoun, Hugh C., Pvt.	F	Captured
Calhoun, Malcom, Pvt.	F	Wounded, "in calf of leg"[7]
Capalini, Lewis, Pvt.	F	Wounded, left knee joint, captured, and died of wounds on June 10, 1862[8]
Capps, Thomas, Pvt.	D	Wounded, chest, captured, and died of wounds
Chistrie, R. J., Pvt.	B	Wounded[9]
Clark, Andrew J., Pvt.	F	Killed
Clewis, Zachariah, Pvt.	D	Wounded
Corbett, David J., Cpl.	E	Wounded
Cromartie, James A., Cpl.	K	Wounded, right side, and captured
Davis, James, Pvt.	K	Captured
Davis, Owen, Pvt.	A	Wounded
De Bouse, George F., Pvt.	E	Wounded, thigh, captured, and died of wounds
Dunham, Jonathan R., Pvt.	K	Captured
Dyer, Samuel I., Pvt.	G	Captured
Edwards, Cornelius, Pvt.	D	Wounded
Edwards, Guilford W., Pvt.	D	Killed
Edwards, Haynes, Pvt.	B	Captured
Edwards, Hinnant, Pvt.	D	Captured
Edwards, John J., Pvt.	H	Killed
Edwards, Neill, Pvt.	D	Wounded, leg[10]
Edwards, Wright, Pvt.	B	Wounded, abdomen, and captured
Fair, Lewis, Pvt.	K	Captured
Ferguson, Daniel, Pvt.	K	Captured
Fisher, Joseph, Pvt.	H	Captured
Flanigan, Alfred, Pvt.	E	Captured
Flanner, Charles, Cpl.	G	Captured
Freeman, Gardner, Pvt.	K	Captured
Frink, William S., Pvt.	H	Wounded
Garriss, Gideon A., Pvt.	E	Captured
Gibson, Duncan M., Pvt.	F	Wounded, head, captured, and died of wounds on June 10, 1862, Yorktown, VA
Gilbert, Thomas F., Pvt.	D	Killed
Graham, Henry P., Pvt.	F	Wounded, "grazed on left thigh," died "at Home" of wounds, June 30, 1862[11]
Green, Daniel, Pvt.	C	Captured
Guyton, Jeremiah, Pvt.	B	Killed

Hackeman, Gerhard D., Pvt.	A	Wounded, right leg, captured, and died of his wounds on June 1, 1862, in Yorktown, VA
Hall, Washington, Pvt.	A	Captured
Hall, William J., Pvt.	A	Wounded, right thigh, and captured
Hammonds, Orren, Pvt.	B	Wounded, head, captured, and died of wounds May 30, 1862
Henderson, John A., Pvt.	F	Wounded, "in calf of right leg"[12]
Hilburn, Calvin L., Pvt.	B	Wounded[13]
Hinson, William J., Pvt.	H	Wounded, leg and captured
Hoener, John, Pvt.	A	Wounded and captured
Huckabee, Alexander A., Pvt.	F	Wounded, "on left side of head"[14]
Hughes, John, Pvt.	F	Captured
Johnston, George A., 1st Lt.	A	Wounded, back or chest, captured, and died of his wounds[15]
Jones, Alexander F., Pvt.	F	Wounded, legs, and captured
Jones, Charles, Cpl.	C	Wounded
Jones, John M., Pvt.	C	Killed
Jordan, David J., Pvt.	B	Wounded, died of wounds June 18, 1862, Petersburg, VA
Kenien, Owen, Pvt.	E	Killed
King, Alexander, Pvt.	K	Captured
King, Samuel J., Cpl.	G	Wounded, throat and right leg, captured, and died of wounds June 4, 1862, Gaines's Mill, VA[16]
Kyle, Henry R., Pvt.	A	Captured
Latter, Edward V., Sgt.	C	Wounded, fibula, and captured
Lawson, Alva, Pvt.	D	Captured
Lay, William J., Sgt.	C	Wounded
Lewis, James B., Pvt.	A	Captured
Lilly, Gabriel R., Cpl.	H	Wounded, left side, captured, and died of wounds on unknown date
Long, James M., Pvt.	C	Killed
Long, Samuel A., 2nd Lt.	C	Wounded, "but fought the battle out"[17]
Long, Wallace W., Pvt.	C	Wounded, right thigh, captured, and died on unknown date
Lovett, Kitchen, Pvt.	D	Wounded, left eye, and captured
McCormack, Murphy C., Pvt.	F	Captured
McDuffie, Murdock, Pvt.	F	Wounded, hand, and captured[18]
McDuffie, William J., Pvt.	K	Captured
McGee, Troy W,. Pvt.	B	Killed
McKeel, Major, Sgt.	H	Captured
McKethan, John M., Pvt.	K	Killed
McKinnon, Deal, Pvt.	F	Captured
McLauchlin, Alexander B., Pvt.	F	Killed
McLauchlin, John M., Pvt.	F	Wounded, hip, and captured
McLean, John F., Pvt.	F	Wounded, hip, and captured
McMillan, John D., Pvt.	K	Captured
McNair, John F., Pvt.	F	Captured
McNeill, Angus H., Pvt.	F	Wounded, hand[19]
McNeill, William H., Pvt.	F	Wounded, "left ankle," captured, and died of wounds June 8, 1862, Yorktown, Va[20]
McNesmith, Neil, Cpl.	F	Captured
McRae, Archibald L., Pvt.	F	Wounded, hip, and captured
Malpass, George W., Pvt.	E	Wounded, shoulder and chest, and captured, died of wounds on June 8, 1862, Fort Columbus, NY

Appendix D: Casualties

Malpass, Lewis H., Pvt.	E	Captured
Malpass, Thaddeus D., Pvt.	E	Wounded
Martin, John G., Pvt.	F	Captured
Maultsby, William J., Cpl.	K	Captured
Meares, Elihu, Cpl.	C	Wounded
Melvin, Henry, Pvt.	K	Captured
Millis, Robert, Pvt.	G	Captured
Moore, Henry, Pvt.	E	Wounded, right leg
Morrison, John B., Pvt.	G	Wounded
Murphy, William H., Pvt.	F	Captured
Nance, John E., Pvt.	B	Wounded, jaw, and captured
Nelson, Wesley H., Pvt.	F	Captured
Newman, Elias, Pvt	H	Wounded
Norton, Elijah Sr., Pvt.	F	Captured
Ortman, Ernest, Pvt.	A	Wounded and captured[21]
Pate, David, Pvt.	B	Captured
Pate, Edward, Pvt.	B	Killed
Patterson, Hugh L., Pvt.	F	Wounded, "in left arm"[22]
Peterson, Haywood L., Pvt.	E	Wounded, thigh
Pigford, Jacob L., Pvt.	E	Wounded, left arm, left foot, or right leg or both
Prevatt, Forney A., Pvt.	D	Wounded, shoulder[23]
Pridgen, Alonzo, Cpl.	E	Wounded, died of wounds on August 28, 1862
Pridgen, Bradley F., Pvt.	E	Killed
Pridgen, Timothy F., Cpl.	K	Captured
Proctor, John, Pvt.	H	Killed
Regan, Authorniles, Pvt.	B	Captured
Regan, Ralph, Pvt.	D	Wounded, "in arm"[24]
Rhodes, William D., Pvt.	C	Wounded, abdomen, captured, and died of wounds on June 8, 1862
Rinaldi, Albert, 1st Sgt.	K	Wounded, left hip and groin, and captured
Roberts, Richard B., Pvt.	B	Wounded, left shoulder, captured, and died of wounds July 24, 1862, near Fort Monroe, VA
Rooks, Archibald B., Pvt.	E	Wounded, side, and captured[25]
Roper, Amos W., Pvt.	F	Wounded, "in left arm"[26]
Schlobohmm, Albert, Pvt.	A	Wounded
Shaw, Daniel P., Pvt.	B	Captured
Sherrell, James M., Pvt.	D	Wounded, right leg, captured, and died of wounds
Sibbit, John, Pvt.	H	Wounded, left ankle, or leg or both, captured, and died of wounds on June 11, 1862, in Yorktown, VA
Simmons, Alexander C., Cpl.	A	Wounded, right shoulder, and captured[27]
Singletary, Harmon W., Pvt.	B	Wounded and died of wounds on June 15, 1862, in Richmond, VA
Singletary, Milton E., Pvt.	B	Captured
Sikes, Willie J., Capt.	B	Killed
Southerland, Daniel K., Pvt.	H	Captured
Stansel, Bunyan, Pvt.	D	Wounded, right leg, and captured
Strickland, Brazil L., Pvt.	C	Wounded, ankle, and captured
Stringfield, David J., Pvt.	E	Captured
Stringfield, James P., Sgt.	E	Captured
Sullivan, Daniel K., Pvt.	K	Captured
Sutton, Martin V. B., Pvt.	K	Captured
Swindall, Chester, Pvt.	K	Captured
Sykes, William H., Pvt.	K	Captured

Tart, Enos, Pvt.	C	Wounded, left thigh, and captured
Taylor, Charles M., Pvt.	E	Captured
Tedder, John W., Pvt.	H	Wounded, left thigh, and captured
Thompson, Needham J., Sgt.	D	Wounded, shoulder[28]
Thrower, Charles N., Pvt.	F	Wounded, "in calf of left leg," and captured[29]
Tolar, Sampson B., Pvt.	K	Wounded
Townsend, Neill, 2nd Lt.	D	Wounded, arm[30]
Trundall, Richard, Pvt.	A	Captured
Vause, Edward K., Pvt.	C	Captured
Vause, Samuel A., Pvt.	C	Captured
Wadkins, Alva M., Pvt.	H	Killed
Ward, Matthew J., 1st Sgt.	C	Killed
Ward, William R., Pvt.	C	Wounded
Weeks, George W., Pvt.	B	Wounded, both thighs, and captured
Whitted, John Mc., Pvt.	G	Captured
Wilkins, Simon P., Pvt.	C	Wounded
Williams, Moses, Pvt.	C	Wounded, right leg, and captured
Williams, Quincey, Pvt.	E	Killed
Williamson, Barnett, Pvt.	C	Wounded and captured
Williamson, Doctor M., Pvt.	C	Wounded
Willis, John S., Pvt.	K	Wounded, thigh, and captured
Wilson, James W., Cpl.	B	Killed
Woodel, Elias, Cpl.	D	Killed
Wright, Samuel, Pvt.	F	Wounded, "right side," and captured[31]
Young, Bryant A., Pvt.	H	Killed

Twenty-eighth North Carolina Troops[1]

Abernathy, J. Henry, Pvt.	C	Captured
Abernathy, John A., Hospt. Stew.	F&S	Captured
Adkins, Robert, Pvt.	A	Captured[2]
Allison, William T., Pvt.	B	Captured
Almond, Ervin, Pvt.	D	Captured
Andrews, Henry C., 1st Sgt.	G	Captured
Apperson, Thomas V., Capt.	F	Wounded, left leg and captured
Armstrong, Merideth T., Pvt.	I	Captured
Ashburn, James W., Pvt.	A	Captured
Atkinson, Charles H., Pvt.	A	Captured
Austin, E. Coleman, Cpl.	C	Captured
Axum, Samuel I., Pvt.	A	Captured
Ballard, James H., Pvt.	E	Captured
Ballard, Miles M., Pvt.	E	Captured
Barbee, James C., Pvt.	D	Captured, and died of typhoid on June 7, 1862, at Fort Columbus, NY
Barger, Allen, Pvt.	C	Captured
Barger, Josiah W., Pvt.	C	Captured
Barger, Marcus, Pvt.	C	Captured
Barham, W. R., Ast. Surg.	F&S	Captured[3]
Beaty, R. M., Pvt.	B	Captured
Bishop, John, Pvt.	G	Captured
Blackwood, Julius T., Pvt.	A	Captured
Blanton, Francis A., Pvt.	H	Captured[4]
Blanton, Thomas J., Pvt.	H	Captured

Appendix D: Casualties 159

Bohannon, Neal, 1st Lt.	I	Captured
Bolch, Arron, Pvt.	C	Captured
Bray, Edward W., Pvt.	A	Captured
Bridges, Preston, Pvt.	H	Captured
Brockwell, William B., Pvt.	G	Captured
Brown, Barnabas, Pvt.	A	Captured
Buchannon, William, Pvt.	I	Captured
Bullin, John A., Pvt.	D	Killed
Bumgarner, Allen L., Pvt.	C	Captured
Bumgarner, David A., Pvt.	C	Captured
Bundy, Henry, Pvt.	I	Captured
Bundy, Nathan, Pvt.	I	Captured
Burgess, Ambrose C, Pvt.	H	Captured
Burris, Lee H., Pvt.	A	Captured
Calvard, Benjamin, Pvt.	F	Wounded, forearm, and captured[5]
Carlton, Sandford B., Pvt.	I	Captured
Carpenter, John T., Pvt.	B	Captured
Carpenter, William H., Pvt.	B	Captured
Carson, John B., Pvt.	B	Captured
Cates, Dennis M., Pvt.	G	Captured
Cheek, Julius M., Pvt.	G	Captured
Cheek, William J. A., Pvt.	G	Captured
Childress, John H., Pvt.	A	Captured
Childress, William H., Pvt.	I	Captured
Cline, Monroe J., Pvt.	C	Captured
Cloninger, James S., Pvt.	B	Captured
Cloninger, Sidney, Pvt.	B	Captured
Cobb, Thompson, Pvt.	H	Captured
Cockerham, Jesse W., Pvt.	A	Captured
Coley, Jesse M., Pvt.	K	Captured
Comer, James Q., Cpl.	I	Captured
Cornelius, John H., 3rd Lt.	F	Wounded, right thigh and captured
Costner, Hiram J., Pvt.	B	Captured
Costner, Jonas L., Pvt.	B	Captured
Crabtree, Simpson, Pvt.	G	Captured
Crabtree, William E., Pvt.	G	Captured
Craige, James F., Pvt.	G	Captured
Crawford, Henry C., Pvt.	G	Captured
Crowell, John M., Pvt.	D	Captured
Crowell, John T., Pvt.	D	Captured
Davis, Albert C., Pvt.	B	Captured
Davis, Daniel, Pvt.	F	Killed
Dickenson, Isaac D., Pvt.	I	Captured
Dobbins, Milas, Pvt.	I	Captured
Dozier, Smith W., Pvt.	I	Captured
Durham, Joseph H., Pvt.	G	Captured
Durham, Robert A., Pvt.	G	Captured
Durham, Thomas M., Pvt.	G	Captured
Eckard, Cyrus, Pvt.	C	Captured, died of typhoid at Fort Columbus, New York, June 22, 1862
Edwards, Adolphus, Pvt.	C	Captured
Edwards, Daniel, Pvt.	A	Captured

Edwards, Edwin S., Sgt. G Captured
Edwards, William D. F., Cpl. G Captured
Eller, Henry P., Pvt. I Captured
Eudy, William, Pvt. K Captured
Everage, Joseph, Pvt. I Captured
Falls, John J., Pvt. B Captured
Farmer, Leon R., Pvt. K Captured
Farris, Enoch H., Pvt. I Captured
Floyd, John A., Pvt. B Captured
Ford, Lauson H., Pvt. B Captured
Foy, Jesse S., Pvt. B Captured
Friday, Andrew S., Pvt. B Captured
Fronebarger, D. A., Pvt. B Captured
Furr, Lauson A., Pvt. K Captured
Gabriel, A. Alonzo, Pvt. C Captured
Gamble, Franklin W., Pvt. B Captured
Gamble, W. A., Pvt. B Killed
Glascoe, Calvin W., Pvt. A Captured
Goins, Philip P., Pvt. C Captured
Green, David O., Pvt. H Captured
Green, Edmond, Pvt. H Captured
Green, James M., Pvt. H Captured
Green, Miles, Pvt. F Captured
Grice, James M., Pvt. C Captured
Grice, John L., Pvt. B Captured
Grigg, William A., Pvt. A Captured[6]
Groves, James L., Pvt. B Captured
Hall, Elisha, Cpl. E Captured
Hall, John W., Pvt. E Captured
Hamrick, Asa, Cpl. H Captured
Harris, John, Pvt. A Captured
Harris, Wiley O., Pvt. B Captured
Hathcock, George W., Mus. K Captured
Hatley, John, Pvt. K Captured
Hayes, Richard T., Pvt. G Captured
Haynes, Anderson H., Pvt. I Captured
Hefner, Serenus, Pvt. C Captured
Hefner, Wilson W., Pvt. C Captured
Hendricks, Cleophus D., Pvt. I Captured
Herman, Daniel M., Pvt. C Captured
Herman, Phanuel J., Pvt. C Captured
Hiatt, George W., Pvt. A Captured
Hicks, Jonathan, Pvt. F Captured
Hilliard, Silas, Pvt. D Captured
Hoffman, John C., Pvt. B Captured
Holler, Lemuel, Pvt. C Captured
Hopkins, John F., Pvt. D Captured
Houston, John M., Pvt. C Captured
Hudspeth, James, Pvt. I Captured
Huffman, Elijah, Pvt. C Captured
Huffman, Elijah J., Pvt. C Captured
Huffman, Marcus, Pvt. C Captured, died of typhoid July 1–2, 1862, at Fort Columbus, NY

Appendix D: Casualties

Huffstetler, Joshua, Pvt.	B	Captured
Huffstetler, William A., Pvt.	B	Captured
Hulin, Newton A., Pvt.	D	Captured
Huneycutt, Henry, Pvt.	D	Captured
Huneycutt, Lindsey L., Pvt.	D	Captured
Huneycutt, Solomon, Pvt.	C	Captured
Hunter, Richard, Pvt.	G	Wounded, died of wounds
Jarvis, Lucket C., Pvt.	I	Captured
Jenkins, Andrew J., Pvt.	B	Captured
Jennings, S. W., Pvt.	I	Captured, died of fever June 28–30, 1862, Davis Island, NY
John, James P., Pvt.	I	Captured
Johnston, George B., Capt.	G	Captured
Jolley, Clingman C., Pvt.	H	Captured[7]
Joyce, Robert H., Pvt.	I	Captured
Joyner, David W., Pvt.	F	Captured
Key, James R., Pvt.	A	Killed
Key, Martin V., Cpl.	A	Killed
Key, R. J., Pvt.	A	Killed
Killian, Joseph E., Pvt.	C	Captured
King, William D., Pvt.	G	Captured
Kirk, Thomas F., Pvt.	D	Captured
Kirk, William D., Pvt.	K	Captured
Kirk, William G., Pvt.	K	Captured
Kirkland, Samuel D., Pvt.	G	Captured
Leagans, Ananias, Pvt.	I	Captured
Leagans, James M., Pvt.	I	Captured
Lefler, Coleman, Pvt.	D	Captured
Lingerfelt, Jacob, Pvt.	B	Captured
Link, Ephraim M., Pvt.	C	Captured
Lovelace, James L., Pvt.	H	Captured
Lowe, Samuel D., Maj.	F&S	Captured
McArver, Franklin H., Pvt.	B	Captured
McAulay, Angus M., Pvt.	E	Captured
McBride, John G., Pvt.	I	Captured
McCaskill, James, Pvt.	E	Captured
McIntyre, Isaiah, Pvt.	K	Captured
McIntyre, John F., Pvt.	K	Captured
McKinley, Steven C., Pvt.	K	Captured
McLure, John J., Pvt.	B	Captured
McSwain, David L., Pvt.	H	Captured
Macy, William L., Pvt.	I	Captured
Marsh, William, Pvt.	A	Captured
Martin, Edward A., Sgt.	G	Captured
Martin, John H. Jr. Pvt.	I	Captured
Martin, Robert N. M. Pvt.	C	Captured, died of typhoid on July 16, 1862, at Fort Columbus, NY
Mauldin, James Pvt.	K	Killed
Mauney, William A. Comm. Sgt.	F&S	Captured
Melton, Zachariah, Pvt.	I	Captured
Michaels, Nicholas, Pvt.	F	Wounded, left hand, and captured
Miller, Arthur K., Pvt.	D	Captured
Milton, George, Pvt.	K	Captured

Mock, John, Pvt.	I	Captured[8]
Moore, John A., Pvt.	C	Wounded, died of wounds on June 10–11, 1862, in Richmond, VA
Morris, Baxter B., Pvt.	G	Wounded, knee or left thigh or both, captured, and died of wounds on June 30, 1862, at Fort Monroe, VA
Morris, Isaac J., Pvt.	G	Captured
Morris, John A., Pvt.	G	Captured
Morrow, Daniel F., Sgt.	G	Captured
Morrow, Richard A., Pvt.	G	Captured
Morton, Jesse A. Sr., Pvt.	K	Captured
Morton, Lemuel, Pvt.	K	Captured
Morton, William G., Pvt.	K	Captured
Motley, Thomas, Pvt.	K	Captured
Neil, Christopher, Pvt.	B	Captured
Nevill, Jesse, Pvt.	G	Captured
Nichols, Abraham S., Pvt.	B	Captured
Nicholson, James G., Pvt.	F	Captured
Page, Henry C., Sgt.	K	Wounded, scalp, and captured
Parks, William C., Pvt.	A	Captured
Parsons, Albert, Pvt.	A	Captured
Patterson, Harrison, Pvt.	A	Captured
Pendergrass, John S., Pvt.	G	Captured
Pennington, Nelson C., Pvt.	D	Captured
Perkins, Michael C., Pvt.	B	Captured
Pettyjohn, James, Pvt.	I	Captured
Pettyjohn, William, Pvt.	I	Captured
Plyler, Henry D., Pvt.	D	Captured
Pool, Henry G., Pvt.	A	Captured
Poovey, David A., Pvt.	C	Captured
Pryor, David, Pvt.	C	Captured
Pryor, Samuel, Pvt.	C	Captured
Pucket, James M., Pvt.	A	Captured
Puckett, Hugh, Pvt.	A	Wounded, right leg, "foot shot off" and captured[9]
Punch, Robert W., Pvt.	C	Wounded
Punch, William S., Pvt.	C	Captured
Rader, William P., Pvt.	C	Captured
Reden, James A., Pvt.	E	Captured
Reece, Evan H., Pvt.	I	Captured
Reid, John, Pvt.	A	Captured
Reynolds, George T., Pvt.	I	Captured
Reynolds, James A., Pvt.	C	Captured
Rhyne, Alexander A., Pvt.	B	Captured
Rhyne, George C., Pvt.	B	Captured
Rink, Henry, Pvt.	C	Wounded, forearm, captured, and died of wounds July 6, 1862, Fort Monroe, VA
Roberson, John A., Pvt.	G	Captured
Roberts, Pleasant H., Pvt.	A	Wounded, thigh, captured, and died of wounds on June 2, 1862, at Gaines's Mill, VA
Rogers, Aaron, Pvt.	K	Captured
Rogers, John W., Sgt.	K	Captured
Rose, Isaac W., Pvt.	I	Captured
Ross, Doctor M., Sgt.	K	Captured
Ross, George P., Pvt.	K	Captured

Royal, Willie D., Mus.	I	Captured
Russell, Joseph C., Pvt.	E	Captured
Ryan, Samuel G., Pvt.	G	Captured
Sanders, Thomas L., Pvt.	B	Captured
Sarvis, John R., Pvt.	B	Captured
Scott, Calvin, 3rd Lt.	G	Wounded and captured
Seaboch, George W., Pvt.	C	Captured
Seaboch, William H., Pvt.	C	Captured
Setzer, Franklin A., Pvt.	C	Captured
Shields, Isaac W., Pvt.	B	Captured
Shores, Alexander F., Cpl.	I	Captured
Short, John, Pvt.	C	Captured, and died on July 20, 1862, at Fort Columbus, NY
Sifford, Daniel M., Pvt.	B	Captured
Sigman, Maxwell A., Pvt.	C	Captured
Sizemore, John E., Pvt.	C	Wounded, captured, and died June 30, 1862, of wounds, Fort Monroe, VA
Smith, Calvin, Pvt.	E	Captured
Smith, Evan, Pvt.	K	Captured
Smith, George, Pvt.	G	Captured
Smith, Mitchell, Pvt.	G	Captured
Smith, Noah, Pvt.	B	Captured
Smith, P. H., Pvt.	B	Captured
Snipes, Jesse B., Pvt.	G	Captured
Speer, William H. A., Capt.	I	Captured
Stanford, William G., Pvt.	G	Wounded and captured
Stantliff, Oliver, Pvt.	A	Captured
Stowe, Beverly F., Pvt.	B	Captured
Stowe, Samuel N., Capt.	B	Captured
Stowe, T. B., Pvt.	B	Captured
Stroup, Moses, Pvt.	B	Captured
Sykes, Johnson C., Pvt.	G	Captured
Tally, Martin V. B., Pvt.	D	Captured
Thomas, William R., Pvt.	B	Captured
Thompson, Calvin C., Pvt.	K	Captured
Thompson, Edmond R., Pvt.	K	Captured
Thompson, Francis W., Pvt.	B	Captured
Throneburg, Marcus A., 2nd Lt.	C	Captured
Tippet, William, Cpl.	E	Captured
Tolbert, Josiah P., Pvt.	K	Captured
Townson, Aaron E., Pvt.	C	Captured
Townson, Solomon, Pvt.	C	Captured[10]
Turner, Enoch, Pvt.	K	Captured
Turner, Ferdinand G., Pvt.	D	Captured
Vickers, Joseph G., Pvt.	G	Captured
Wagner, Noah P., Pvt.	C	Captured
Wagner, Thomas J., Pvt.	C	Captured
Waisner, David W., Pvt.	E	Captured
Ward, William J., Pvt.	G	Captured
Weatherman, Robert W., 1st Sgt.	I	Captured
Weaver, James M., Pvt.	I	Captured
White, E. M., Pvt.	B	Captured
Whitehead, James S., Pvt.	I	Captured

Whitley, George, Pvt.	K	Captured
Williams, George D., Pvt.	F	Captured
Williams, Isaac, 1st Sgt.	E	Captured
Wilson, George W., Pvt.	H	Captured
Wishon, Samuel A., Pvt.	I	Captured
Wyatt, Wyley A., Pvt.	B	Captured

Thirty-third North Carolina Troops[1]

Ball, Martin V., Pvt.	F	Captured
Barnhardt, Rufus W., Pvt.	C	Captured
Brady, Richard B., Pvt.	E	Wounded, right hand and shoulder[2]
Brown, Martin, Pvt.	D	Captured
Cass, Noah, Pvt.	A	Deserted
Dillon, Michael, Pvt.	A	Captured
Emory, John, Pvt.	F	Captured
Fulton, John, Pvt.	I	Captured
Gardner, James W., Pvt.	B	Captured
Gray, William H., Pvt.	F	Captured
Guy, John N., Pvt.	A	Wounded, "fingers of right hand," and captured[3]
Hine, William C., Pvt.	I	Captured[4]
Lane, James F., Pvt.	I	Captured
Mitchell, William J., Pvt.	G	Captured
Murph, John M., Pvt.	A	Captured
O'Neal, Robert H., Pvt.	B	Captured
Propst, John A., Pvt.	C	Wounded, left arm
Riddick, William H., Pvt.	E	Captured
Sawyer, William I., Pvt.	F	Captured
Shaffner, John F., Surg.	F&S	Captured
Sterling, Duncan J., Pvt.	G	Captured
Summerlin, James M., Pvt.	B	Captured
Vainright, William, Pvt.	B	Captured
Ward, Joseph H., Cpl.	A	Captured

Thirty-seventh North Carolina Troops[1]

Abernathy, William R. D., Pvt.	H	Wounded, "shot in arm," captured, and died of typhoid on June 18, 1862, at Fort Columbus, NY[2]
Adams, Charles, Pvt.	A	Wounded, left arm, and captured
Adams, Lowrie, Pvt.	I	Wounded, "foot"[3]
Anderson, A. M., Pvt.	F	Captured
Anderson, Harrison, Pvt.	F	Captured
Anderson, Wesley, Pvt.	F	Killed
Armstrong, John B., Pvt.	H	Killed
Armstrong, Rufus, Pvt.	H	"Missing"[4]
Austin, David A., Pvt.	G	Captured
Austin, Jehua N., Pvt.	G	Killed
Barber, William M., Lt. Col.	F&S	Wounded, neck[5]
Barker, Abraham, Pvt.	A	Captured
Barlow, John B., Pvt.	F	Captured
Barlow, Larkin C., Pvt.	F	Killed
Barnes, Brinsley, Pvt.	G	Killed[6]

Appendix D: Casualties

Barnes, George W., Pvt.	G	Captured
Barnes, L. A., Pvt.	I	"Missing"[7]
Baucom, George W., Cpl.	D	Captured
Bell, Archibald L., Pvt.	F	Wounded, thumb
Bell, George, Pvt.	H	Wounded, "shot in shoulder, and captured[8]
Bingham, Jeptha K., Pvt.	K	Killed, "mortally wounded in head"[9]
Black, George, Pvt.	A	Captured
Black, Joseph P., Pvt.	I	Wounded, thigh, captured, and died of wounds on June 10, 1862, at Gaines's Mill, VA
Blair, William T., Pvt.	E	Captured
Blankenship, Thomas E., Pvt	I	Wounded, back, captured, and died of "phthisis pulmonalis" on September 23, 1862, at Fort Columbus, NY
Blevins, William H. Pvt.	A	Captured
Bost, Jackson L., 2nd Lt.	D	Captured
Brimer, James P., Pvt.	H	Wounded, "in side severely"[10]
Brown, Archer, Pvt.	G	Wounded, severely[11]
Brown, Oliver, Pvt.	H	Killed, "Shot in body badly"[12]
Bryant, George, Pvt.	A	Wounded, hip[13]
Bumgarner, John M., Pvt.	G	Wounded
Bumgarner, Joseph A., Pvt.	F	Captured
Burns, Samuel A., Sgt.	I	Captured
Calloway, Eli, Pvt.	A	Captured
Canady, Laban, Pvt.	H	Captured
Cannon, James S., Pvt.	H	Wounded, right elbow
Cardwell, James L., Pvt.	F	Wounded, lungs and right thigh, captured, and died of wounds on May 30, 1862
Carlton, Lindsey H., Mus.	B	Captured
Carter, Columbus R., Pvt.	A	Captured
Chapman, Richard, Pvt.	G	Wounded
Chapman, Thomas H., Sgt.	G	Wounded, "shot through jaw, passing out through mouth" and captured[14]
Clemmer, Lewis J., Pvt.	H	Captured
Clemmer, Perry E., Pvt.	H	Wounded, neck and chest, captured, died of wounds June 16, 1862
Cloniger, Emanuel, Pvt.	H	Wounded, hand[15]
Clontz, Abraham C., Pvt.	I	Killed
Coffey, James C., Pvt.	E	Captured
Coffey, John E., Pvt.	E	Captured
Coffey, Thomas N., Pvt.	E	Captured
Coldiron, Benjamin C., Pvt.	A	Wounded, "perforating wound of brain, through right eye," captured, and died on June 6 or June 11, 1862, of wounds[16]
Collins, Lawson D., Pvt.	D	Captured
Conley, W. D., Pvt.	H	Wounded, leg[17]
Cox, Leander A., Pvt.	A	Wounded, right thigh, captured, and died of "typhoid fever" at Portsmith's Grove, RI, July 8, 1862
Cox, William, Sr., Pvt.	A	Captured
Craven, George, Pvt.	A	Wounded, right knee, captured, and died June 12 or June 23, 1862, of wounds[18]
Crouch, Lawson, Pvt.	G	Wounded, "slightly ... in jaw"[19]
Davis, William J., Pvt.	A	Wounded, arm[20]
Deal, Noah, Pvt.	G	Wounded, neck[21]

Dees, Kenneth M., Cpl.	D	Captured
Dees, William R., Pvt.	D	Captured[22]
Dotson, Abner C., Pvt.	E	Captured
Douglass, George Y., Pvt.	K	Captured, died of unknown causes, July 29, 1862, at Ft. Columbus, NY
Dula, Linsey, Pvt.	F	Captured[23]
Durby, Reuben, Sgt.	A	Wounded, "shot in leg, missing"[24]
Eason, John W., Pvt.	D	Captured
Echard, Henry F., Pvt.	G	Wounded, "shot through jaws and half inch of tongue cut off"[25]
Eggers, Brizilla, Pvt.	E	Captured
Eggers, Johiel S., 3rd Lt.	E	Captured
Eggers, Richard E., Sgt.	E	Captured
Eldrich, Jacob, Pvt.	A	Captured
Eldrich, John, Pvt.	A	Killed
Eldrich, David, Pvt.	A	Captured, died July 9, 1862, Fort Columbus, NY, of "pneumonia & diarrhoea following measles"
Elmore, Jesse, Pvt.	H	Captured
Evans, Abram, Pvt.	K	Killed
Evans, David K., Pvt.	K	Wounded, "severely in shoulder and arm," and died of wounds June 23, 1862, Richmond, VA[26]
Farthing, James M., Cpl.	E	Captured
Farthing, William Y., Capt.	E	Captured[27]
Fincher, Henry H., Pvt.	D	Captured
Fite, Henry C., 3rd Lt.	H	Wounded, arm[28]
Fite, James H., Pvt.	H	Wounded, "in hand slightly"[29]
Flanagan, Benjamin M., Pvt.	I	Captured
Flannery, Joseph D., Pvt.	E	Captured
Ford, William G., Pvt.	H	Wounded, shoulder[30]
Fox, Moses G., Pvt.	G	Killed
Fox, William Sr., Pvt.	G	Killed
Furguson, George F., Pvt.	H	Captured
Furguson, Robert, Pvt.	H	Wounded, neck, captured, and died of wounds
Gardner, Ransom J., Pvt.	D	Captured
Gentry, Andrew C., Pvt.	A	Wounded, mouth, captured, and died of wounds
Gentry, Robert T., Pvt.	A	Wounded, chest, head, side, and arm, captured, and died of wounds on June 27, 1862, at Fort Monroe, VA
Gilbreath, George R., 2nd Lt.	F	Wounded, head, and died of wounds on May 31, 1862, in Richmond, VA
Glenn, Henry H., Pvt.	E	Captured
Gordon, James P., Pvt.	I	Wounded, hip
Grady, Henry C., Cpl.	D	Captured
Green, Alfred, Pvt.	E	Captured
Green, Burzilla, Pvt.	E	Captured
Green, Silas, Pvt.	E	Captured
Green, Solomon, Pvt.	B	Captured
Green, William, Cpl.	E	Captured
Griffin, Phillip C., Pvt.	D	Captured
Griffin, Stanley J., Pvt.	D	Captured
Grubb, John, Pvt.	K	Captured
Gryder, Adam A., Pvt.	G	Wounded, hand[31]
Gurley, William D., Pvt.	I	Wounded, "in leg"[32]
Halsey, Ira M., Pvt.	K	Wounded, "right fore-finger shot off"[33]

Appendix D: Casualties

Ham, Thomas, Pvt.	A	Wounded
Hanner, Simpson A., Pvt.	F	Wounded, thigh, and captured
Harden, William, Pvt.	E	Captured
Harrington, John, Pvt.	G	Captured
Hartley, William, Pvt.	E	Captured
Hasty, Andrew J., Pvt.	D	Killed
Hasty, Kenneth M., Pvt.	D	Captured
Henderson, John A., Pvt.	A	Captured
Hendrick, Henry H., Pvt.	A	Wounded, cheek, and captured[34]
Henry, Berry G., Pvt.	I	Wounded, "slightly in hand"[35]
Hicks, David, Pvt.	E	Captured
Higginson, John, Pvt.	I	Captured
Hill, William, Pvt.	D	Captured
Hilliard, Harrison H., Pvt.	E	Captured
Hilliard, James R., Pvt.	E	Captured
Hinchey, Richard M., Pvt.	F	Killed
Horne, Thomas J., Pvt.	D	Captured
Howell, John O., Pvt.	F	Captured
Hucks, Samuel L., Pvt.	C	Captured
Hurley, William H., Pvt.	A	Wounded, right knee, captured, and died of wounds, June 8, 1862
Jenkins, John, Pvt.	H	Wounded, "shot in body badly"[36]
Johnson, William R. Pvt.	E	Captured
Johnston, James B., Cpl.	K	Wounded, "slightly in foot"[37]
Jones, Isham H., Pvt.	K	Captured
Jones, William D., Pvt.	K	Captured
Jones, William R., Pvt.	K	Captured
Kerley, Hiram, Pvt.	G	Wounded, died of wounds on May 27, 1862
Kirby, Benjamin H., Pvt.	F	Captured
Kissian, William M., Pvt.	I	Wounded, "foot"[38]
Kizer, William L., Pvt.	D	Wounded, captured, and died at Fort Columbus, New York, July 8, 1862
Knight, Levi H., Pvt.	E	Captured
Lane, Robert M., Pvt.	A	Captured
Liles, Dennis A., Pvt	D	Captured
Little, Ellis P., Pvt.	D	Captured
Little, Patrick, Pvt.	D	Captured
Livingston, John E., Pvt.	D	Captured, and died of typhoid June 28, 1862, at Fort Columbus, NY
Long, Felix, Pvt.	K	Killed, "mortally wounded in side"[39]
Lowery, James T., Pvt.	D	Captured
Lynch, John W., Pvt.	H	Captured
McCormick, Robert B., Pvt.	D	Captured
McCracken, William D., Pvt.	G	Captured, died of disease January 1, 1863
McGinnas, George L., Pvt.	H	Killed
McKee, George W., Pvt.	H	Wounded, "in head slightly"[40]
Manus, Nathan E., Pvt.	D	Captured[41]
Mash, Thomas, Pvt.	A	Wounded, "gluteal region" or "the second Vertebra or both"
Maston, William J., Pvt.	F	Wounded, "slightly in breast"[42]
Miller, Calvin C., Mus.	B	Captured
Miller, Lowery, Pvt.	A	Wounded, side, and captured[43]
Miller, William R., Pvt.	K	Killed

Montgomery, James M., Pvt.	I	Captured
Morris, William G., Capt.	H	Wounded, neck[44]
Morrison, David, Pvt.	H	"Missing"[45]
Mullus, Martin V., Pvt.	A	Wounded, rectum, testicles, and left thigh, captured, and died of "tetanus" June 5–9, 1862
Munday, James W., Pvt.	E	Captured
Nash, Abner, Pvt.	D	Captured
Neal, James, Pvt.	H	Captured
Newsom, Edmond T., Pvt.	D	Captured
Nicholson, John B., Pvt.	I	Wounded, neck and left shoulder, and captured.
Owens, Daniel L., Pvt.	F	Wounded, side, captured, and died "of two shots in side" on unknown date
Parker, Elijah J., Pvt.	D	Wounded
Parson, Marcus D. L., Pvt.	K	Wounded, right thigh, and captured
Pasoin, J. H., Pvt.	H	Wounded, "shot in arm badly"[46]
Patrick, George W., Pvt.	E	Captured
Patterson, Eli, Pvt.	I	Wounded, "slightly in hand"[47]
Paysour, Phillip H., Pvt.	H	Wounded, right hip, and captured
Perry, Jonathan, Pvt.	A	Wounded, elbow, and died of wounds September 2, 1862, in Richmond, VA[48]
Phillips, Archer A., Pvt.	G	Captured, died August 15, 1862, of disease
Phillips, James, Pvt.	I	"Missing"[49]
Phillips, Jordan B., Sgt.	E	Captured
Pollard, Thomas, Pvt.	F	Wounded, "finger shot off"[50]
Presnell, Harrison C., Pvt.	G	Wounded, hand, and captured[51]
Price, John Jr., Pvt.	K	Wounded, "right fore-finger shot off"[52]
Price, Redmond, Pvt.	E	Captured
Ragan, Robert F., Pvt.	H	Wounded, "in face"[53]
Rape, Samuel M., Pvt.	D	Captured, died of typhoid July 4–6, 1862, at Fort Columbus, NY
Reece, Hugh, Pvt.	E	Captured
Reed, John A., Pvt.	G	Captured, died of disease on August 30, 1862
Reid, John L., Pvt.	C	Wounded, hip and finger[54]
Rhyne, Henry M., Pvt.	H	Wounded, "shot in arm, badly"[55]
Rhyne, Peyton S., Pvt.	H	Wounded, tongue, jaw, and left cheek, and captured
Richardson, James, Pvt.	K	Captured
Robnett, Abner E., Pvt.	G	Captured
Robnett, James W., Pvt.	G	Killed
Robnett, Jesse A., Pvt.	G	Wounded, both thighs, and captured
Robnett, Joel B., Pvt.	G	Killed
Robnett, John C., Pvt.	G	Killed
Robnett, William P., Pvt.	G	Killed
Rushing, Felix G., Pvt.	D	Captured, died of typhoid, July 3, 1862, at Fort Columbus, NY
Russell, Sterling H., Pvt.	I	Wounded, left thigh, captured, and died of wounds, June 28, 1862, Fort Monroe, VA
Rutledge, Ruburtus G., Pvt.	H	Wounded, left leg, and captured
Sale, Francis M., Sgt.	F	Wounded, elbow, and captured
Sexton, Reuben, Pvt.	A	Wounded, shoulder, and captured
Sharp, Thomas A., Pvt.	I	Wounded, "slightly in hand"[56]
Shew, William P., Pvt.	F	Wounded
Shoe, Jacob, Pvt.	I	Wounded, both arms, and captured
Shull, Joseph C., Pvt.	E	Captured

Appendix D: Casualties

Shull, Nathaniel C., Pvt.	E	Captured
Sloane, Thomas A., Pvt.	C	Captured
Smith, Bennett, Pvt.	E	Captured
Smith, John E., Pvt.	B	Captured[57]
Spears, Jeptha J., Pvt.	I	Killed
Stamper, Joshua, Pvt.	A	Captured
Stamper, William H., Pvt.	K	Wounded
Steele, Robert L., 1st Lt.	G	Captured
Stegall, John, Pvt.	D	Captured
Stevens, Thomas, Pvt.	E	Captured
Stinson, David W., Pvt.	I	Wounded, left side, captured, and died of wounds, June 10, 1862
Stowe, James A., Pvt.	H	Killed
Stuart, William A., 3rd Lt.	A	Wounded, elbow, and captured
Summy, Andrew, Pvt.	H	Killed
Taggart, James S., Pvt.	I	Wounded, "severely in thigh"[58]
Teague, Vandiver S., Pvt.	G	Wounded, left elbow
Teaster, J. Harrison, Pvt.	E	Captured
Thomas, William, Pvt.	D	Captured
Thomasson, John A., Pvt.	H	Wounded, "in arm slightly"[59]
Townsend, George, Pvt.	E	Captured, died of typhoid June 3, 1862, Fort Columbus, NY
Treadaway, Moses, Pvt.	F	Captured
Treadway, John, Pvt.	D	Captured
Trivett, John E., Cpl.	E	Captured
Tucker, George T., Pvt.	D	Captured
Tucker, Jesse M., Pvt.	D	Captured
Tucker, Robert B., Pvt.	H	Captured
Vannoy, James H., Pvt.	A	Captured
Walker, Leondias J., Pvt.	D	Captured, died of typhoid July 6, 1862, at Fort Columbus, NY
Walker, Robert, Pvt.	I	Missing, but would return to company[60]
Walker, William A., Pvt.	A	Captured
Walker, William C., Cpl	G	Wounded, head, hip, and or abdomen, captured, and died of wounds on June 2, 1862
Wallace, Elbert Pvt., Pvt.	F	Wounded, "severely in head"[61]
Wallace, John G., Pvt.	F	Wounded, "severely in shoulder"[62]
Ward, John, Pvt.	A	Wounded, "heel shot off by a ball," captured, and died of wounds[63]
Watson, Pinkey W., Pvt.	H	Killed
Watts, John, Pvt.	G	Captured, died of disease, June 30, 1862, Fort Delaware, DE
Weaston, John, Pvt.	H	Wounded, shoulder[64]
Weaver, John, Pvt.	A	Wounded, "shot in leg," captured, and died of wounds[65]
Welch, William, Pvt.	A	Wounded, captured, and died of wounds
Wiles, William, Pvt.	F	Killed
Williams, Thomas R., Pvt.	E	Captured[66]
Williamson, George W., Pvt.	I	Wounded, "severely in arm and shoulder"[67]
Wilson, Hiram, Pvt.	E	Captured
Wilson, John J., Cpl.	I	Wounded, "slightly in arm"[68]
Wilson, Thomas A., Pvt.	H	Captured
Winkler, Thomas, Pvt.	G	Captured
Withers, John L., Pvt.	H	Wounded, "shot in shoulder"[69]

Wolf, Elam B., Pvt.	I	Killed
Worsham, Francis M., Pvt.	C	Wounded, hip and finger[70]
Worsham, Rufus R., Pvt.	C	Wounded, "slightly ... in finger"[71]
Wyatt, John, Pvt.	A	Captured
Young, Albert P., Pvt.	I	Captured

Latham's Battery (Branch Artillery)[1]

Anderson, H. B., Pvt.	Captured
Burgess, Zepheniah W., Cpl.	Wounded, left temple and eye, and captured[2]
Gaskins, Henry, Pvt.	Wounded, leg (amputated), captured
Hall, William H., Pvt.	Captured
Hardy, Allen, Pvt.	Wounded[3]
Hawkins, William H., Pvt.	Wounded[4]
Jackson, Noah, Pvt.	Captured
Lee, Daniel S., Pvt.	Wounded and captured
McCafferty, William, Pvt.	Captured
Malpass, George W., Pvt.	Captured
Malpass, James, Pvt.	Wounded and captured
Malpass, Windell, Pvt.	Captured
Miller, Wiley P., Cpl.	Captured
Sleight, Barney W., Sgt.	Captured
Smith, William, Pvt.	Wounded, captured, and died of wounds on August 27, 1862, Gordonsville, VA
Taylor, William I., Pvt.	Wounded
Tindale, Richard, Pvt.	Wounded and captured
Williams, Curtis, Pvt.	Captured

Federal Casualities

Second Maine Volunteers[1]

Bergdoll, Joseph, Pvt.	D	Wounded[2]
Berry, Isaac, Pvt.	F	Wounded[3]
Bridges, Elijah, Pvt.	K	Wounded
Burgtoll, Joseph, Pvt.	D	Wounded
Crook, Phillip, Pvt.	C	Wounded
Davis, Samuel N., Pvt.	B	Wounded, left arm, chest[4]
Durgen, John F., Pvt.	H	Wounded
Dyer, Daniel C., Pvt.	I	Killed
Dyer, Samuel, Pvt.	D	Wounded
Ellis, Charles J., Sgt. Maj.	F&S	Wounded, jaw[5]
Ellis, Crawford S., Pvt.	B	Wounded[6]
Farrell, Charles, Pvt.	I	Wounded, thigh[7]
Griffin, Benjamin, Pvt.	B	Wounded[8]
Hammett, Walter P., Pvt.	H	Wounded[9]
Haskell, Winthrope B., Pvt.	B	Wounded[10]
Hogan, Michael, Pvt.	I	Wounded, slightly[11]
Jordan, William T., Pvt.	I	Wounded
McKay, Alexander, Pvt.	D	Wounded
McKinser, F. D., Pvt.	D	Killed
Mahoney, Timothy, Pvt.	I	Wounded

Appendix D: Casualties 171

Moore, John, Pvt.	E	Killed
Murch, Simeon C., Sgt.	B	Killed[12]
Murphy, Jeremiah, Pvt.	D	Wounded[13]
Nickerson, Frederick D., Pvt.	D	Killed[14]
Philbrock, Joseph, Pvt.	C	Wounded[15]
Pollard, Henry M., Pvt.	G	Killed
Prescott, Henry S., Pvt.	B	Wounded
Ray, Joshua, Pvt.	E	Wounded
Rowe, James L., Sgt.	E	Wounded and died of wounds on June 6, 1862[16]
Smart, Benjamin F., Sgt.	K	Killed
Smith, James, Pvt.	H	Wounded, shoulder[17]
Snow, A. J., Cpl.	C	Wounded[18]
Sylvester, Joseph H., Sgt.	B	Wounded, leg[19]
Thomas, Joel, Pvt.	B	Mortally wounded[20]
Tilden, Charles W., Capt.	B	Wounded, throat[21]
Wentworth, John, Pvt.	H	Wounded
Wilson, Asa, Pvt.	F	Wounded, "ear shot off"[22]

Third Massachusetts Artillery[1]

Robertson, J. P., Pvt.   Wounded

Ninth Massachusetts Infantry[1]

Armstrong, William, Pvt.	G	Wounded
Conlan, Lawrence, Sgt.	I	Wounded
Lennert, John, Pvt.		Wounded
Leonard, John, Pvt.	C	Wounded
McGrath, William, Pvt.	H	Wounded
McGuire, John D., Pvt.	C	Wounded
McLaughlin, Jason, Pvt.		Wounded
Miller, George, Pvt.		Wounded
O'Brien, Michael, Pvt.	B	Wounded
Regan, Daniel J., Sgt.	G	Killed
Shehan, John, Pvt.		Wounded
Spillant, John, Pvt.		Wounded
Smith, Samuel, Pvt.	E	Wounded

Twenty-second Massachusetts Volunteer Infantry[1]

Coleman, Thomas, Pvt.   E   Wounded

Thirteenth New York Volunteer Infantry[1]

Cook, Daniel, Pvt.	B	Wounded
Shiller, Joseph, Pvt.		Wounded
Vantyne, Chester W., Pvt.		Wounded

Fourteenth New York Volunteer Infantry[1]

Beardsley, Daniel H., Pvt.		Wounded
Ellis, William E., Sgt.		Wounded
Evans, Daniel, Pvt.		Wounded
Morrow, Joseph, Pvt.	E	Wounded

Twenty-fifth New York Volunteer Infantry[1]

Atkins, Charles, Cpl.	H	Killed
Barrett, P. R., Sgt.	C	Wounded
Batchelder, G. W., Sgt.	F	Wounded
Benedict, Anthony, Pvt.	C	Wounded
Brener, J., Pvt.	D	Captured
Brown, Jason, Pvt.	F	Captured
Bruse, James, Pvt.	F	Captured
Burgin, Daniel, Pvt.	E	Killed
Burns, Patrick, Pvt.	F	Wounded
Burns, William, Pvt.	E	Killed
Carroll, John, Pvt.	H	Wounded
Cash, Whildon, Pvt.	G	Captured
Cassidy, Richard, Pvt.	D	Wounded
Clancy, James, Pvt.	G	Killed
Clark, Henry B., Sgt.	K	Killed
Cody, Thomas, Pvt.	A	Wounded
Coe, John, Pvt.	I	Killed
Coglan, Thomas, 1st Lt.	D	Wounded
Conklin, John, Pvt.	D	Wounded
Conners, William, Pvt.	I	Wounded
Conroy, Thomas, Cpl.	I	Captured
Corniff, M., Pvt.	K	Captured
Corning, William, Pvt.	E	Wounded
Costello, James, Pvt.	G	Killed
Creed, Jeremiah, Pvt.	C	Wounded
Crossey, William, Pvt.	F	Captured
Curran, Benjamin, Sgt.	F	Captured
Darley, William, Pvt.	E	Wounded
Dean, Joe, Pvt.	F	Captured
Delanny, Thomas, Pvt.	K	Killed
Deming, Hugh, Pvt.	B	Wounded
Ditzer, Frank, Pvt.	D	Wounded
Downey, James, Pvt.	B	Wounded
Douglar, George, Pvt.	F	Captured
Edgeworth, Richard, Pvt.	B	Wounded, right arm amputated[2]
Edmonson, Edmond B., Cpl.	D	Wounded
Emerson, Napoleon, Sgt.	I	Wounded
Enrich, Henry, Pvt.	E	Killed
Evans, William D., Pvt.	G	Captured
Farrell, Dominick, Pvt.	B	Wounded
Fenno, C. E., Sgt.	I	Killed[3]
Finnigan, Patrick, Pvt.	A	Killed
Fisk, George E., Lt.	A	Killed[4]
Fitzgerald, Thomas, Pvt.	D	Captured
Flaherty, Eugene, Cpl.	I	Wounded
Flaherty, John, Pvt.	I	Wounded
Flood, Owen, Pvt.	I	Wounded
Frank, George, Pvt.	G	Captured
Garnet, Peter, Pvt.	C	Captured
Garrighty, Michael, Pvt.	A	Wounded
Garvey, Luke, Pvt.	E	Wounded

Appendix D: Casualties

Gavitt, Amor, Pvt.	E	Captured
Graham, Peter, Pvt.	H	Wounded
Haffey, Francis, Sgt.	G	Captured
Haplin, Charles, 2nd Lt.	K	Killed
Harrington, Timothy, Cpl.	G	Killed
Harris, Benjamin F., Capt.	I	Captured
Hayes, James, Pvt.	A	Killed
Hayes, James, Pvt.	B	Wounded[5]
Hedden, James, Pvt.	C	Captured
Henderson, John, Pvt.	G	Captured
Hessylsstyn, ____, Lt.	E	Captured
Hicks, Patrick, 2nd Lt.	I	Wounded
Hill, James, Pvt.	C	Captured
Hill, John W., Pvt.	A	Killed
Hogan, Edward, Pvt.	H	Wounded
Holland, Timothy, Pvt.	H	Wounded
Jackson, William E., Cpl.	D	Killed
Jacobs, Morris, Pvt.	D	Captured
Johnson, Charles A., Col.	F&S	Wounded, leg[6]
Johnson, James, Pvt.	G	Wounded
Kane, Thomas, Pvt.	F	Wounded
Kelt, John, Pvt.	D	Wounded
Kendrick, Patrick, Pvt.	G	Captured
Kennedy, James, Cpl.	I	Wounded
Kennedy, John, Pvt.	B	Captured
Kenny, Patrick, Pvt.	E	Killed
Laughlin, Michael, Pvt.	B	Wounded
Learin, Owen, Pvt.	G	Captured
Leonard, William, Pvt.	G	Captured
Leorelle, Frank, Pvt.	K	Captured
Lerallous, Felix Bugler	K	Captured
Lynch, John, Pvt.	F	Captured
McAurea, Edward, Pvt.	G	Captured
McCafferty, James, Pvt.	G	Captured
McCaffrey, James, Pvt.	K	Captured
McCue, Thomas, 1st Sgt.	G	Killed
McDonough, John, Pvt.	E	Wounded
McGovern, Bernard, Pvt.	K	Captured
McGovern, Owen, Pvt.	I	Wounded
McGrath, Lawrence, Pvt.	D	Killed
McGrath, Michael, Pvt.	D	Wounded
McGuire, Charles, Pvt.	H	Wounded, leg[7]
Mack, John, Pvt.	D	Wounded
McKee, Jason, Sgt.	I	Wounded
McKnight, George, Pvt.	F	Captured
McLogue, John, Pvt.	C	Captured
McMahon, Michael, Capt.	C	Killed
McMather, Gilbert, Pvt.	F	Wounded
McNally, P., Pvt.	D	Wounded
McQuade, Felix, Pvt.	C	Captured
Malid, Michael, Pvt.	G	Captured
Manny, Michael, Pvt.	B	Killed
Martin, John, Pvt.	G	Captured

Matear, Patrick, Pvt.	B	Captured
Moffatt, Sgt.	B	Wounded
Monahan, James, Pvt.	B	Wounded
Moore, Charles, Pvt.	A	Wounded
Morton, Cpl.	B	Wounded
Murphy, Morris, Pvt.	K	Captured
Nelson, Richard, Cpl.	C	Wounded
O'Brien, Lawrence, Pvt.	G	Captured
O'Connell, Daniel, Pvt.	C	Wounded
O'Neill, James, Pvt.	A	Wounded
O'Sherle, Jacob, Pvt.	K	Captured
Oterell, James, Pvt.	K	Killed
Pendergrast, Daniel, Pvt.	K	Killed[8]
Pittman, George, Pvt.	F	Captured
Pluckett, Edward, Pvt.	F	Captured
Pollard, William, Pvt.	D	Wounded
Quinn, John, Pvt.	K	Killed
Reagan, Michael, Pvt.	D	Captured
Reilly, Thomas, Pvt.	A	Wounded
Riley, John, Pvt.	G	Captured
Riley, Lawrence, Pvt.	G	Captured
Ross, William, Pvt.	H	Wounded
Ryan, Thomas, Pvt.	F	Captured
Ryan, Thomas, Pvt.	K	Captured
Savage, Henry F., Lt. Col.	F&S	Wounded, arm[9]
Schroder, John, Pvt.	D	Wounded
Sherry, Thomas, Pvt.	F	Captured
Silsby, G. T., Sgt.	D	Captured
Smith, Charles F., Pvt.	I	Killed
Smith, Thomas, Pvt.	H	Wounded
Solopeter, Daniel, Pvt.	F	Killed
Sullivan, Patrick, Pvt.	G	Captured
Thompson, Thomas P., 2nd Lt.	B	Killed
Tooly, Terence, Pvt.	B	Captured
Trimble, John, Pvt.	F	Captured
Tyter, Henry, Pvt.	I	Wounded
Van Kovanburgh, Peter, Pvt.	E	Captured
Wagner, Christopher, Pvt.	D	Captured
Warner, Percival, Cpl.	G	Captured
Welch, David, Pvt.	D	Wounded
Welch, John, Sgt.	E	Captured
Whist, Christopher, Pvt.	E	Wounded
White, John, Pvt.	F	Captured
Zachus, John, Sgt.	E	Wounded
Zaeder, Solomon, Pvt.	K	Captured

Forty-fourth New York Volunteer Infantry[1]

Allen, William B., Pvt.	G	Killed, buried in the Cold Harbor National Cemetery
Anthony, Jay M., Pvt.	A	Wounded, "leg, slight"[2]
Babcock, Elisha, Pvt.	F	Wounded
Baker, Edward, Pvt.	C	Killed, buried in the Cold Harbor National Cemetery
Banks, G. D., Pvt.	E	Wounded, "left arm, amputated"[3]

Appendix D: Casualties   175

Barnes, Addison, Pvt.	G	Wounded[4]
Blair, Charles H., Pvt.	H	Wounded, "breast"[5]
Borel, Charles L., Pvt.		Wounded
Brooks, Seward, Pvt.	G	Wounded
Butler, John, Pvt.	G	Killed, buried in the Cold Harbor National Cemetery
Carey, William, Pvt.	F	Wounded, "slight"[6]
Cannady, D., Pvt.	C	Wounded, "left leg, dangerously"[7]
Chandler, Samuel W., Cpl.	F	Wounded, body[8]
Chapin, E P., Maj.	F&S	Wounded, back
Cleary, William, Pvt.		Wounded
Cole, William W., Pvt.	A	Killed, buried in the Cold Harbor National Cemetery
Cook, Warren D., Pvt.	H	Killed
Dack, Garret, Pvt.	G	Killed
Daily, W. J., Pvt.	H	Wounded, "leg"[9]
Delahanty, Joseph, Pvt.	F	Wounded
Densmore, Ransford, Pvt.	E	Wounded[10]
Depuy, Thomas R., Pvt.	E	Wounded[11]
Dumass, Moses, Pvt.	C	Wounded, "right leg"[12]
Dunham, Josiah, Pvt.	F	Killed
Dunner, Josiah, Pvt.		Wounded
Evans, Jonas, Pvt.	G	Wounded[13]
Fellows, Henry, Pvt.	G	Killed
Forman, J., Pvt.		Wounded
Fox, Jacob, Lt.	A	Wounded, shoulder[14]
Frair, Frederick O., Pvt.	I	Wounded, "abdomen, slight"[15]
Gilkenow, G. W., Pvt.		Wounded
Goold, Jason S., Pvt.	B	Wounded, "head, slight"[16]
Graver, Anthony G., Pvt.	I	Wounded[17]
Griffin, A. M., Pvt.	G	Wounded[18]
Guernsey, Thomas, Pvt.	G	Killed
Hagens, John, Pvt.	F	Killed, buried in the Cold Harbor National Cemetery
Hanks, George, Pvt.		Wounded
Haskell, Norman, Pvt.	E	Killed
Harris, Joseph, Cpl.	H	Wounded, "breast, severe"[19]
Hickok, T. H., Pvt.	H	Wounded, "head"[20]
Hill, George V., Pvt.	G	Wounded[21]
Hislock, Frank, Pvt.		Wounded
Hoes, Theodore, Pvt.	C	Wounded, "right hand, slight"[22]
Holt, John B., Cpl.	G	Wounded[23]
Hooker, Hull, Pvt.	H	Wounded
Irish, Oliver K., Pvt.	A	Killed, buried at the Cold Harbor National Cemetery
Isaac, J. H., Pvt.		Wounded
Johnston, John, Pvt.		Wounded
Knox, Edward B., Adj.	F&S	Wounded, wrist[24]
Lawless, John H., Pvt.	E	Killed, buried in the Cold Harbor National Cemetery
Leland, Lewis J., Pvt.	F	Wounded, finger[25]
Leonard, John H., Pvt.	E	Wounded[26]
McClellan, William, Pvt.		Wounded
McCormack, Samue, Pvt.	C	Wounded, "left wrist"[27]
McCue, Jason, Pvt.		Wounded
McCutchen, J., Pvt.	A	Wounded, "leg, slight"[28]
Marshall, William D., Pvt.	G	Killed
Miller, Lewis L., Pvt.	B	Killed

Moaff, Jason, Pvt.		Wounded
Morse, Perry, Pvt.	H	Wounded
Morse, Willis, Pvt.	H	Wounded, "head"[29]
Muncy, K. A., Pvt.	H	Wounded, "thigh"[30]
Nelligan, Theodore, Pvt.	F	Wounded
Nolan, William, Pvt.	G	Killed, buried in the Cold Harbor National Cemetery
Ostrander, Philip, Pvt.	F	Wounded, "slight"[31]
Patridge, Eugnen, Pvt.	C	Wounded, "left leg, slight"[32]
Peaslie, H., Cpl.	G	Killed, buried in the Cold Harbor National Cemetery
Pitcher, Henry, Pvt.	E	Killed, buried in the Cold Harbor National Cemetery
Ramsey, John A., Pvt.	H	Wounded
Roberts, William C., Pvt.	F	Wounded
Robinson, John J., Pvt.	F	Killed, buried in the Cold Harbor National Cemetery
Satterly, M., Cpl.	C	Killed
Siger, J. M., Cpl.	A	Wounded, "head, severe"[33]
Skillen, R. M., Cpl.	A	Wounded, "hand, slight"[34]
Smith, Bernard, Pvt.	C	Wounded, "head, dangerously"[35]
Smith, Horatio A., Pvt.	B	Wounded, "left arm, slight"[36]
Stoddard, E. R., Pvt.	B	Killed, "shot in head"[37]
Thrall, John, Pvt.	G	Wounded[38]
Tinkham, Albert B., Sgt.	A	Wounded, elbow[39]
Van Trump, W. H., Pvt.	F	Killed
Van Zandit, G. W., Pvt.	F	Killed, buried in the Cold Harbor National Cemetery
Vanderpool, Andrew, Pvt.	G	Killed
Vase, Benjamin, Pvt.	F	Killed
Wallrader, Philip H., Pvt.		Wounded
Weinstein, Peter, Pvt.	E	Wounded
Weldon, Thomas, Pvt.	B	Killed
Whiteman, George, H.	G	Wounded
Williams, George T., Pvt.	F	Wounded
Wood, John, Pvt.	F	Wounded
Wooden, William H., Pvt.		Wounded
Young, Floyd D., Pvt.	C	Wounded
Young, James, Cpl.	F	Killed

Sixth Pennsylvania Cavalry[1]

Aulrich, Daniel, Pvt.		Wounded
Zayzer, John, Pvt.		Wounded

Sixty-second Pennsylvania Volunteer Infantry[1]

Arnsburg, George, Pvt.	I	Wounded
Field, Ira, Jr., Pvt.	I	Wounded
Harley, David, Pvt.	F	Wounded
Kaylor, John, Pvt.	I	Wounded
McSparrin, James W., Pvt.	I	Wounded
Reed, William, Pvt.	D	Wounded

Eighty-third Pennsylvania Volunteer Infantry[1]

Briggs, Benjamin F., Pvt.	G	Wounded
Cheeseman, Miner, Pvt.	E	Wounded

Hulbert, Egbert D., Sgt.	K	Wounded, foot[2]
McBride, Frank, Pvt.	K	Wounded, foot[3]
McCalmonty, Alexander T., Pvt.	G	Wounded
Schriser, J., Pvt.		Wounded

First United States Sharpshooters[1]

Allen, Lewis J., Sgt.	Wounded
Billings, Benjamin H., Pvt.	Wounded
Davis, James S., Pvt.	Wounded
Dawson, W. L., Pvt.	Wounded
Donner, Martin, Pvt.	Wounded
Fallen, Hammond, Pvt.	Wounded
Lewis, Peter, Pvt.	Wounded
Lorarage, Clinton, Pvt.	Wounded
Richardson, Hiram T., Cpl.	Wounded
Sheppard, C. J., Lt.	Wounded

Second United States Artillery[1]

Cope, W., Pvt.	M	Wounded
Francis, Joseph J., Pvt.	M	Wounded

Sixth United States Cavalry[1]

Doyle, James, Sgt.	Wounded
Smith, H. C., Pvt.	Wounded

Notes

Chapter 1

1. Theodore Stern, "Powhatan Confederacy," *Dictionary of American History* (New York: Charles Scribner's Sons, 1976), 5:385; Robert B. Lancaster, *A Sketch of the Early History of Hanover County and Its Large and Important Contributions to the American Revolution* (Richmond, VA: Whittet and Shepperson, 1976), 11–12; *Richmond Times,* August 23, 1942; *Concise Dictionary of American Biography* (New York: Charles Scribner's Sons, 1997), 2:1191; Steve Rajtar, *Indian War Sites: A Guidebook to Battlefields, Monuments, and Memorials* (Jefferson, NC: McFarland and Company, 1999), 248.

2. Ibid., 12–13; VaGenWeb Hanover County, Virginia, Genealogy Project.

3. Lancaster, *A Sketch of the Early History of Hanover County,* 12, 21; *Concise Dictionary of American Biography,* 1:543, 644–645, 909, 916.

4. Lancaster, *A Sketch of the Early History of Hanover County,* 79; *Concise Dictionary of American Biography,* 1:221; 2:1069.

5. William K. Scarborough, "Edmund Ruffin," *The Confederacy* (New York: Simon & Schuster Macmillan, 1993), 915–917; Lancaster, *A Sketch of the Early History of Hanover County,* 71.

6. Kenneth L. Stiles, "William Carter Wickham," *The Confederacy,* 1165–1167; Lancaster, *A Sketch of the Early History of Hanover County,* 80.

7. "Hanover Tavern." Lancaster, *A Sketch of the Early History of Hanover County,* 75.

8. Charles W. Turner, "The Virginia Central at War, 1961–1865," *The Journal of Southern History* 12.4 (November 1946): 527; Charles W. Turner, "The Richmond, Fredericksburg and Potomac, 1861–1865," *Civil War History* 7 (1961): 255.

Chapter 2

1. McClellan's telegram to his wife, Mary Ellen McClellan, reads: "Have arrived here all well. Navy fully prepared to sink Merrimac. I only hope she may appear tomorrow. The grass will not grow under my feet." The telegram was sent from Fort Monroe at "11 1/2 pm." Stephen W. Sears, ed., *The Civil War Papers of George B. McClellan: Selected Correspondence, 1860–1865* (New York: Da Capo Press, 1989), 225; Stephen Sears, *To the Gates of Richmond: The Peninsula Campaign* (New York: Ticknor and Fields, 1992), 24.

2. Steven H. Newton, *Joseph E. Johnston and the Defense of Richmond* (Lawrence: University Press of Kansas, 1998), 32–33; Michael B. Chesson, "Richmond, Virginia," *The Confederacy* (New York: Simon and Schuster Macmillan, 1993), 908–910.

3. The inactivity of the Army of the Potomac was not entirely McClellan's fault. He had taken some offensive maneuvers, occupying Munson's Hill and Upton's Hill, just across the river from Washington, D. C. Some of his inability to assume offensive operations came from his superior, Winfield Scott, general in chief of the armies of the United States, who was opposed to any advance into Virginia. Russel H. Beatie, *Army of the Potomac: McClellan Takes Command, September 1861–February 1862* (Cambridge, MA: Da Capo Press, 2004), 239–257.

4. For more information on the Occoquan-Cedar Run plan, see Beatie, *McClellan Takes Command,* 367–377.

5. Beatie places the months of August or September as the period of time that McDowell advanced the idea with McClellan. The idea was not McDowell's alone. Another Union general, Samuel P. Heintzelman, also developed a Peninsula campaign to take Richmond. *Ibid.,* 375, 379.

6. Longstreet argued for a similar move during the Gettysburg campaign. See Sears, *The Civil War Papers of ... McClellan,* 167–168.

7. Beatie, *McClellan Takes Command,* 387; Sears, *The Civil War Papers of ... McClellan,* 162–170.

8. Beatie, *McClellan Takes Command*, 398–399, 402; Stephen W. Sears, *George B. McClellan: The Young Napoleon* (New York: Da Capo Press, 1999), 136–147.

9. McClellan had replaced Scott as general in chief on November 1, 1861. John H. Eicher and David J. Eicher, *Civil War High Commands* (Stanford, CA: Stanford University Press, 2001), 372; Beatie, *McClellan Takes Command*, 433–434.

10. Clarence E. Macartney, *Lincoln and His Generals* (Philadelphia: Dorrance and Company, Publishers, 1925), 74–75; John Niven, *Salmon P. Chase: A Biography* (New York: Oxford University, 1995), 275–277; Sears, *McClellan*, 140–143; Sears, *The Civil War Papers of ... McClellan*, 152–154. Beatie writes that "McClellan apparently went to the meeting at the White House in a foul humor. In an uncharacteristic way he brimmed with hostility for McDowell, whom, he believed, had betrayed him and wanted to replace him as commander of the army." *McClellan Takes Command*, 455.

11. Roy P. Basler, *The Collected Works of Abraham Lincoln* 5 vols. (New Brunswick, NJ: Rutgers University Press, 1953), 5:111, 115, 120; Sears, *The Civil War Papers of ... McClellan*, 149.

12. Bruce Catton, *Mr. Lincoln's Army* (New York: Doubleday and Company, 1962), 83; McClellan was writing to Samuel L. M. Barlow, a New York lawyer, railroad executive, and Democratic Party leader. Sears, *The Civil War Papers of ... McClellan*, 154; Clifford Dowdey, *The Seven Days: The Emergence of Lee* (Lincoln: University of Nebraska Press, 1964), 33; Benjamin P. Thomas and Harold M. Hyman, *Stanton: The Life and Times of Lincoln's Secretary of War* (New York: Alfred A. Knopf, 1962), 175; the assistant secretary of war had been sent to the Midwest to explore the possibility of moving troops from the Army of the Potomac. McClellan stated that he wanted "to take about 70,000 infantry, 250 guns, 2500 cavalry—at least 3 bridge trains." Sears, *The Civil War Papers of ... McClellan*, 158.

13. Basler, *The Collected Works of ... Lincoln*, 5:118; Sears, *The Civil War Papers of ... McClellan*, 162–170; Sears noted that "After receiving Lincoln's War Order No. 1 on Friday, Jan. 31, and obtaining permission to respond ... [McClellan] spent the weekend revising and expanding the draft he had prepared earlier." *Ibid.*, 171; Allan Nevins, *The War for the Union* (New York: Charles Scribner's Sons, 1960), 2:42; John E. Clark, *Railroads in the Civil War: The Impact of Management on Victory and Defeat* (Baton Rouge: Louisiana State University Press, 2001), 20. Nevins believed that McClellan's response could have been made verbally, or possibly not at all.

14. Sears, *The Civil War Papers of ... McClellan*, 56–157; Thomas and Hyman, *Stanton*, 177.

15. William Wallace "Willie" Lincoln was born on December 21, 1862, and was the Lincolns' favorite child. Willie became sick after Christmas 1861, mostly likely with typhoid, and died on February 20, 1862. His funeral took place at the White House, and he was buried at the Oak Hill Cemetery in Georgetown. After the assassination of his father, Willie's remains were exhumed, placed on board the Lincoln funeral train, and reinterred with his father in Springfield, Illinois. While Willie was sick, his parents seldom left his side, and the ordeal might explain some of Lincoln's behavior. See Margaret Leech, *Reveille in Washington, 1860–1865* (New York: Harper Collins, 1941, 1980), 160–161; Sears, *George B. McClellan*, 158–160; *New York Tribune*, January 18, 1862; for information on Gurley, see Nevins, *The War for the Union*, 2:44; Wadsworth to Bryant, February 3, 1862, quoted in *Ibid.*, 2:45.

16. U. S. War Department, *The War of the Rebellion: A Compilation of the Official Records of the Union and Confederate Armies* 70 Volumes (Washington: Government Printing Office, 1880–1901), Vol. 11, 3:57–58; Basler, *The Collected Works of ... Lincoln*, 5:150. Lincoln's order went on to specify that the movement would begin on or before March 18. *Ibid.*, 151; Wayne Mahood, *General Wadsworth: the Life and Times of Brevet Major General James S. Wadsworth* (Cambridge, MA: Da Capo, 2003), chapters 8 and 9. McClellan's ideas about corps commanders, by October 1861, were: I Corps—Sumner; II Corps—McDowell; III Corps—Heintzelman; IV Corps—Fitz John Porter; V Corps—Franklin, and VI—Andrew Porter. Beatie, *McClellan Takes Command*, 179.

17. Sears, *George B. McClellan*, 165; Nevins, *The War for the Union*, 46; Lincoln did not appoint a new general in chief until Henry Halleck was appointed on July 23, 1862. Eicher and Eicher, *Civil War High Commanders*, 274.

18. Johnston faced innumerable difficulties in his withdrawal, including moving or leaving behind massive amounts of stores and munitions. The Confederates were also forced to abandon many cannons too large to be withdrawn without detection. Newton, *Joseph E. Johnston*, 52; Joseph L. Harsh, *Confederate Tide Rising: Robert E. Lee and the Making of Southern Strategy, 1861–1862* (Kent, OH: Kent State University Press, 1998), 27.

19. Newton, *Joseph E. Johnston*, 3.

20. Sears, *The Civil War Papers of ... McClellan*, 200, 213; Sears, *McClellan*, 163–164; Sears, *To the Gates of Richmond*, 17; *Philadelphia Inquirer*, reprinted in the *Janesville Daily Gazette*, Janesville, Wisconsin, March 18, 1862; *New York Tribune*, March 15, 1862; McClellan was writing to Samuel L. M. Barlow, 16 March 1862.

21. Sears, *The Civil War Papers of ... McClellan*, 168. In McClellan's February 3 report to Lin-

coln, he considered the use of Fort Monroe "the worst."

22. Sears, *To the Gates of Richmond*, 22; Thomas and Hyman, *Stanton*, 186; Hitchcock was the grandson of Ethan Allen and a veteran of the Mexican War. According to Nevins, Hitchcock confided in his diary on April 13, 1862, that he had received an offer from Stanton to replace the slow and siege-minded McClellan. "Stanton added that the President wished it, and that if Hitchcock said the word, he could have the order in two minutes." Nevins, *The War for the Union*, 2:61. Hitchcock's answer is recorded in Leech, *Reveille in Washington*, 205, 210.

23. Harsh, *Confederate Tide Rising*, 36. Official Records Vol. 11, 3:3; Sears, *The Civil War Papers of ... McClellan*, 79–80.

24. Johnston's first attempt at arguing for a movement across the Potomac came on April 14. The second time, in a personal letter to Lee, Johnston wrote: "We are engaged in a species of warfare at which we can never win ... [McClellan] would depend for success on artillery and engineering.... We can compete with him in neither.... We can have no success while McClellan is allowed, as he is by our defensive, to choose his mode of warfare.... We must therefore change our course, collect all the troops we have in the east and cross the Potomac with them, while Beauregard, with all we have in the west, invades Ohio.... Our troops have always wished for the offensive, and so does the country." *Official Records*, Vol. 11, 3:477. Lee responded on May 1: the "feasibility" of "advancing a column to the Potomac with all the troops that can be made available" had been considered for some time. Harsh, *Confederate Tide Rising*, 38. See also *Official Records*, Vol. 11, 3:485; Sears, *The Civil War Correspondence of ... McClellan*, 79, 81.

25. Leech, *Reveille in Washington*, 206; *Official Records* Vol. 11, pt. 2, 57–62; *Ibid*. Vol. 11, pt. 3, 54–55, 57; Sears, *To the Gates of Richmond*, 34. "Wadsworth's veracity was later impeached by the N. Y. *World*, and he replied in a letter to the N. Y. *Times*" (in *Tribune*, May 21, 1863). Nevins, *The War for the Union*, 2:59. Leech writes that Wadsworth had inspected his troops just 10 days prior to April 1, and found the number of soldiers "amply sufficient." *Reveille in Washington*, 208.

26. Thomas J. Rowland, "'Heaven Save a Country Governed By Such Counsels!' The Safety of Washington and the Peninsula Campaign," *Civil War History* 42, no. 1 (1996): 8.

27. Sears, *The Civil War Papers of ... McClellan*, 228–229, 230.

28. Leech, *Reveille in Washington*, 208–209.

29. James I. Robertson, *Stonewall Jackson: The Man, the Soldier, the Legend* (New York: Macmillan, 1997), 330.

30. Joseph E. Johnston, *Narrative of Military Operations* (New York: D. Appleton, 1874), 106.

31. Sears, *To the Gates of Richmond*, 32–33; Bruce Catton, *Terrible Swift Sword* (New York: Simon and Schuster, 1985), 190–191; Eicher and Eicher, *Civil War High Commanders*, 243.

32. Basler, *The Collected Works of ... Lincoln*, 5:184–85.

33. Quoted in Macartney, *Lincoln and His Generals*, 84.

34. Nevins, *The War for the Union*, 57–58; Douglas S. Freeman, *R. E. Lee* 4 Volumes (New York: C. Scribner's Sons, 1934–1935), 2:17–19; William J. Miller "No American Sevastopol," *America's Civil War* 13, no. 2 (May 2000): 30–38.

35. Freeman *R. E. Lee*, 2:8–12.

36. Clark Larsen, "A succession of attempts on President Abraham Lincoln's life led to the development of the Secret Service, " *Military History* 18, no. 1 (April 2001): 12–14; Nevins, *The War for the Union*, 1:371, 2:42. In June 1862, Pinkerton estimated the Army of Northern Virginia contained 180,000 men. See Brian K. Burton, *Extraordinary Circumstances: The Seven Days Battles* (Bloomington: Indiana University Press, 2001), 15.

37. Sears, *The Civil War Papers of ... McClellan*, 252; the quote about sickness is attributed to Brig. Gen. Andrew Humphreys; see Miller, "No American Sevastopol," 35.

38. Harsh, *Confederate Tide Rising*, 39.

39. Basler, *The Collected Works of ... Lincoln*, 5:220.

40. Sears, *To the Gates of Richmond*, 109–112; William J. Miller, "'I Only Wait for the River': McClellan and his Engineers on the Chickahominy," *The Richmond Campaign of 1862: The Peninsula and the Seven Days*. Gary W. Gallagher, ed. (Chapel Hill: University of North Carolina Press, 2000), 48–49.

41. Thomas and Hyman, *Stanton*, 195–196; Basler, *The Collected Works of ... Lincoln*, 5:232; *Official Records*, Vol. 10, 1:30.

42. James I. Robertson, "Shenandoah Valley Campaign of Jackson," *The Confederacy* 963–966; Gary Schreckengost, "Stonewall's Triumphant Return to Winchester," *America's Civil War* 13, no. 3 (July 2000): 26–33.

43. Thomas and Hyman, *Stanton*, 196; Gary W. Gallagher, *The Shenandoah Valley Campaign of 1862* (Chapel Hill: University of North Carolina Press, 2003), 8; Nevins, *The War for the Union*, 2:125; Leech, *Reveille in Washington*, 214.

44. Lincoln's actions show a commander who was more interested in the offensive rather than the defensive measures to save Washington. See Gallagher, *The Shenandoah Valley Campaign*, 10; Basler, *The Collected Works of ... Lincoln*, 5:232–233.

45. *Official Records*, Vol. 12 pt. 3, 220–221.

46. McDowell to C. A. Heckster, June 17, 1862, Barlow Papers, Hunting Library, quoted in Nevins, *The War for the Union*, 2:128.

47. Sears, *The Civil War Papers of ... McClellan*, 275–6; Nevins writes: "McClellan still cherished the idea of a conspiracy. He said in Boston in February, 1863, that the cabal against him had gained great strength when he lay ill of fever. He thought the fears of the President for Washington had been adroitly excited by men who knew the city was really safe, and who did not wish the Peninsula campaign to succeed, for that would mean the end of the influence of ultra-radical Republicans." *The War for Union*, 128.

48. Harsh, *Confederate Tide Rising*, 41. The debate regarding McClellan's plan to change his base from the York and Pamunkey rivers to the James River has been the subject of much debate. Lincoln's orders to McClellan tied the general to a certain sphere of operations, and removed from him the ability to change that base if that had been McClellan's aim.

Chapter 3

1. Newton, *Joseph E. Johnston and the Defense of Richmond*, 86–87.
2. Blair Howard, Mary Burham, and Bill Burham, *The Virginia Handbook* (Edison, NJ: Hunter Publishing, 2001), 85–86; *Official Records*, Vol. 12, 1:434.
3. *Ibid.*, Vol. 12, 3:66, 80.
4. *Ibid.*, Vol. 12, 3:80.
5. For Walter Taylor's response to Field's telegrams, see *Ibid.*, Vol. 12, 3:850–851.
6. *Ibid.*, Vol. 12, 1:429.
7. *Ibid.*, Vol. 12, 1:434.
8. *Ibid.*, Vol. 12, 1:430, 438.
9. *Ibid.*, Vol. 12, 1:431, 438.
10. *Ibid.*, Vol. 12, 1:428, 434.
11. Rebecca Campbell Light, ed., *The War at Our Doors: The Civil War Diaries of the Bernard Sisters of Virginia* (Fredericksburg, VA: The American History Company, 1998), 28–28; John Hennessy "Fredericksburg in the War," *Blue and Gray Magazine* 22, no. 1 (Winter 2005): 10.
12. *Official Records*, Vol. 12, 1:435, 3:856, 859.
13. *Ibid.*, Vol. 12, 3:859. Jackson did give thought to Ewell's going to Fredericksburg. See *Ibid.*, Vol. 12, 3:863–4.
14. *Ibid.*, Vol. 12, 3:97–8, 99.
15. *Ibid.*, Vol. 11, 3:458; *Ibid.* Vol. 12, 3:859, 867. Newton notes in *Joseph E. Johnston and the Defense of Richmond*, 127, "Anderson obviously considered himself the commander of one of the Confederacy's many small independent armies, answerable only to the commanding general. Lee neither corrected him ... nor ever informed him that [Joseph E.] Johnston was his official superior.... On the other hand, Lee informed both Jackson and Ewell of Anderson's appointment in advance and ordered the three generals to communicate with each other."
16. *Official Records*, Vol. 12, 3:117–8. McDowell's informants were "four very intelligent men–two of them Pennsylvanians, one a Virginian, and one a Marylander... ." These men informed McDowell that the Confederates planned to "make a stand" at Hanover Junction or Hanover Court House. *Ibid.*, Vol. 12, 3:124, 132, 135; Hennessy, "Fredericksburg in the War," 10.
17. Robert E. Lee to Theophilus Holmes, May 13, 1862, quoted in Harsh, *Confederate Tide Rising*, 218. See note 95; Freeman, *R. E. Lee*, 2:51.
18. *Official Records*, Vol. 12, 3:142, 144, 160, 169–170, 885, 886.
19. *Ibid.*, Vol. 12, 3:888.
20. James S. Brawely, "The Public and Military Career of Lawrence O'Bryan Branch." Master's thesis. Chapel Hill: University of North Carolina 1951), 159.
21. *Official Records*, Vol. 12, 3:890. In a second message to Branch on May 15, Ewell again stressed the necessity to limit baggage, instructing Branch that he could not "bring tents; tent-flies without poles, or tents cut down to that size, and only a few as are indispensable. No mess-chest, trunks, &c. It is better to leave these things where you are than throw them away after starting. We can get along without anything but food and ammunition." *Ibid.*, 892.
22. John B. Alexander to his wife, May 14, 1862 (John B. Alexander Papers, University of North Carolina, Charlotte); Thomas and Hyman, *Stanton*, 195; Basler, *The Collected Works of ... Lincoln*, 5:218.
23. *Ibid.*, 5:219–220; For McClellan's rebuttal to Lincoln concerning McDowell, see Sears, *The Civil War Papers of ... McClellan*, 271–2.
24. William G. Morris to his wife, May 22, 1862 (William G. Morris Letters, Southern Historical Collection, University of North Carolina, Chapel Hill); Brawley, "The Public Life and Military Career of Lawrence O'Bryan Branch," 163; *Official Records*, Vol. 12, 3:898.
25. *Ibid.*, Vol. 12, 3:202, 203, 207, 215.
26. *Ibid.*, Vol. 11, 3:535, 537.
27. *Ibid.*, Vol. 11, 3:540–1; Kenneth L. Stiles, *4th Virginia Cavalry* (Lynchburg, VA: H. E. Howard, 1985), 11.
28. *Official Records*, Vol. 11, 3:544 Anderson addresses Branch as "Major-General." *Ibid.*, Vol. 12, 3:243.
29. *Ibid.*, Vol. 11, 3:550–1.

Chapter 4

1. William H. Powell, *The Fifth Army Corps: A Record of Operations During the Civil War in*

the United States of America, 1861–1865 (Reprint, Dayton, OH: Morningside Bookshop, 1984), 27.

2. Undated memorandum by Fitz John Porter, reel 3 (container 7), Porter Papers; Eicher and Eicher, *Civil War High Commands*, 269, 369.

3. Ibid., 521.

4. Eric J. Wittenberg, *"We Have It Damn Hard Out Here": The Civil War Letters of Sergeant Thomas W. Smith, 6th Pennsylvania Cavalry* (Kent, OH: Kent State University Press, 1999), 2; Eicher and Eicher, *Civil War High Commands*, 266–67.

5. Janet B. Hewettt, Noah A. Trudeau, and Bryce A. Suderow, ed., *Supplement to the Official Records of the Union and Confederate Armies.* (Wilmington, NC: Broadfoot, 1994, Vol. 11, 352; Wittenburg, *"We Have It Damn Hard Out Here,"* 34; *Official Records*, Vol. 11, 3:667; Edward G. Longacre, *Lincoln's Cavalrymen: A History of the Mounted Forces of the Army of the Potomac, 1861–1865* (Mechanicsburg, PA: Stackpole Books, 2000), 83–86; Fitz John Porter to Gouverneur K. Warren, May 23, 1862, Warren Papers, Box 20, Folder 4, New York State Library. The Thirteenth New York received orders to report to Old Church on May 22. Warren Papers, Box 20, Folder 4; *Rochester Union and Advertiser*, June 13, 1862; Eicher and Eicher, *Civil War High Commands*, 554–555.

6. *Supplement to the Official Records*, Vol. 11, 356.

7. Porter to Warren, May 25, 1862, Warren Papers, NYSL; *Official Records*, Vol. 11, 3:677.

8. Judith McGuire, *Diary of a Southern Refugee During the War, By a Lady of Virginia.* (Lincoln: University of Nebraska Press, 1995), 135–137. Mrs. Willoughby Newton was born Mary S. Brockenbrough. Her husband was a lawyer, as well as a state and congressional representative. Mr. Newton was a member of the state house from 1861–1863. Mrs. Newton was soon to play another part in the war, a part remembered for generations and recorded in poems and paintings. On J.E.B. Stuart's ride around McClellan's army in June 1862, Captain William Latane of Company F, Ninth Virginia Cavalry, was killed, the only soldier to lose his life during the ride. The body was borne to Westwood and placed in the care of Mrs. Catherine Brockenbrough and Mrs. Willoughby Newton. "Nineteenth-century women were accustomed to preparing bodies for burial, and these women had slaves to construct a coffin and dig a grave. But because they were in "enemy county," the women were unable to find a clergyman to perform the burial service. So Mrs. Newton took charge and read the service at the family graveyard while the women and children from the neighborhood looked on." Emory M. Thomas, *Bold Dragoon: The Life of J.E.B. Stuart* (Norman: University of Oklahoma Press, 1999), 117–118.

See also "The Death and Burial of Captain William Latane." *Southern Historical Society Papers* Vol. 39, (April 1914): 87–90, and Lancaster, *A Sketch of the Early History of Hanover County*, 75–76.

9. Edwin W. Stone, *Rhode Island in the Rebellion* (Providence, R.I.: G. H. Whitney, 1864), 92.

10. *Rochester Union and Advertiser*, June 13, 1862.

11. Edwin C. Fishel, *The Secret War for the Union: The Untold Story of Military Intelligence in the Civil War* (Boston: Houghton-Mifflin Trade and Reference, 1996), 155. Had McClellan believed Dr. Pollock in regard to the size of the Confederate force, he likely would have sent more than just Porter's V Corps.

12. Donald B. Koonce, ed., *Doctor to the Front: The Recollections of Confederate Surgeon Thomas Fanning Wood 1861–1865* (Knoxville: University of Tennessee Press, 2000), 26; Allen P. Speer, *Voices from Cemetery Hill: The Civil War Diary, Reports, and Letters of Colonel William Henry Asbury Speer, 1861–1864* (Johnson City, TN: The Overmountain Press, 1997), 46.

13. Some sources say three days' rations. See Oliver W. Norton, *Army Letters 1861–1865* (Chicago: C. L. Deming, 1903), 82; Amos M. Judson, *History of the Eighty-third Regiment of Pennsylvania Volunteers* (Erie, PA: B. F. Lynn, Publisher, 1865), 48; Porter to Warren, May 26, 1862, Warren Papers, NYSL; *Official Records*, Vol. 11, 1:682, 702; Stone, *Rhode Island in the Rebellion*, 92–93; *Rochester (NY) Democrat and American*, June 9, 1862.

14. *Official Records*, Vol. 11, 1:723, 725, 739; Norton, *Army Letters*, 82; *Rochester (NY) Democrat and American*, June 9, 1862; John O'Connell Memoir, Civil War Miscellaneous Boxes, United States Army Military History Institute.

15. *Official Records*, Vol. 11, 1:685; Stiles, *4th Virginia Cavalry*, 10.

16. McGuire, *Diary of a Southern Refugee*, 139; *Official Records*, Vol. 11, 1:741; Jeffery C. Lowe and Sam Hodges, eds., *Letters to Amanda: The Civil War Letters of Marion Hill Fitzpatrick, Army of Northern Virginia* (Macon, GA: Mercer University Press, 1998), 9.

17. *Official Records*, Vol. 11, 1:741; Speer, *Voices from Cemetery Hill*, 47–48.

18. Eicher and Eicher, *Civil War High Commanders*, 366; undated memorandum by Fitz John Porter, Porter Papers, reel 3 (container 7), Library of Congress; William B. Styple, ed., *Writing and Fighting the Civil War: Soldier Correspondence to the New York Sunday Mercury* (Kearny, N. J., Belle Grove Publishing Company, 2000), 97; *New York Times*, June 7, 1862; *Rochester (NY) Union and Advertiser*, June 19, 1862.

19. *Official Records*, Vol. 11, 1:702.

20. Charles A. Johnson was brevetted brigadier general on March 13, 1865, for his serv-

ice at Hanover. Eicher and Eicher, *Civil War High Commands*, 320; *Indiana* (PA) *Messenger*, June 4, 1862; *New York Times*, June 7, 1862; *Rochester* (NY) *Democrat and American*, June 10, 1862.

21. *Official Records*, Vol. 11, 1:743; *State Journal* (NC), June 4, 1862; *Rochester* (NY) *Democrat and American*, June 10, 1862; Styple, *Writing and Fighting the Civil War*, 99.

22. *Official Records*, Vol. 11, 1:694.

23. Speer, *Voices from Cemetery Hill*, 52–53; Letter from Jonas Cloninger to Father, August 27, 1862, Bell Wiley Collection, Emory University.

24. According to Stiles, *4th Virginia Cavalry*, there were 75 Federal prisoners, 12.

25. *Official Records*, Vol. 11, 1:723; Historical Sketch of the 12th, http://www.dmna.state.ny.us/historic/reghist/civil/infantry/12thInf/12thInfHistSketch.htm; *Official Records*, Vol. 11, 1:726; Norton, *Army Letters*, 83; *Erie* (PA) *Weekly Gazette*, June 12, 1862. The role of Berdan's Sharpshooters is not entirely clear. Berdan's report, written on May 30, is extremely short. Concerning the regiment's role in the first fight, Berdan writes: "In the forenoon my regiment was deployed in the edge of the woods in front of the enemy's battery, to co-operate with the Twenty-fifth New York on the right and another regiment on the left. They all advanced together through the open field upon which the enemy retired." Nowhere in the report of the Twenty-fifth New York is there mention of participation in the attack of Butterfield's brigade. *Official Records*, Vol. 11, 1:701, 716.

26. Historical Sketch of the 12th, http://www.dmna.state.ny.us/historic/reghist/civil/infantry/12thInf/12thInfHistSketch.htm; *Official Records*, Vol. 11, 1:694, 696, 734; Speer, *Voices from Cemetery Hill*, 54. There was much dispute between the Seventeenth New York and the Eighty-third Pennsylvania regarding the capture of the Confederate cannon. Both regiments claimed capture, and the Seventeenth was credited with the capture in a letter by McClellan. This cannon was the first captured by the Army of the Potomac in battle. The story of a lone gunner being killed just as the Federals swarmed around the guns is dubious. According to Manarin and Jordan, no gunners were killed, and only one, Pvt. William Smith, later died of his wounds. Louis H. Manarin and Weymouth T. Jordan, eds. *North Carolina Troops, 1861–1865: A Roster* (Raleigh: North Carolina Department of Archives and History, 1961– present), 1:465–478.

27. Speer, *Voices from Cemetery Hill*, 54; *Official Records*, Vol. 11, 1:723.

28. *Ibid.*, Vol. 11, 1:725, 726, 734.

29. *Ibid.*, Vol. 11, 1:697, 745.

30. Speer, *Voices from Cemetery Hill*, 55–56; Jonas Cloninger to Father, August 27, 1862, Bell Wiley papers.

31. Michael C. Hardy, *The Thirty-seventh North Carolina Troops: Tar Heels in the Army of Northern Virginia* (Jefferson: McFarland and Company, 2003), 57; *Official Records*, Vol. 11: 1:689, 692.

32. Wittenberg, "We Have It Damn Hard Out Here," 36–37.

Chapter 5

1. *Supplement to the Army Official Records*, Vol. 11, 367; William M. Barber was born in Rowan County, North Carolina, in 1834. He attended St. James College in Hagerstown, Maryland, before being admitted to the bar in North Carolina in 1859. At the time of the war, he was practicing law in Wilkes County, North Carolina. On September 24, 1861, Barber became captain of the Western Carolina Stars, and on November 20, lieutenant colonel of the Thirty-seventh North Carolina. Barber was mortally wounded on September 30, 1864, at Jones Farm, Virginia, and died on October 3, 1864, in Petersburg, Virginia. See Hardy, *The Thirty-seventh North Carolina Troops*, 14, 107, 211.

2. William S. Powell, "Charles Cochrane Lee," *Dictionary of North Carolina Biography*. 6. (Chapel Hill: University of North Carolina Press, 1991), 43. Charles C. Lee's father was Stephen Lee, colonel of the Sixteenth North Carolina Troops (Sixth North Carolina Volunteers).

3. Robert K. Krick, *Lee's Colonels* (Dayton, OH: Morningside Bookshop, 1979), 71; *Supplement to the Official Records of the Union and Confederate Armies*, Vol. 11, 361–2; Erza J. Warner, *Generals in Gray: Lives of the Confederate Commanders* (Baton Rouge: Louisiana State University Press, 1959), 140. Hoke ended the war as a major general. For more information on Hoke, see Daniel W. Barefoot, *General Robert F. Hoke: Lee's Modest Warrior* (Winston-Salem, NC: John F. Blair, 1996)

4. Martindale's other two regiments, the Eighteenth Massachusetts and the Thirteenth New York, were not under Martindale's command during the battle. The Eighteenth Massachusetts was "on detached service," and the Thirteenth New York was "on picket duty" and accompanied Warren's brigade. *Official Records*, Vol. 11, 1:702.

5. Colonel Gove was later killed at Gaines's Mill, Virginia, on June 27, 1862.

6. *Official Records*, Vol. 11, 1:702.

7. Cpl. Joseph Simonds to sister Susie, May 28, 1862. Lewis Leigh, Book 49, United States Army Military History Institute; John L. Parker, *Henry Wilson's Regiment—History of the Twenty-Second Massachusetts Infantry, the Second Company Sharpshooters and the Third Light Battery,*

in the War of Rebellion (Boston: Rand Avery Co., 1887), 106.

8. *State Journal*, September 3, 1862. Colonel Barber's name is sometimes found spelled "Barbour." The family insists that the former is correct, and that is how the name is spelled on the colonel's grave marker in Wilkesboro, North Carolina.

9. *Official Records*, Vol. 11, 1:696.

10. Krick, *Lee's Colonels*, 357, 371; *Supplement to the Official Records of the Union and Confederate Armies*, Vol. 11, 356; *Raleigh Register*, June 25, 1862.

11. *Official Records*, Vol. 11, 1:696; *Wilmington Journal*, June 12, 1862; Alfred Davenport, *Camp and Field Life of the Fifth New York Volunteer Infantry* (New York: Dick and Fitzgerald, 1879), 186; *Raleigh Register*, June 7, 1862.

12. James H. Muncay, *Second to None: The Story of the 2d Maine Volunteer Infantry, "The Bangor Regiment"* (Charborough, MA: Harp Publications, 1992), 44–45. The Second Maine enlisted to serve for two years, except for 120 men who signed on for three years. After the two-year men went home, the 120 that were left mutinied and refused to fight, claiming that they had enlisted to serve only in the Second Maine. These 120 men were assigned to the Twentieth Maine and participated, for the most part heroically, in the battle of Gettysburg.

13. *Official Records*, Vol. 11, 1:708; *Bangor Daily Whig and Courier*, June 5, 1862.

14. *Official Records*, Vol. 11, 1:703.

15. Ibid., Vol. 11, 1:708; 713–714; Joseph Simonds to Susie May 28, 1862, USAMHI.

16. *New York Times*, June 7, 1862; *Official Records*, Vol. 11, 1:703–704; Powell, *The Fifth Army Corps*, 10–11.

17. Krick, *Lee's Colonels*, 90; *Supplement to the Official Records*, Vol. 11, 366; *Wilmington Journal*, June 5, 1862; *Raleigh Register*, June 7, 1862.

18. Wood, *Doctor to the Front*, 26.

19. *Official Records*, Vol. 11, 1:704, 708.

20. Ibid., Vol. 11, 1:728; Eugene A. Nash, *A History of the Forty-Fourth, New York Volunteer Infantry, in the Civil War, 1861–1865* (Chicago: R. R. Donnelley & Sons Co., 1911), 74.

21. *Official Records*, Vol. 11, 1: 741.

22. Joseph H. Saunders to mother, June 6, 1862. Saunders Family Papers, Southern Historical Collection, University of North Carolina, Chapel Hill; *Rochester* (NY) *Democrat and American*, June 6, 1862. *New York Times*, June 4, 1862. No official report has been found for the Thirty-third North Carolina and the battle of Hanover Court House and Slash Church.

23. *New York Times* June 13, 1862.

24. *Buffalo* (NY) *Morning Express*, June 6, 1862; *Official Records*, Vol. 11, 1:728; *National Tribune*, March 21, 1901.

25. *Raleigh Register*, 25 June 1862. No official report for the battle of Hanover Court House and Slash Church has been found for the Twelfth North Carolina.

26. *Supplement to the Army Official Records*, Vol. 11, 173.

27. *Official Records*, Vol. 11, 1:704; Nash, *A History of the Forty-Fourth Regiment*, 75. Martindale makes no mention in his report of a conversation with Colonel Stryker at this point in the battle.

28. *Wilmington Journal Weekly*, June 12, 1862; *Supplement to the Official Records of the Union and Confederate Armies*, Vol. 11, 367; *Rochester Democrat and American*, June 9, 1862; An official report for the Eighteenth North Carolina has never been found.

29. Styple, *Writing and Fighting the Civil War*, 97; *Official Records*, Vol. 11, 1:716.

30. *Official Records*, Vol. 11, 1:709; *Bangor Daily Whig and Courier*, June 10, 1862; *Fayetteville Observer*, June 16, 1862. It is interesting to note that Roberts's report does not include the order to fix bayonets. This comes from General Martindale's report.

31. *Wilmington Journal Weekly*, June 12, 1862; Wood, *Doctor to the Front*, 27.

32. Mundy *Second to None* 139; *Official Records*, Vol. 11, 1:709.

33. William G. Morris to wife, May 27, 1862, Morris Letters, Southern Historical Collection, University of North Carolina, Chapel Hill; *Supplement to the Official Records of the Union and Confederate Armies*, Vol. 11, 367; *Weekly Catawba Journal*, June 10, 1862.

34. *Official Records*, Vol. 11, 1:709; Styple, *Writing and Fighting the Civil War*, 97–98; *New York Times*, June 7, 1862; Nash, *A History of the Forty-fourth Regiment*, 77.

35. *Morning Express*, June 6, 1862; *Official Records*, Vol. 11, 1:705, 717; Nash, *A History of the Forty-fourth Regiment*, 75–76; *Steubenville Herald*, June 2, 1897.

36. Hardy, *The Thirty-seventh North Carolina Troops*, 62–63; *Raleigh Register*, June 7, 1862.

37. *Bangor Daily Whig and Courier*, June 4, 1862, June 5, 1862; June 10, 1862; Mundy *Second to None*, 141; *New York Times*, June 7, 1862.

38. *Official Records*, Vol. 11, 1:682, 700, 717–718.

39. Ibid., 1:709, 718, 720; *Oneida Weekly Herald*, June 17, 1862.

40. Parker, *Henry Wilson's Regiment*, 107–108; *Official Records*, Vol. 11, 1:745.

41. *Raleigh Register*, September 3, 1862; *National Tribune*, June 10, 1901; *Official Records*, Vol. 11, 1:697, 719, 721. According to one source, Colonel Cass "was seriously ill" when the order came to march early on the morning of May 27, "and the regiment marched away under command of Lieut. Col. Guiney. They had not gone far, however, when the colonel came galloping

along and took charge. He simply could not stand back and let his regiment go into its first battle without being on the spot." Frank J. Flynn, *"The Fighting Ninth" for Fifty Years and the Semicentennial Celebration* (Boston: n.p., 1911), 15–16.

42. Davenport, *Camp and Field Life of the Fifth New York Volunteer Infantry*, 185; Eicher and Eicher, *Civil War High Commands*, 219; *National Tribune*, January 24, 1884.

43. *Official Reports*, Vol. 11, 1:742; *Raleigh Weekly Standard*, July 2, 1862; *Supplement to the Official Records*, Vol. 11, 365; Williams, *History of Jones County, Georgia, 1807–1907*, 519. Branch originally said that he had only one ambulance and one ammunition wagon. For Branch, that might have been personally true, but it seems that other regiments under his command, the Twenty-eighth and Thirty-third North Carolina and the Forty-fifth Georgia, had their own wagons.

44. Louis Shaffner, "A Civil War Surgeon's Diary." *North Carolina Medical Journal* 27, no. 9 (September 1966): 410.

45. *Raleigh Register*, June 7, 1862; Davenport, *Camp and Field Life of the Fifth New York Infantry*, 186. This account of the charge of the Fifth New York is far more detailed than the description Colonel Warren wrote in his report: "The Fifth New York Volunteers and the First Connecticut were formed in line of battle and moved promptly forward under their respective commanders, as did Weeden's battery, but before they could reach the enemy he broke and fled under the fire of other portions of our forces." It is likely that the true movement of the Fifth New York lies somewhere between the two reports. *Official Reports*, Vol. 11, 1:736.

46. *National Tribune*, January 24, 1884; *Rochester Union and Advertiser*, June 13, 1862; W. J. H. Bellamy Diary, Southern Historical Collection, University of North Carolina, Chapel Hill.

47. Michael Schellhammer, *The 83rd Pennsylvania Volunteers in the Civil War* (Jefferson, NC: McFarland and Company, 2003), 74–75; *Official Records*, Vol. 11, 1:734–735.

48. *Ibid.*, Vol. 11, 1:720; *National Tribune*, January 24, 1884.

49. *Official Records* Vol. 11, 1:720, 742; *National Tribune*, January 24, 1884.

50. *Steubenville Herald*, June 2, 1897.

51. Norton, *Army Letters, 1861–1865*, 85.

Chapter 6

1. Stone, *Rhode Island in the Rebellion*, 95.
2. Bell I. Wiley, *The Life of Billy Yank* (New York: Bob Merrills, 1951), 148.
3. *The Catawba Weekly Journal*, June 10, 1862; *A Survey of Civil War Sites in Hanover County, Virginia* (2002), 6.

4. Cowles, *History of the Fifth Mass. Battery*, 274–5; *National Tribune*, January 24, 1884.
5. *Ibid.*
6. *Rochester Union and Advertiser*, June 13, 1862; *Official Records*, Vol. 11, 1:742.
7. H. H. Cunningham, *Doctors in Gray: The Confederate Medical Service* (Baton Rouge: Louisiana State University Press, 1986), 114.
8. Herbert M. Schiller, "Health and Medicine: Battle Injuries," in *The Confederacy* (New York: Simon & Schuster Macmillan, 1993), 515; *Catawba Weekly Journal*, June 10, 1862.
9. Gregory Coco, *The Civil War Infantryman: In Camp, on the March, and in Battle*, (Gettysburg, PA: Thomas Publishers, 1996), 141; Schellhammer, *The 83rd Pennsylvania Volunteers in the Civil War*, 77; *Raleigh Weekly Standard*, July 7, 1862.
10. *Rochester Union and Advertiser*, June 13, 1862; Tripler was author of *Manual of the Medical Officer of the Army of the United States*, (1858); *Official Records*, Vol. 11, 1:187.
11. J. Franklin Dyer, *The Journal of a Civil War Surgeon*, edited by Michael B. Chesson (Lincoln, NC: University of Nebraska Press, 2003), 22; Styple, *Writing and Fighting the Civil War*, 98.
12. *Rochester Democrat and American*, June 10, 1862; *Erie Weekly Gazette*, June 12, 1862.
13. *Bangor Daily Whig and Courier*, June 7, 1862.

Chapter 7

1. Davenport, *Camp and Field Life of the Fifth New York*, 187.
2. John J. Hennessy, *Fighting with the Eighteenth Massachusetts: The Civil War Memoir of Thomas H. Mann* (Baton Rouge: Louisiana State University Press, 2000), 67.
3. "The Diary of Lewis Bramer, Jr.," http://skaneateles.org/1braner1.html; Norton, *Army Letters, 1861–1865*, 85; Styple, *Writing and Fighting the Civil War*, 98; Cowles, *History of the Fifth Massachusetts Battery*, 1902), 275.
4. *Oneida Weekly Herald*, June 17, 1862; Davenport, *Camp and Field Life of the Fifth New York Volunteer Infantry*, 187; Speer, *Voices from Cemetery Hill*, 59.
5. *Rochester Union and Advertiser*, June 13, 1862; Judson, *History of the Eighty-third Regiment Pennsylvania Volunteers*, 37; Norton, *Army Letters, 1861–1865*, 85; *Erie Weekly Gazette*, June 12, 1862; *Dedham Gazette*, June 7, 1862.
6. Luther C. Furst Diary, Harrisburg CWRT Collection, USAMHI.
7. Cowles, *History of the Fifth Massachusetts Battery*, 275; Norton, *Army Letters 1861–1865*, 86; Schellhammer, *The 83rd Pennsylvania Volunteers*, 78; *National Tribune*, January 24, 1884; *North*

Bridgewater Gazette, June 14, 1862; *Rochester Union and American,* June 9, 1862, June 13, 1862; Furst, Diary, USAMHI.

8. Flynn, *The Fighting Ninth,* 16; Samito, *Commanding Boston's Irish 9th,* 105; Parker, *Henry Wilson's Regiment,* 110–111; Cowles, *History of the Fifth Massachusetts Battery,* 273.

9. Speer, *Voices from Cemetery Hill,* 56–57. It is unclear just what moon Speer reported seeing. According to the U. S. Naval Observatory, the moon was full on May 13, two weeks prior to the battle, and the moon was new on May 27. Jonas Cloninger, Bell Wiley Collection, Emory University.

10. *Catawba Weekly Journal,* June 10, 1861. Surgeon Robert Gibbon had a brother in the Twenty-eighth, Nicholas Gibbon, assistant commissary of substance. A third brother, John Gibbon, was a major general in the Federal army. Manarin and Jordan, eds. *North Carolina Troops,* 8:111; Eicher and Eicher, *Civil War High Commands,* 253.

11. *Official Records,* Vol. 11, 1:712.

12. *Ibid.*; Parker, *Henry Wilson's Regiment,* 110. It was on the return of this expedition that the flag of Company D, Forty-fifth Georgia, was captured.

13. General Emory, in his report, states that two companies of the Seventeenth New York were assigned to the operation, while Colonel Lansing reports five companies. *Official Records,* Vol. 11, 1:686, 693, 695, 726.

14. *Ibid.,* Vol. 11, 1:686, 689.

15. *Ibid.,* Vol. 11, 1:690.

16. Wittenberg, "We Have It Damn Hard Out Here," 37.

17. *Rochester Union and Advertiser,* June 13, 1862.

18. *Dedham Gazette,* June 7, 1862; Joseph Simonds to Susie, May 28, 1862, Lewis Leigh Collection, USAMHI; *Philadelphia Press,* June 2, 1862.

19. Speer, *Voices From Cemetery Hill,* 60–61.

20. Shaffner, "A Civil War Surgeon's Diary," 410.

21. *Official Records,* Vol. 11, 1:35, 679.

22. Sears, *The Civil War Papers of ... McClellan,* 279; *Official Records,* Vol. 11, 1:36; David R. Barbee, "The Musical Mr. Lincoln," *Abraham Lincoln Quarterly* 5 (December 1949): 450–51; *Bangor Daily Whig and Courier,* June 10, 1862; *Rochester Union and Advertiser,* June 13, 1862; Furst, Diary, USAMHI. The telegraph had been located at the headquarters of the Army of the Potomac until Stanton assumed office. While McClellan was away one day, Stanton had the telegraph moved to the War Department and set up in an office in the second-floor library. Leech, *Reveille in Washington,* 199.

23. *Official Records,* Vol. 11, 1:693.

24. *Ibid.,* Vol. 11 1:690–691.

25. *Ibid.,* Vol. 11, 1:736–739; *Supplement to the Official Records,* Vol. 2, 1:358.

26. *Official Records,* Vol. 11, 1:37.

27. Cowles, *History of the Fifth Massachusetts Battery,* 276; Nash, *44th New York Volunteer Infantry,* 77; *Rochester Union and Advertiser,* June 9, 1862, June 13, 1862; Styple, *Writing and Fighting the Civil War,* 98; Judson, *History of the Eighty-third Regiment Pennsylvania Volunteers,* 37. Lt. Amos M. Judson wrote: "One result of this affair was the large numbers of contrabands that followed us back to camp. They remained in the Regiment a long time afterwards, and participated in all its marches, fatigues and in not a few of its dangers. Many have since enlisted in the army and have done their share in the work of overthrowing the rebellion and striking off the shackles from their long enslaved race."

28. "The Diary of Lewis Bramer, Jr." http://skaneateless.org/1bramer1.html; *Rochester Union and Advertiser,* June 13, 1862; Styple, *Writing and Fighting the Civil War,* 98.

29. *Official Records,* Vol. 11, 1:685.

Chapter 8

1. Wood, *Doctor to the Front,* 27; Williams, *History of Jones County, Georgia,* 519.

2. *Official Records,* Vol. 11, 1: 742; *Supplement to the Official Records of the Union and Confederate Armies,* Vol. 11, 364; J. G. DeRoulhac Hamilton, ed., et al., "The Diary of Bartlett Yancey Malone." *The James Sprunt Historical Publications.* 16:2 (1919): 20.

3. *Biblical Recorder,* June 11, 1862.

4. At a meeting in Richmond on April 18, 1862, the citizens passed a resolution to "secure quarters for the wounded." Emory M. Thomas, *The Confederate State of Richmond: A Biography of the Capital* (Baton Rouge: Louisiana State University Press, 1998), 90. For a good description of Confederate hospitals, see Cunningham, *Doctors in Gray,* 45–69.

5. *Richmond Examiner,* April 2, 1862; *Official Records,* Vol. 11, 3:504.

6. Thomas, *The Confederate State of Richmond,* 92–94.

7. *Official Records,* Vol. 12, 3:232, 233, 266, 268. Jerry J. Coggeshall, in his 1999 thesis "Hanover Courthouse: The Union's Tactical Victory and Strategic Failure," speculated that McDowell "was trying to discourage Lincoln and Stanton from sending any more of his troops from Fredericksburg to the Valley. If McCall and King were busy demonstrating south of Fredericksburg it would be unwise, and inconvenient, to send them into the valley after Jackson." Jerry J. Coggeshall, "Hanover Court House: The Union's Tactical Victory and Strategic Failure." Master's thesis. (Old Dominion University, 1999), 30.

8. *Official Records,* Vol. 11, 3:557.

9. Gregg's brigade was composed of the First, First Rifles, Twelfth, Thirteenth, and Fourteenth South Carolina regiments. Field's brigade now contained the Fortieth, Forty-seventh, Fifty-fifth, and Sixtieth Virginia Regiments, along with the Twenty-second Virginia Battalion. Pender's brigade was composed of the Sixteenth, Twenty-second, Thirty-fourth, and Thirty-eighth North Carolina Regiments. The First, Seventh, and Fourteenth Tennessee, the Nineteenth Georgia, and the Fifth Alabama Battalion comprised Archer's brigade. See James I. Robertson, Jr., *General A. P. Hill: The Story of a Confederate Warrior* (New York: Random House, 1987), 59–64; *Confederate Veteran* 23 (1915), 161.

10. *Official Records,* Vol. 11, 1:741–742.

11. These figures were derived from Appendix D in the back of this book. The returns for the Twenty-eighth North Carolina show only 2 men wounded, with 14 both wounded and captured, a number far too low to be in keeping with the size of the regiment and its activities during the battle.

Chapter 9

1. *New York Sunday Mercury,* June 15, 1862.
2. Brayton Harris, *Blue and Gray in Black and White: Newspapers in the Civil War* (Washington: Brassey's, 1999), 14–15; Norman Rourke, "The Newsmen," *Civil War Times Illustrated* 40, no. 6 (December 2001): 15.
3. *New York Times,* May 29, 1862.
4. *Brooklyn Eagle,* May 31, 1862; Rourke "The Newsman," 17.
5. *Philadelphia Press,* June 2, 1862.
6. *New York Times,* June 4, 1862.
7. *Ibid.,* June 7, 1862.
8. *Rochester Union and Advertiser,* June 9, 1862; *Bangor Daily Whig and Courier,* June 10, 1862; *Erie Weekly Gazette,* June 6, 1862.
9. *Bangor Daily Whig and Courier,* June 4, 1862.
10. *Ibid.,* June 5, 1862.
11. *National Tribune,* June 10, 1901.
12. *Ibid.,* March 21, 1901.
13. Rourke "The Newsman," 17; *Richmond Whig,* quoted in the *Fayetteville Observer,* June 4, 1862.
14. *Richmond Enquirer* and *Richmond Examiner,* quoted in the *Fayetteville Observer,* June 4, 1862.
15. *Richmond Dispatch,* quoted in the *Fayetteville Observer,* June 4, 1862.
16. *Western Carolinian,* June 6, 1862.
17. *Fayetteville Observer,* June 9, 1862.
18. *Biblical Recorder,* June 11, 1862.

19. *State Journal,* September 3, 1862; *Weekly Register,* June 4, 1862, June 11, 1862; *Spirit of the Age,* June 16, 1862; *State Journal,* June 18, 1862.

20. The "Hanover" letter appeared in the *North Carolina Standard* on June 4, the *Peoples Press,* on June 6, and the *Spirit of the Age* on June 9.

21. *Spirit of the Age,* June 9, 1862.

22. Octavius A. Wiggins, "Thirty-seventh Regiment," in Walter Clark, ed. *Histories of the Several Regiments and Battalions from North Carolina in the Great War, 1861–1865.* 5 vols. (Raleigh, NC: E. M. Uzzell, 1901) 3: 24. The identity of the officer in the Thirty-third is unknown, and this account appears only in Wiggins's narrative.

23. *The Weekly Catawba Journal,* June 19, 1862.

24. No evidence has surfaced indicating whether the court of inquiry requested by Branch was ever held. Since Colonel Lee was killed a month after the battles of Hanover Court House and Peake's Turnout, and Branch was killed during the battle of Sharpsburg in September, it is likely that Branch decided to drop the matter altogether or had not had the opportunity to pursue the inquiry before he died barely three and a half months after the battle that called his competence into question.

Chapter 10

1. William G. Morris to wife, May 30, 1862, Morris Papers; UNC-Chapel Hill; John B. Alexander to wife, June 2, 1862, Alexander Letters, UNC-Charlotte.

2. Branch, in a letter to Richard C. Morgan, assistant adjutant general for A. P. Hill, that Latham's Battery "reported to me from North Carolina only the evening before I left Hanover Court-House, with only half enough men for the efficient service of the guns and with horses entirely untrained." *Supplement to Official Records,* 11:360.

3. *Ibid.,* 11:365–6.
4. *Ibid.,* 11:361.
5. *Ibid.,* 11:366.

6. It is also probable that the Twelfth North Carolina was armed with smoothbore muskets, and these men were never able to come close enough to the Federal lines to do any damage.

7. *Official Records,* Vol. 11, 1:742; It is possible that portions of the Twelfth North Carolina also worked at stopping the pursuing Federals.

8. *Ibid.,* Vol. 11, 1:682.
9. *Ibid.,* Vol. 11, 1:682.

10. Joseph E. Johnston to Wigfall, November 12, 1863, Wigfall Family Papers, Library of Congress.

11. D. H. Hill wrote on about seeing Johnston and Smith on the afternoon of May 29, and recalled the enthusiasm of the general. See Newton, *Johnston and the Defense of Richmond*, 169; Johnston, *Narrative*, 138.

Chapter 11

1. For more information about all the military action in Hanover County in 1861–1865, see *A Survey of Civil War Sites in Hanover County, Virginia*.
2. Lancaster, *A Sketch of the Early History of Hanover County, Virginia*, 21. In 2004, there were 38 structures, battlefields, districts, and sites from Hanover County on the National Register of Historic Places.

Appendix D

Seventh North Carolina State Troops

1. Unless otherwise noted, this list is compiled from Manarin and Jordan, eds. *North Carolina Troops*, Vol. 4:405–515.
2. This soldier's name does not appear on the roster in Manarin and Jordan, eds. *North Carolina Troops*, Vol. 4. He was reported wounded and captured in the *Petersburg Express*, reprinted in the Raleigh *Weekly Standard*, July 7, 1862.

Twelfth North Carolina Troops

1. Unless otherwise noted, this list is compiled from Manarin and Jordan, eds. *North Carolina Troops*, Vol. 5:114–246.
2. Pvt. William P. Bugg, Company C, was discharged on August 26, 1862, due to the wound he received at Hanover Court House. *Ibid.*, 148.
3. Pvt. Lewis W. Hedgpeth is listed as a member of Company I in Raleigh *Weekly Standard*, 7 Jun. 1862. He served as a member of 2nd Company H, Twelfth North Carolina Troops. *Ibid.*, 216.
4. The records state that Pvt. Thomas Robertson, Company C, was exchanged prior to June 4, 1862, but died at "Gaines." *Ibid.*, 154.
5. This information comes from the *Petersburg Express*, reprinted in the Raleigh *Weekly Standard*, June 7, 1862.
6. Pvt. Henry A. Todd was a member of the 2nd Company H. *Ibid.*, 217.
7. Pvt. Bently Wilkerson, Company B, was reported in a Federal hospital in Gaines's Mill, Virginia, on June 5, 1862. The "Roll of Honor indicates that he was killed in the battle of Hanover Court House." Federal records do not "indicate his subsequent disposition." *Ibid.*, 139.
8. Pvt. Andrew Wilson served in the 1st Company H, Twelfth North Carolina State Troops, until transferring to the 2nd Company H, Twelfth North Carolina State Troops, on May 1, 1862. *Ibid.*, 218.

Eighteenth North Carolina Troops

1. Unless otherwise noted, this list compiled from Manarin and Jordan, eds. *North Carolina Troops*, Vol. 6:305–424.
2. Fayetteville *Observer*, June 9, 1862.
3. *Ibid.*
4. *Ibid.*
5. *Ibid.*
6. *Ibid.*
7. *Ibid.*
8. Raleigh *Weekly Standard*, 7 July 1862.
9. "R. J. Chistrie" does not appear on the roster of the Eighteenth North Carolina found in *North Carolina Troops*, Vol. 5, but is listed as a casualty in *Fayetteville Observer*, June 9, 1862.
10. "Neill Edwards" does not appear on the roster of the Eighteenth North Carolina found in *North Carolina Troops*, Vol. 5, but is listed as a casualty in *Fayetteville Observer*, June 9, 1862.
11. *Ibid.*
12. *Ibid.*
13. *Ibid.*
14. *Ibid.*
15. *North Carolina Troops*, Vol. 5, states Lt. George A. Johnston was wounded in the back, while the *Petersburg Express*, reprinted in the Raleigh *Weekly Standard*, July 7, 1862, states that Johnston had a "perforating wound of chest...."
16. Raleigh *Weekly Standard*, 7 July 1862, states that Cpl. Samuel King died on June 11, 1862.
17. *Fayetteville Observer*, 16 June 1862.
18. *Ibid.*, June 9, 1862.
19. *Ibid.*
20. *Ibid.*
21. *Ibid.*
22. *Ibid.*
23. *Ibid.*
24. *Ibid.*
25. According to the *Raleigh Weekly Standard*, July 7, 1862, Archibald B. Rooks was wounded in the chest.
26. *Fayetteville Observer*, June 9, 1862.
27. Pvt. Alexander Simmons was discharged on April 5, 1862, due to his wounds. Manarin and Jordan, eds. *North Carolina Troops*, Vol. 5:319.

28. *Fayetteville Observer,* June 9, 1862.
29. *Ibid.*
30. *Ibid.*
31. *Ibid.*

Twenty-eighth North Carolina Troops

1. Unless otherwise noted, this list is compiled from Manarin and Jordan, eds. *North Carolina Troops,* Vol. 8:110–231; *Fayetteville Observer,* June 9, 1862; and *Spirit of the Age,* June 16, 1862.
2. Federal records do not support Pvt. Robert Adkins's being captured on May 27, 1862. Manarin and Jordan, eds., *North Carolina Troops,* Vol. 8:113.
3. North Carolina newspapers, according to *North Carolina Troops,* state that Assistant Surgeon Barham was captured "while in attendance on some of our wounded men, who had been necessarily left behind. Federal records do not support this. Manarin and Jordan, eds., *North Carolina Troops,* Vol. 8:111.
4. Pvt. Francis A. Blanton was declared exchanged on August 5, 1862, and died of unknown causes on August 6, 1862, in a hospital in Petersburg, Virginia. *Ibid.,* 197.
5. Pvt. Benjamin Calvard was discharged on January 3, 1864, by reason of his wounds sustained at Hanover Court House. *Ibid.,* 176.
6. Pvt. William A. Grigg died in a hospital in Petersburg, Va, on August 13, 1862, of typhoid. *Ibid.,* 117.
7. Pvt. Clingman C. Jolley was paroled and transferred for exchange, where on August 4, 1862, he died "on a steamboat coming up the James River to Richmond." *Ibid.,* 202–203.
8. Pvt. John Mock was received for exchange on August 5, 1862, and hospitalized in Richmond on August 7, 1862. He died of "phthisis" on August 11, 1862. *Ibid.,* 215.
9. *Spirit of the Age,* June 16, 1862.
10. Pvt. Solomon Townson was declared exchanged on August 5, 1862, and died of typhoid on August 10, 1862, in a hospital "in Virginia." Manarin and Jordan, eds., *North Carolina Troops,* Vol. 8:152.

Thirty-third North Carolina Troops

1. Unless otherwise noted, this list is compiled from Manarin and Jordan, eds., *North Carolina Troops,* Vol. 9:118–224.
2. Pvt. Richard B. Brady was discharged on October 17, 1863, due to the wounds he received at Hanover Court House. *Ibid.,* 173.
3. *Raleigh Weekly Standard,* July 7, 1862.
4. Company records indicate that Pvt. William C. Hines was captured on May 27, 1862, at Hanover Court House, Virginia. Federal records do not substantiate these reports. Manarin and Jordan, eds., *North Carolina Troops,* Vol. 9:225.

Thirty-seventh North Carolina Troops

1. Unless otherwise noted, this list is compiled from Manarin and Jordan, eds., *North Carolina Troops,* Vol. 9:468–604.
2. *Raleigh Weekly Register,* June 18, 1862.
3. *State Journal,* July 2, 1862.
4. "Rufus Armstrong," Company H, does not appear in Manarin and Jordan, eds., *North Carolina Troops,* Vol. 9, but is listed as a casualty belonging to this regiment in the *Raleigh Weekly Register,* June 18, 1862.
5. *State Journal,* July 2, 1862.
6. It is unclear if Pvt. Brinsley Barnes died of disease on May 20, 1862, or was killed on May 27, 1762, at Hanover. Manarin and Jordan, eds., *North Carolina Troops,* Vol. 9:552.
7. "L. A. Barnes" Company I, does not appear in *Ibid.,* but is listed as a casualty belonging to this regiment in the *Raleigh Weekly Register,* June 18, 1862.
8. *Ibid.*
9. *Ibid.*
10. *State Journal,* July 2, 1862.
11. *Raleigh Weekly Register,* June 18, 1862.
12. *Ibid.*
13. *State Journal,* July 2, 1862.
14. *Raleigh Weekly Register,* June 18, 1862.
15. *Ibid.*
16. *Ibid.,* July 7, 1862.
17. "W. D. Conley" Company I, does not appear in Manarin and Jordan, eds., *North Carolina Troops,* Vol. 9, but is listed as a casualty belonging to this regiment in the *Raleigh Weekly Register,* June 18, 1862.
18. *State Journal,* July 2, 1862, reports that Craven was wounded in both legs.
19. *Raleigh Weekly Register,* 18 June 1862.
20. *State Journal,* 2 July 1862.
21. *Ibid.*
22. Pvt. William R. Dees, Company D, was declared exchanged on August 5, 1862, and died on August 18, 1862, of "ty[phoid] febris" in a hospital in Petersburg, Virginia. Manarin and Jordan, eds. *North Carolina Troops,* Vol. 9:512.
23. Pvt. Linsey Dula was declared exchanged on August 5, 1862, and died of unknown causes on August 8, 1862, in Richmond, VA. *Ibid.,* 541.
24. "Sergt. Reuben Durby," Company A, does not appear in Manarin and Jordan, eds., *North Carolina Troops,* Vol. 9, but is listed as a casualty in the *Raleigh Weekly Register,* June 18, 1862.

25. *Ibid.*
26. *State Journal,* July 2, 1862.
27. Capt. William Y Farthing was declared exchanged on November 10, 1862, and on November 12, he wrote his letter of resignation. That resignation was accepted on November 28, 1862, the same day he died of "pleuritis" in a hospital in Winchester, Virginia. Manarin and Jordan, eds., *North Carolina Troops,* Vol. 9:523.
28. *State Journal,* July 2, 1862.
29. *Ibid.*
30. *Ibid.*
31. *Ibid.*
32. *Ibid.*
33. *Raleigh Weekly Register,* June 18, 1862.
34. *State Journal,* July 2, 1862.
35. *Ibid.*
36. "John Jenkins" Company H, does not appear in Manarin and Jordan, eds., *North Carolina Troops,* Vol. 9, but is listed as a casualty belonging to this regiment in the *Raleigh Weekly Register,* June 18, 1862.
37. *State Journal,* July 2, 1862.
38. *Ibid.*
39. *Raleigh Weekly Register,* June 18, 1862.
40. "G. W. McKee" does not appear in the roster in Manarin and Jordan, eds., *North Carolina Troops,* Vol. 9. He is listed as being a casualty in the *State Journal,* July 2, 1862.
41. Pvt. Nathan E. Manus was declared exchanged on August 5, 1862. He died that same day in a hospital in Petersburg, Virginia, of typhoid. Manarin and Jordan, eds., *North Carolina Troops,* Vol. 9:517.
42. *State Journal,* July 2, 1862.
43. *Ibid.*
44. *Ibid.*
45. Pvt. David Morrison is reported as missing by the *Raleigh Weekly Register,* June 18, 1862. According to Manarin and Jordan, eds., *North Carolina Troops,* Vol. 9:574–574, he did not enlist until August 12, 1862.
46. "J. H. Pasoin," Company H, does not appear in *Ibid.*, but is listed as a casualty belonging to this regiment in the *Raleigh Weekly Register,* June 18, 1862. It is possible that this could be Pvt. Phillip H. Payscur, Company H, also wounded on May 27, 1862.
47. *State Journal,* July 2, 1862.
48. *Ibid.*
49. "James Phillips,' Company I, does not appear in Manarin and Jordan, eds., *North Carolina Troops,* Vol. 9, but is listed as a casualty belonging to this regiment in the *Raleigh Weekly Register,* June 18, 1862.
50. *Ibid.*
51. *State Journal,* July 2, 1862.
52. *Raleigh Weekly Register,* June 18, 1862.
53. *State Journal,* July 2, 1862.
54. *Ibid.*
55. *Raleigh Weekly Register,* June 18, 1862.
56. *State Journal,* July 2, 1862.
57. Pvt. John E. Smith, Company B, contracted some unknown disease while a prisoner of war at Fort Delaware, Delaware. On August 5, 1862, the day he was declared exchanged, he died in a hospital in Richmond, Virginia. Manarin and Jordan, eds., *North Carolina Troops,* Vol. 9:498.
58. *State Journal,* July 2, 1862.
59. *Ibid.*
60. *Raleigh Weekly Register,* June 18, 1862.
61. *State Journal,* July 2, 1862.
62. *Ibid.*
63. *Raleigh Weekly Register,* June 18, 1862.
64. "John Weaston" does not appear in the roster in Manarin and Jordan, eds., *North Carolina Troops,* Vol. 9. He is listed as being a casualty in the *State Journal,* July 2, 1862.
65. *Raleigh Weekly Register,* June 18, 1862.
66. Pvt. Thomas R. Williams was declared exchanged on August 5, 1862, and died of "debilitas" on August 6, 1862, in a hospital in Petersburg, Virginia. Manarin and Jordan, eds., *North Carolina Troops,* Vol. 9:537.
67. *State Journal,* July 2, 1862.
68. *Ibid.*
69. *Raleigh Weekly Register,* June 18, 1862.
70. *State Journal,* July 2, 1862.
71. *Raleigh Weekly Register,* June 18, 1862.

Latham's Battery (Branch Artillery)

1. Unless otherwise noted, this list is compiled from Manarin and Jordan, eds., *North Carolina Troops,* Vol. 1:464–478.
2. *Petersburg Express,* reprinted in the *Raleigh Weekly Standard,* July 7, 1862.
3. *Ibid.*
4. *Fayetteville Observer,* June 16, 1862.

Second Maine Volunteers

1. Unless otherwise noted, this list is taken from the *New York Times,* June 4, 1862.
2. *Bangor Daily Whig and Courier,* June 8, 1862.
3. *Ibid.*
4. Munday, *Second to None,* 142.
5. *Ibid.,* 141.
6. *Bangor Daily Whig and Courier,* June 8, 1862.
7. *Ibid.*; Mundy, *Second to None,* 143.
8. Bangor *Daily Whig and Courier,* June 8, 1862.
9. *Ibid.*
10. *Ibid.*
11. *New York Times,* June 7, 1862.
12. Mundy, *Second to None,* 141.
13. *Bangor Daily Whig and Courier,* June 8, 1862.

14. *Ibid.*
15. *Ibid.*
16. Mundy, *Second to None,* 141.
17. *Bangor Daily Whig and Courier,* June 10, 1862.
18. *Ibid.,* June 8, 1862.
19. *Ibid.*; Mundy, *Second to None,* 142.
20. *Ibid.*
21. *Bangor Daily Whig and Courier,* June 8, 1862; Munday, *Second to None,* 142.
22. *Bangor Daily Whig and Courier,* June 8, 1862; Mundy, *Second to None,* 141.

Third Massachusetts Artillery

1. This list is taken from the *New York Times,* June 4, 1862.

Ninth Massachusetts Infantry

1. This list is taken from the *New York Times,* June 4, 1862.

Twenty-Second Massachusetts Volunteer Infantry

1. This list is taken from the *New York Times,* June 4, 1862.

Thirteenth New York Volunteer Infantry

1. This list is taken from the *New York Times,* June 4, 1862.

Fourteenth New York Volunteer Infantry

1. This list is taken from the *New York Times,* June 4, 1862.

Twenty-fifth New York Volunteer Infantry

1. Unless otherwise noted, this list is taken from the *New York Times,* June 4, 1862.
2. Styple, *Writing and Fighting the Civil War,* 99.
3. This is most likely Edgar Fenno, a sergeant in Company I.
4. Styple, *Writing and Fighting the Civil War,* 97.
5. It is unclear just who this reportedly wounded soldier is. The only James Hayes in the Twenty-fifth New York was in Company A, and he was killed.
6. Styple, *Writing and Fighting the Civil War,* 97.

7. *Ibid.*
8. The *New York Times* casualty list names this person as Dion Pendergrast, but no soldier by that name could be found.
9. Styple, *Writing and Fighting the Civil War,* 97.

Forty-fourth New York Volunteer Infantry

1. Unless otherwise noted, this list is taken from the *New York Times,* June 4, 1862.
2. *Ibid.,* June 7, 1862.
3. *Ibid.*
4. *Ibid.*
5. *Ibid.*
6. *Ibid.*
7. *Ibid.*
8. *Steubenville Herald,* June 2, 1897.
9. *New York Times,* June 7, 1862.
10. *Ibid.*
11. *Ibid.*
12. *Ibid.*
13. *Ibid.*
14. *Morning Express,* June 6, 1862.
15. *New York Times,* June 7, 1862.
16. *Ibid.*
17. *Ibid.*
18. *Ibid.*
19. *Ibid.*
20. *Ibid.*
21. *Ibid.*
22. *Ibid.*
23. *Ibid.*
24. *Morning Express,* June 6, 1862.
25. *Steubenville Herald,* June 2, 1897.
26. *New York Times,* June 7, 1862.
27. *Ibid.*
28. *Ibid.*
29. *Ibid.*
30. *Ibid.*
31. *Ibid.*
32. *Ibid.*
33. *Morning Express,* June 6, 1862; *New York Times,* June 7, 1862.
34. *Ibid.*
35. *Ibid.*
36. *Ibid.*
37. *Herkimer Journal,* June 12, 1862.
38. *New York Times,* June 7, 1862.
39. *Morning Express,* June 6, 1862. The *New York Times* reported that Tinkham's wound was to the "left arm" and "severe." *New York Times,* June 7, 1862.

Sixth Pennsylvania Cavalry

1. This list is taken from the *New York Times,* June 4, 1862.

Sixty-second Pennsylvania Volunteer Infantry

1. This list is taken from the *New York Times*, June 4, 1862.

Eighty-third Pennsylvania Volunteer Infantry

1. Unless otherwise noted, this list is taken from the *New York Times*, June 4, 1862.
2. Norton, *Army Letters*, 84.
3. *Ibid.*

First United States Sharpshooters

1. This list is taken from the *New York Times*, June 4, 1862.

Second United States Artillery

1. This list is taken from the *New York Times*, June 4, 1862.

Sixth United States Cavalry

1. This list is taken from the *New York Times*, June 4, 1862.

Bibliography

Manuscripts

Emory University
   Bell Wiley Collection

Library of Congress
   Fitz John Porter Papers
   Wigfall Family Papers

New York State Library
   Gouverneur K. Warren Papers

North Carolina Department of Cultural Resources, Department of Archives and History
   Noah Collins Papers

Richmond National Battlefield Park, Richmond
   Charles C. Braurn Letters

Southern Historical Collection, University of North Carolina, Chapel Hill
   W. J. H. Bellamy Diary
   Saunders Family Papers

United States Army Military History Institute.
   John O'Connell Memoir, Civil War Miscellaneous Boxes
   Luther C. Furst Diary, Harrisburg Civil War Round Table Collection.

University of North Carolina, Charlotte
   John B. Alexander Papers

Published Works

Adams, George W. *Doctors in Blue*. Baton Rouge: Louisiana State University Press, 1952, 1996.

Barefoot, Daniel W. *General Robert F. Hoke: Lee's Modest Warrior*. Winston-Salem, NC: John F. Blair, Publisher, 2001.

Beatie, Russel H. *Army of the Potomac: Birth of Command, November 1860–September 1862*. Cambridge, MA: Da Capo Press, 2002.

———. *Army of the Potomac: McClellan Takes Command, September 1861–February 1862.* Cambridge, MA: Da Capo Press, 2004.
Bissell, Eleanor. "Underground Railway." *The Lancaster Legend*, March–April 2001, 1–6.
Burton, Brian K. *Extraordinary Circumstances: The Seven Days Battles.* Bloomington: Indiana University Press, 2001.
Carter, Robert G. *Four Brothers in Blue, or, Sunshine and Shadows of the War of the Rebellion.* University of Texas Press, 1913, 1978.
Catton, Bruce. *The Army of the Potomac: Mr. Lincoln's Army.* New York: Doubleday and Company, 1951, 1962.
———. *Terrible Swift Sword.* New York: Simon and Schuster, 1985.
Charles Scribner's Sons. *Dictionary of American History* 10 Vols. New York: Charles Scribner's Sons, 1976.
Clark, Lewis H. *Military History of Wayne County, N. Y.: The County in the Civil War.* Sodus, NY: Lewis H. Clark, Hulett and Gaylord, 1883.
Clark, Walter, ed. *Histories of the Several Regiments and Battalions from North Carolina in the Great War, 1861–1865.* 5 vols. Raleigh, NC: E. M. Uzzell, 1901.
Coco, Gregory A. *The Civil War Infantryman: In Camp, on the March, and in Battle.* Gettysburg, PA: Thomas Publications, 1996.
Concise Dictionary of American History. 2 vols. New York: Charles Scribner's Sons, 1997.
Cullen, Joseph P. *The Peninsula Campaign of 1862.* Harrisburg, PA: Stackpole Books, 1973.
Cunningham, H. H. *Doctors in Gray.* Baton Rouge: Louisiana State University Press, 1958, 1986.
Davenport, Alfred. *Camp and Field of the Fifth New York Volunteer Inf. (Duryee Zouaves).* New York: Dick and Fitzgerald, 1879.
Dowdey, Clifford. *The Seven Days: The Emergence of Lee.* Lincoln: University of Nebraska Press, 1964.
Dyer, J. Franklin. *The Journal of a Civil War Surgeon.* Edited by Michael B. Chesson. Lincoln: University of Nebraska Press, 2003.
Eicher, John H., and David J. Eicher. *Civil War High Commands.* Stanford, CA: Stanford University Press, 2001.
Eisenschiml, Otto. *The Celebrated Case of Fitz John Porter: An American Dreyfus Affair.* Indianapolis: Bobbs-Merrill, 1950.
Fishel, Edwin C. *The Secret War for the Union: The Untold Story of Military Intelligence in the Civil War.* Boston: Houghton-Mifflin Trade and Reference, 1996.
Flynn, Frank J. *"The Fighting Ninth" for Fifty Years and the Semicentennial Celebration.* Boston: n.p., 1911.
Freeman, Douglas S. *R. E. Lee.* New York: C. Scribner's Sons, 1934–1935.
Gabbert, John M. *Military Operations in Hanover County, Virginia, 1861–1865.* Roanoke, VA: J. M. Gabbert, 1989.
Gallegher, Gary W., ed. *The Richmond Campaign of 1862: The Peninsula and the Seven Days.* Chapel Hill: University of North Carolina Press, 2000.
———. *The Shenandoah Valley Campaign of 1862.* Chapel Hill: University of North Carolina Press, 2003.
Govan, Gilbert E., and James Livingston. *Joseph E. Johnston: A Different Valor.* Westport, CT: Greenwood, 1973.
Hamilton, J. G. deRoulhac, Henry McGilbert Wogstaff, and William Whatley Pierson, eds. "The Diary of Bartlett Yancey Malone." *The James Sprunt Historical Publications*, 16:2 (1919), 5–59.

Hanover County Historical Society. *Old Homes of Hanover County, Virginia.* Hanover, VA: Hanover County Historical Society, 1983.

Hardy, Michael C. *The Thirty-seventh North Carolina Troops: Tar Heels in the Army of Northern Virginia.* Jefferson, N.C.: McFarland, 2003.

Harris, Brayton. *Blue and Gray in Black and White: Newspapers in the Civil War.* Washington: Brassey's, 1999.

Harsh, Joseph L. *Confederate Tide Rising: Robert E. Lee and the Making of Southern Strategy, 1861–1862.* Kent, OH: Kent State University Press, 1998.

Hassler, Warren W. Jr. *Commanders of the Army of the Potomac.* Baton Rouge: Louisiana State University Press, 1962.

Haydock, Michael D. "The Court-Martial of Fitz John Porter" *American History* 33, no. 6 (February 1999): 48–57.

Hennessy, John J., ed. *Fighting with the Eighteenth Massachusetts: The Civil War Memoir of Thomas H. Mann.* Baton Rouge: Louisiana State University Press, 2000.

_____. "Fredericksburg in the War." *Blue and Gray,* Vol. 22, no. 1 (Winter 2005).

Hewett, Janet B., Noah Andre Trudeau, and Bryce A. Suderow, eds., *Supplement to the Official Records of the Union and Confederate Armies.* Wilmington, NC: Broadfoot, 1994.

Johnson, Robert U., and Clarence C. Buel, eds. *Battles and Leaders of the Civil War.* 4 vols. New York: Thomas Yoseloff, 1956.

Jordon, David M. *"Happiness Is Not My Companion": The Life of General G. K. Warren.* Bloomington: Indiana University Press, 2001.

Judson, Amos H. *History of the Eighty-third Regiment Pennsylvania Volunteers.* Dayton, OH: Morningside, 1865, 1986.

Koonce, Donald B., ed. *Doctor to the Front: The Recollections of Confederate Surgeon Thomas Fanning Wood, 1861–1865.* Knoxville: University of Tennessee Press, 2000.

Krick, Robert K. *Lee's Colonels.* Dayton, OH: Morningside Bookshop, 1979.

Lancaster, Robert B. *A Sketch of the Early History of Hanover County and Its Large and Important Contributions to the American Revolution.* Richmond, VA: Whittet and Shepperson, 1976.

Larsen, Clark. "A succession of attempts on President Abraham Lincoln's life led to the development of the Secret Service. " *Military History* 18, no. 1 (April 2001): 12–14.

Lash, Jeffery N. "Joseph E. Johnston and the Virginia Railways, 1861–1862." *Civil War History* 35 (1989): 5–27.

Leech, Margaret. *Reveille in Washington, 1860–1865.* New York: Harper and Row, 1941, 1980.

Light, Rebecca Campbell, ed. *The War at Our Doors: The Civil War Diaries of the Bernard Sisters of Virginia.* Fredericksburg, VA: American History Company, 1998.

Longacre, Edward G. *Lincoln's Cavalrymen: A History of the Mounted Forces of the Army of the Potomac, 1861–1865.* Mechanicsburg, PA: Stackpole Books, 2000.

Lowe, Jeffery C., and Sam Hodges, eds. *Letters to Amanda: The Civil War Letters of Marion H. Fitzpatrick, Army of Northern Virginia.* Macon, GA: Mercer University Press, 1998.

Luther E. Cowles. *History of the Fifth Massachusetts Battery.* Boston: Luther E. Cowles, publisher, 1902.

Macartney, Clarence E. *Lincoln and His Generals.* Philadelphia: Dorrance and Company, Publishers, 1925.

Macmillan Compendium. *The Confederacy.* New York: Simon and Schuster Macmillan, 1993.

MacNamara, M. H. *The Irish Ninth in Bivouac and Battle: or Virginia and Maryland Campaigns.* Boston: Lee and Shepard, 1867.

Mahood, Wayne. *General Wadsworth. The Life and Times of Brevet Major General James S. Wadsworth*. Cambridge, MA: Da Capo Press, 2003.

Manarin, Louis H., and Weymouth T. Jordan, eds. *North Carolina Troops, 1861–1865: A Roster*. 11 Vols. Raleigh, NC: North Carolina Department of Archives and History, 1961-present.

Markle, Donald E. *Spies and Spymasters of the Civil War*. New York: Hippocrene Books, 1994.

McGuire, Judith W. *Diary of a Southern Refugee During the War by a Lady of Virginia*. Lincoln: University of Nebraska Press, 1995.

Miller, William J., ed. "'I Only Wait for the River': McClellan and his Engineers on the Chickahominy" in *The Richmond Campaign of 1862: The Peninsula and the Seven Days*, edited by Gary W. Gallagher. Chapel Hill: University of North Carolina Press, 2000, 44–65.

_____. "No American Sevastopol." *America's Civil War* 13, no. 2 (May 2000): 30–38.

_____. *Prelude to the Seven Days: The Peninsula Campaign of 1862*. 3 Vols. Campbell, CA: Savas Woodbury, 1997.

Munday, James H. *Second to None: The Story of the 2d Maine Volunteers, "The Bangor Regiment."* Scarborough, ME: Harp Publishers, 1992.

Nash, Eugene A. *A History of the Forty-Fourth Regiment, New York Volunteer Infantry, in the Civil War. 1861–1865*. Chicago: R. R. Donnelley & Sons, 1911.

Nevins, Allan. *The War for the Union*. 4 Vol. New York: Charles Scribner's Sons, 1960.

Newton, Steven H. *Joseph E. Johnston and the Defense of Richmond*. Lawrence: University Press of Kansas, 1998.

Niven, John. *Salmon P. Chase: A Biography*. New York: Oxford University, 1995.

Norton, Oliver Willcox. *Army Letters, 1861–1865*. Dayton, OH: Morningside, 1903, 1990.

Nosworthy, Brent. *Bloody Crucible of Courage: Fighting Methods and Combat Experience of the Civil War*. New York: Carroll & Graf, 2003.

Parker, John L. *Henry Wilson's Regiment History of the Twenty-second Massachusetts Infantry, the Second Company Sharpshooters and the Third Light Battery, in the War of the Rebellion*. Boston: Rand Avery Co., 1887.

Phisterer, Frederick, comp. *New York in the War of the Rebellion*. Vol. 3. Albany, NY: Weed and Parsons, 1890.

Powell, William H. *The Fifth Army Corps: A Record of Operations During the Civil War in the United States of America, 1861–1865*. Reprint, Dayton, OH: Morningside Bookshop, 1984.

Rafuse, Ethan S. "McClellan, von Clausewitz, and the Politics of War." *Columbiad* 1, no. 3 (1997): 23–37.

Rajtar, Steve. *Indian War Sites: A Guidebook to Battlefields, Monuments, and Memorials*. Jefferson, NC: McFarland, 1999.

Reese, Timothy J. *Sykes' Regular Infantry Division, 1861–1864*. Jefferson, NC: McFarland, 1990.

Ripley, William Y. M. *Vermont Riflemen in the War for the Union 1861 to 1865: A History of Company F, 1st USSS*. Rutland: Tuttle, printers, 1883.

Robertson, James I. *General A. P. Hill: The Story of a Confederate Warrior*. New York: Random House, 1987.

_____. *Stonewall Jackson: The Man, the Soldier, the Legend*. New York: Macmillan, 1997.

Rourke, Norman. "The Newsmen." *Civil War Times Illustrated* 40, no. 6 (December 2001): 14–22.

Rowland, Thomas J. "'Heaven Save a County Governed By Such Counsels!' The Safety of Washington and the Peninsula Campaign." *Civil War History* 42 (1996): 5–17.

Samito, Christian G. *Commanding Boston's Irish Ninth: The Civil War Letters of Colonel Patrick R. Guiney. Ninth Massachusetts Volunteer Infantry*. New York: Fordman, 1998.

Schellhammer, Michael. *The 83rd Pennsylvania Volunteers in the Civil War*. Jefferson, NC: McFarland, 2003.

Schreckengost, Gary "Stonewall's Triumphant Return to Winchester." *America's Civil War*, 13, no. 3 (July 2000): 26–33.

Sears, Stephen W. *George B. McClellan: The Young Napoleon*. New York: Da Capo Press, 1999.

_____. *To the Gates of Richmond: The Peninsula Campaign*. New York: Ticknor & Fields, 1983.

_____, ed. *The Civil War Papers of George B. McClellan: Selected Correspondence, 1860–1865*. New York: Da Capo Press, 1992.

Shaffner, Louis. "A Civil War Surgeon's Diary." *North Carolina Medical Journal* 27 (September 1966): 409–15.

Speer, Allen P. *Voices from Cemetery Hill: The Civil War Diary, Reports, and Letters of Colonel William Henry Asbury Speer (1861–1864)*. Johnston City, TN: The Overmountain Press, 1997.

Stanley, R. H., and George O. Hall. *Eastern Maine and the Rebellion: Being an Account of the Principal Events in Eastern Maine During the War: contains accounts of Mobs, Riots, Destruction of Newspapers, War Meetings, Drafts, Confederate Raids, Peace Meetings, Celebrations, Soldiers' Letters, and Scenes and Incidents at the Front, Never Before in Print*. Bangor: Maine: R. H. Stanley, 1887.

Stevens, William, ed. *Dictionary of North Carolina Biography*. 6 vols. Chapel Hill: University of North Carolina Press, 1979.

Stone, Edwin W. *Rhode Island in the Rebellion*. Providence, RI: G. H. Whitney, 1864.

Styple, William B., ed. *Writing and Fighting the Civil War: Soldier Correspondence to the New York Mercury*. Kearny, N.J.: Belle Grove, 2000.

Symonds, Craig L. *Joseph E. Johnston: A Civil War Biography*. New York: W. W. Norton, 1994.

Tevis, C. V. *The History of the Fighting Fourteenth: Published in Commemoration of the Anniversary of the Muster of the Regiment into the United States Service*. Brooklyn: Brooklyn Eagle, 1991.

Thomas, Emory M. *Bold Dragoon: The Life of J. E. B. Stuart*. Norman: University of Oklahoma Press, 1999.

_____. *The Confederate State of Richmond: A Biography of the Capital*. Baton Rouge: Louisiana State University Press, 1971, 1998.

Turner, Charles W. "The Richmond, Fredericksburg, and Potomac, 1861–1865." *Civil War History* 7 (1961): 255–263.

_____. "The Virginia Central at War, 1861–1865." *The Journal of Southern History* 12, no. 4 (November 1946): 510–533.

Warner, Ezra J. *Generals in Gray: Live of the Confederate Commanders*. Baton Rouge: Louisiana State University, 1959.

Wiggins, Octavius A. "Thirty-seventh Regiment" in *Histories of the Several Regiments and Battalions from North Carolina in the Great War, 1861 to 1865*, edited by Walter Clark. Raleigh, NC: E. M. Uzzell, 1901.

Wiley, Bell I. *The Life of Billy Yank*. New York: Bob Merrills, 1951.

Williams, Carolyn White. *History of Jones County, Georgia: For One Hundred Years, Specifically 1807–1907*. Macon, GA: J. W. Burke, 1957.

Wittenberg, Eric J. *"We Have It Damn Hard Out Here:" The Civil War Letters of Sergeant Thomas W. Smith, 6th Pennsylvania Cavalry*. Kent, OH: Kent State University Press, 1999.

Newspapers

Bangor Daily Whig and Courier (ME)
Biblical Recorder (NC)
Brooklyn Eagle (NY)
Buffalo Morning Express (NY)
Dedham Gazette (MA)
Fayetteville Observer (NC)
Herkimer Journal (NY)
Morning Express (NY)
National Tribune (Washington D. C.)
New York Tribune
New York Times
Oneida Weekly Herald (NY)
Raleigh State Journal (NC)
Raleigh Register (NC)
Richmond Examiner (VA)
Richmond Times (VA)
Rochester Democrat and American (NY)
Rochester Union and Advertiser (NY)
Spirit of the Age (NC)
The State Journal (NC)
Steubenville Herald (OH)
The Sunny South (GA)
Weekly Catawba Journal (NC)
Weekly Raleigh Register (NC)
Weekly Standard (NC)
Wilmington Journal Weekly (NC)

Theses and Dissertations

Alexander, William K. "'Fought Them Like Tigers': The Life and Times of the Thirty-third North Carolina Infantry Regiment." Master's thesis: Western Carolina University, 2003.
Brawley, James Shober. "The Public and Military Career of Lawrence O'Bryan Branch." Master's thesis: University of North Carolina at Chapel Hill, 1951.
Coggeshall, Jerry J. "Hanover Court House: The Union's Tactical Victory and Strategic Failure." Master's thesis: Old Dominion University, 1999.
Dozier, Graham Town. "The Eighteenth North Carolina Infantry Regiment, C.S.A." Master's thesis: Virginia Polytechnic Institute, 1992.
Gianneschi, Matthew Everett. "A Man from Mecklenburg: 1st Sergeant John Tally and the 'Hornet's Nest Riflemen,' North Carolina, 37th Regiment, Company I." Master's thesis: University of Denver, 1998.
McDaid, William K. "Four Years of Arduous Service: The History of the Branch-Lane Brigade in the Civil War." Ph.D. diss.: Michigan State University, 1987.
Phillips, Kenneth Edwards. "James Henry Lane and the War for Southern Independence." Master's thesis: Auburn University, 1982

Index

Numbers in ***bold italics*** indicate pages with photographs.

Abercrombie, John J. 22, 34
Abernathy, John A. 87 158
Adams, W. J. 121, 122
Alexandria, VA 12, 46
Anderson, Joseph R. 12, 28, 31, 38, 39, 41, 42, 43 113, 129, 147
Appomattox, VA 137
Aquia Creek 29, 33, 37, 41, 42
Archer, James J. 113
Army of the Potomac 1, 11, 12, 14, 16, 17, 18, 20, 21, 26, 27, 28, 31, 47, 48, 96
Ashcake, VA 53, 149
Ashcraft, John 65, 124
Ashland, VA 2, 5, 65, 89, 92, 103, 105, 108, 109, 111, 118, 123, 131, 146, 147, 148, 149, 151
Augur, Christopher C. 35, 36, 37
Austin, Henry 96

Baltimore and Ohio Railroad 17
Banks, Nathaniel B. 17, 18, 23, 25, 28, 29, 30, 37, 38, 39, 40, 41, 117
Barber, William M. 67, 70, 74, 85, 90, 124, 164
Barnes, Clark 83
Barringer, William D. 123
Barry, William F. 48
Bayard, George D. 36
Beaver Dam Creek, VA 96, 135, 137
Bellamy, William J.H. 90, 112
Benson, Henry 57, 58, 60, 63, 64, 104, 117

Berdan, Hiram 47, 53, 60, 119, 142, 146
Bernard, Helen 36
Bissell, Eliad L. 77
Blair, Charles H. 81
Blair, Montgomery ***15***
Blenker, Louis 24
Bohannon, Neal 103
Bramer, Lewis, Jr. 99, 110
Branch, Lawrence O'B. 1, 2, 38, ***39***, 40, 41, 42, 43, 45, 48, 49, 50, 53, 60, 67, 69, 74, 76, 80, 87, 89, 91, 94, 95, 107, 111, 113, 114, 122, 124, 125, 126, 129, 130, 131, 132, 135, 137, 139, 141, 147, 149, 151
Branch's brigade 28, 31, 38, 40, 129, 137
Britt, Amos 83
Brook Church, VA 111, 113
Bryant, William C. 17
Buchanan, Robert C. 47, 142
Buell, Don Carlos 14, 23
Burnside, Ambrose 25, 38
Butterfield, Daniel 46, 52, 60, 61, 62, 63, 64, 75, 90, 94, 103, 117, 121, 122, 130, 133, 134, 135, 138, 142, 147

Cameron, Simon 16, 115
Campbell, Reuben P. 67, 90, 91, 127, 150
Casey, Silas 28
Cass, Thomas 87, 91
Centreville, VA 14, 27
Chambers, Daniel W. 112, 124
Chambliss, William P. 108, 109, 148
Chandler, Samuel W. 85
Chaplin, Daniel 86

Chapin, E.P. 85, 175
Chapman, William 47, 142
Charlottesville, VA. 9, 39
Chase, Salmon P. 13, 14, 15, 29, 40
Chattanooga, TN 17
Chickahominy River 27, 28, 42, 48, 107, 129, 135, 137
Clark, Harry 58
Clark, Henry C. 111
Cloninger, Jonas S. 60, 65, 103
Cold Harbor National Cemetery 139, 174, 175, 176
Cold Harbor, VA 137
Cooper, Samuel 35
Corps: (I) 18, 22, 23, 24, 43, 46, 48, 50; (II) 18, 96; (III) 18, 21, 46; (IV) 18; (V) 1, 45, 46, 51, 99, 109, 110, 113, 116, 121, 132, 133, 137, 145; (VI) 46, 47
Cowan, Robert H. 74, 76, 81, 83, 131, 149, 150
Crenshaw's Virginia Battery 38
Curtis, Samuel R. 23

Dahlgren, John A. 14, 28
Davenport, Alfred 90
Davidson's Letcher Battery 38
Davis, B.B. 35
Davis, Jefferson 25, ***26***, 31, 43, 112, 117, 135
Davis, William J. 112
Davis Island, NY 161
Dennison, William 19
Dillingham, Robert 102
Douglas, Beverly B. 43
Dumfries, VA 19
Duryea, Abram 89

201

Dyer, Samuel 83

Edwards, Neill 83
Eighteenth Massachusetts Infantry 46, 99, 101, 106, 141
Eighteenth North Carolina Troops 38, 50, 74, 76, 80, 81, 82, 83, 84, 85, 90, 91, 96, 102, 106, 111, 112, 122, 123, 124, 126, 131, 138, 139, 141, 149, 150, 154
Eighth Illinois Cavalry 47
Eighty-third Pennsylvania Infantry 47, 52, 60, 62, 63, 64, 90, 92, 96, 97, 100, 101, 102, 110, 117, 119, 122, 142, 176
Eleventh United States Infantry 47
Ellis, Charles J. 86, 170
Eltham's Landing, VA 27
Emory, William H. 47, 52, 65, 143, 145, 147, 148
Evans, David K. 112
Ewell, Richard S. 30, 31, 33, 37, 38, 39, 40, 41

Fairfax Court House, VA 21, 22
Falmouth, VA 35, 36
Farthing, William Y. 124, 166
Field, Charles 31, 33, 35, 36, 37, 38, 89, 111, 113
Fifth Alabama Battalion 35
Fifth New York Infantry 47, 48, 50, 88, 90, 99, 100, 142, 145
Fifth United States Artillery: Battery D 47, 64, 72, 74, 88, 117, 142; Battery I 47, 64, 117, 143
Fifth United States Cavalry 47, 49, 52, 65, 66, 104, 105, 108, 143, 147
Fifty-fifth Virginia Infantry 33, 35
First Connecticut Heavy Artillery 47, 48, 50, 90, 142, 145
First North Carolina Volunteers 54, 67, 69
First Pennsylvania Cavalry 35, 36
First Rhode Island Light Artillery, Battery C 1, 47, 48, 50, 52, 93, 142, 145

First South Carolina Infantry 38
First United States Cavalry 49, 104
First United States Sharpshooters 47, 53, 60, 117, 119, 142, 177
Fiske, George E. 58, 172
Fitzpatrick, Marion H. 53
Fort Columbus, NY 156, 158, 159, 160, 161, 163, 164, 165, 166, 167, 168, 169
Fort Delaware, DE 169
Fortieth Pennsylvania Infantry 80
Fortieth Virginia Infantry 33, 35
Fortress Monroe, VA 11, 13, 21, 22, 25, 46, 157, 162, 163, 166, 168
Forty-fifth Georgia Infantry 1, 38, 43, 53, 80, 89, 102, 111, 123, 127, 141, 149, 150
Forty-first New York Infantry 45
Forty-fourth New York Infantry 46, 52, 75, 77, 78, 80, 81, 84, 85, 90, 100, 109, 110, 119, 120, 121, 131, 133, 134, 135, 142, 174
Forty-ninth Georgia Infantry 38
Forty-seventh Virginia Infantry 33
Forty-third Virginia Infantry 109
Fourteenth Massachusetts Infantry 45
Fourteenth New York Infantry 46, 86, 87, 89, 100, 117, 119, 121, 142, 171
Fourteenth South Carolina Infantry 38
Fourteenth United States Infantry 47, 142
Fourth Louisiana Battalion 38
Fourth Michigan Infantry 45, 46, 87, 120, 121, 141
Fourth United States Infantry 47, 142
Fourth Virginia Cavalry 8, 43, 53, 60, 67, 109, 127, 141
Franklin, William B. 14, 15, 18, 46
Fredericksburg, VA 1, 9, 24, 28, 29, 30, 31, 33, 34, 35, 36, 37, 38, 39, 40, 41, 42, 43, 72, 109, 113, 134, 147

Fremont, John C. 24, 25, 30, 37
Front Royal, VA 31, 42, 43
Furst, Luther C. 101

Garnsey, Frank A. 86
Gerley, William 112
Gibbon, Robert 94, 95, 103
Gilbert, Edwin S. 58, 81, 97
Goldsborough, Louis M. 14
Gordon, J.P. 112
Gordonsville, VA 9, 16, 31, 38, 39, 40, 41, 170
Gove, Jesse A. 69, 70, 72, 73, 87, 103, 104, 116, 147
Grant, Ulysses S. 23, 69
Greeley, Horace 17
Gregg, Maxcy 31, 38, 113
Grier, William N. 49
Griffin, Charles 47, 64, 71, 94, 117, 142
Grows, David H. 94, 100
Gurley, John A. 17

Halleck, Henry W. 14, 23
Hamilton, Charles S. *15*, 21
Hanover County Confederate Monument *138*
Hanover County, VA 5–9, 137, 138
Hanover Court House, VA 2, 41, 42, 43, 47, 48, 49, 53, 54, 58, 63, 64, 66, 69, 72, 73, 74, 80, 86, 89, 94, 97, 99, 104, 107, 110, 113, 115, 116, 117, 118, 120, 121, 123, 127, 131, 132, 134, 135, 137, 138, 140, 145, 146, 147, 149, 150
Hanover Junction, VA 43
Hanover Tavern *8*, 9, 138
Hardeman, Robert 89
Hardeman, Thomas 53, 127, 149, 150
Harley, J.P. 87, 120, 122
Harpers Ferry, VA 17, 21, 30
Harris, Ira 25
Harrison, J.E. 105, 147
Hart, Moses N. 84
Hasty, Andrew J. 65
Haupt, Herman 28
Heintzelman, Samuel P. 18, 46
Heth, Henry 26
Hickerson, Charles N. 71, 90
Hill, Ambrose P. 113, 149, 151
Hill, Daniel H. 54, 67
Hitchcock, Ethan Allen 21, 22
Hitchcock, James B. 78, 121, 122

Hoke, Robert F. 68, 68, 76, 150
Hollywood Cemetery, Richmond, VA 139
Holmes, Theophilus 38
Hooker, Joseph 22
Horner, Frederick 80
Houghton, Olivia C. 84
Hulbert, Egbert D. 62, 96
Hunger, Benjamin 25
Hunter, Henry J. 47

Jackson, Thomas J. "Stonewall" 23, 24, 26, 28, 29, 30, 31, 33, 37, 38, 39, 40, 43, 53, 129
James River 5, 12, 13, 25
Jameson, Charles D. 72
Johnson, Charles A. 54, 57, 58, 81, 84, 117, 119, 146
Johnson, Edward 26
Johnston, George 54
Johnston, Joseph E. *19*, 21, 25, 26, 27, 28, 33, 38, 41, 42, 43, 114, 129, 135, 149, 151
Jones, Owen 36
Jordan, Johnny 86
Judson, Amos 52

Kane, Michael 102
Kelleher, Richard 72, 86, 120
Kernstown, VA 23
Keyes, Erasmus D. 18, 25, 28, 117
Kilpatrick, Judson 36
King, Samuel 96, 113
Kinney, Thomas H. 54, 58, 94, 137
Kinney farm 1, 2, 54, 57, 58, *60*, 86, 89, 94, 95, 103, 106, 133, 137, 138
Knox, Edward B. 85, 175

Lane, James H. 53, 54, 57, 58, 60, 62, 67, 69, 74, 76, 86, 87, 124, 125, 127, 130, 131, 133, 149, 150, 151
Lansing, Henry S. 62, 103, 104, 117
Latham's battery 39, 53, 71, 76, 91, 117, 123, 126, 127, 141, 149, 150, 170
Lebanon Church 2, 67, 71, 89, 125, 130, ***139***
Lee, Charles C. 2, 67, 69, 70, 71, 74, 76, 80, 83, 84, 85, 87, 114, 124, 125, 126, 127, 130, 149, 150

Lee, Robert E. 25, 26, 31, 37, 38, 39, 40, 43, 126, 135
Lee, William H.F. 35, 36, 37
Leesburg, VA 19
Letcher, John 112
Lewisburg, VA 26
Ligon's Factory Hospital, Richmond, VA 112
Lincoln, Abraham 12, 14, ***15***, 16, 17, 18, 19, 22, 23, 24, 26, 27, 28, 29, 30, 31, 41, 43, 108, 109, 113, 115
Louisa Railroad *see* Virginia Central Railroad
Lovill, Edward F. 124
Lowe, Samuel D. 103, 161
Lowe, Thaddeus S.C. 48
Luray, VA 40
Lynchburg Railroad 17

Madison Court House, VA 40
Magruder, John B. 25
Manassas, VA 8, 14, 15, 16, 18, 19, 20, 21, 22, 23, 24, 26, 34, 72
Mann, Thomas H. 99
Marcy, Randolph B. 109
Marshall, Elisha 52
Marshall, Humphrey 26, 90, 91
Marston, Frank W. 80
Martindale, John H. 45, 46, 54, 57, 66, 69, 70, 71, 72, 73, 74, 75, 78, 80, 81, 83, 84, 85, 86, 90, 99, 110, 120, 133, 134, 135, 141, 146, 147
Martin's battery 75, 80, 86
Massachusetts Light Artillery 47, 94, 100, 101, 102, 109, 117, 142, 171
Mattapony River 5, 39
May, Alexander 101
McBride, Frank 62
McClellan, George B. 1, 11, 12, ***13***, 14, 15, 16, 17, 18, 19, 20, 22, 23, 24, 25, 26, 27, 28, 29, 30, 31, 33, 38, 41, 42, 43, 45, 46, 48, 50, 51, 107, 108, 109, 113, 115, 132, 135, 137, 151
McDowell, Irving 1, 12, 13, 14, 15, 18, 22, 23, 24, 25, 28, 29, 30, 33, 34, 35, 37, 38, 39, 41, 42, 43, 48, 50, 51, 109, 113, 117, 118, 123, 135
McIntosh's Pee Dee Battery 38
McLane, John W. 52, 90, 91, 117

McMahon, Michael 58, 173
McQuade, James 46, 86, 87, 142, 147
Mechanicsville, VA 43, 48, 117, 137
Meigs, Montgomery C. 15
Middleton, VA 29, 42
Mines, John F. 97, 98
Morell, George W. 46, 47, 52, 53, 54, 64, 74, 80, 87, 116, 121, 132, 134, 141, 146, 147
Morris, Thomas E. 62
Morris, Thomas F. 104
Morris, William G. 83, 168
Morrow, Daniel 54
Mount Jackson, VA 23
Muirhead, Henry P. 103

New Bern, NC 40, 67, 80
Newton, Mrs. Willoughby 49, 50
Nicholson, William T. 85, 125
Nineteenth Massachusetts Infantry 96
Ninth Massachusetts Infantry 45, 46, 87, 88, 89, 91, 102, 110, 117, 120, 121, 141, 171
Ninth Virginia Cavalry 33, 35, 43, 50
Norfolk, VA 27, 39
North Anna River 5, 137
Norton, Oliver W. 52, 62, 92, 99

Occoquan River 12
O'Connell, John 52
Old Church 53, 129
Orange and Alexandria Railroad 17, 40

Pamunkey River 5, 27, 39, 41, 43, 48, 50, 52, 66, 86, 105, 106, 129, 145, 146, 147
Parker, Elijah J. 65
Parker, John L. 87
Patrick, Marsena R. 29
Peacock, N. 112
Peake's Turnout 1, 2, 65, 66, 67, ***70***, 85, 86, 94, 97, 99, 110, 115, 118, 120, 129, 137, 138, 140, 146, 149
Pender, Dorsey 113
Perry, David M. 100
Petersburg, VA 156
Phillips, Charles A. 101
Pigford, Jacob M. 96, 157
Pinkerton, Allan 20, 26, 27
Pollard, Abigail L. 97

Pope, John 23
Porter, Andrew 14
Porter, Fitz John 1, 14, 45, 46, 47, 48, 49, 50, 51, 52, 54, 55, 56, 57, 58, 60, 64, 66, 72, 74, 80, 86, 90, 96, 100, *101*, 103, 107, 108, 109, 110, 113, 116, 118, 120, 130, 132, 133, 134, 135, 137, 141, 145
Portsmith's Grove, RI 165
Potomac River 17, 18, 19, 28, 29
Potts, J. R. 53, 60, 64
Prevatt, Elias 83
Privett, Forney 83

Radcliffe, James D. 74
Raleigh, NC 112, 123
Randolph, George W. 112, 113
Rappahannock River 13, 19, 25, 28, 33, 35, 38, 39, 41, 113
Regan, Daniel J. 91
Rice, James C. 81, 84, 85, 92
Richmond and Danville Railroad 12, 16
Richmond and Petersburg Railroad 12
Richmond and York River Railroad 12, 28
Richmond, Fredericksburg, and Potomac Railroad 9, 12, 17, 43, 108, 109, 112, 116, 147
Richmond, VA 1, 5, 8, 9, 11, 12, 13, 14, 16, 19, 20, 21, 22, 23, 25, 26, 27, 28, 29, 30, 31, 33, 35, 37, 38, 39, 40, 43, 69, 107, 109, 111, 112, 117, 119, 122, 124, 129, 131, 135, 145, 147, 154, 157, 162, 166, 168
Roberts, Charles W. 72, 75, 81, 82, 83, 84, 86, 87, 107, 119
Roberts, Pleasant H. 59, 162
Robertson, Beverly H. 89, 127, 150
Robnett, Joel B. 85
Robnett, John C. 85
Robnett, William P. 85
Royall, William B. 65
Rush, Richard H. 47, 48, 49, 66, 109, 147

Sampson, Walter S. 70
Saunders, Joseph H. 76
Savage, Henry F. 57, 77, 78, 174

Schutt, Frank B. 85
Scott, Thomas A. 14
Scott, Winfield 21
Second Maine Infantry 45, 46, 52, 57, 69, 70, 72, 74, 75, 78, 80, 81, 82, 83, 84, 85, 86, 87, 89, 97, 107, 110, 117, 119, 120, 131, 134, 135, 141
Second Massachusetts Sharpshooters 102
Second New York Cavalry 35, 36
Second United States Artillery, Battery M 58, 69, 70, 71, 104, 177
Second United States Cavalry, Troop I 45
Second United States Infantry 47, 142
Sergeant, Daniel F. 72
Seven Pines, VA 28, 43
Seventeenth New York Infantry 46, 57, 60, 62, 63, 64, 103, 104, 108, 117, *132*, *133*, 142
Seventeenth United States Infantry 47, 142
Seventh North Carolina State Troops 38, 67, 68, 80, 91, 92, 94, 112, 127, 131, 141, 150, 151, 153
Seward, William H. 14, 15, 29
Shadwell, VA 9
Shaffner, John 89, 107, 164
Shenandoah Valley, VA 1, 23, 24, 26, 28, 29, 30, 37, 39, 40, 43, 129
Sheridan, Philip H. 137
Sherman, William T. 45
Shields, James 24, 28, 30, 41, 42
Shriver, Jacob T. 62
Sigel, Franz 23
Sikes, Willie J. 83
Simmons, Alexander 112
Simonds, Joseph 70, 73
Sixteenth Michigan Infantry 46, 60, 62, 90, 117, 142
Sixth North Carolina State Troops 111
Sixth Pennsylvania Cavalry 3, 47, 48, 49, 52, 65, 103, 104, 105, 108, 109, 130, 143, 145, 176
Sixth United States Cavalry 47, 52, 104, 105, 108, 109, 116, 143, 147, 177

Sixth United States Infantry 47, 142
Sixtieth Virginia Infantry 33
Sixty-second Pennsylvania Infantry 46, 87, 89, 117, 119, 121, 141, 176
Skillen, Charles H. 86
Slash Church 1, 2, *42*, 43, 50, 53, 67, 89, 130, 139, 149
Slaughter, Montgomery 37
Smart, Benjamin F. 83, 171
Smith, James H. 83, 171
Smith, Thomas W. 105, 106
South Anna River, VA 104, 108, 109, 137, 145, 147
Southside Railroad 17
Speer, William H.A. 54, 58, 63, 64, 103, 106, 107, 163
Stansel, Buntan 96
Stanton, Edwin 13, *15*, 16, 17, 21, 22, 23, 27, 28, 29, 31, 33, 37, 38, 39, 41, 107, 108, 109, 115, 132
Staunton, VA 26
Stoneman, George 47, 74, 134, 147, 148
Stowe, Samuel 65, 163
Strasburg, VA 29, 42
Stryker, Stephen W. 75, 78, 80, 81, 85
Stuart, J.E.B. 137, 138
Summey, Andrew 85
Sumner, Edwin V. 18, 22, 29
Sykes, George 47, 142, 148

Taliaferro's Mill 50, 53, 54, 129, 130, 133, 149
Taylorsviile, VA 64
Tenth United States Infantry 142
Third North Carolina State Troops 74
Third United States Artillery: Battery E 45; Battery L 47, 143; Battery M 47, 143
Third United States Infantry 47, 142
Thirteenth New York Infantry 45, 46, 48, 52, 89, 90, 91, 92, 94, 96, 100, 102, 106, 107, 110, 118, 119, 141, 171
Thirteenth South Carolina Infantry 38
Thirty-eighth North Carolina Troops 38, 89
Thirty-fourth North Carolina Troops 38

Index

Thirty-seventh North Carolina Troops 2, 39, 41, 50, 53, 65, 67, 70, 71, 74, 76, 80, 81, 83, 84, 85, 87, 90, 91, 102, 105, 111, 112, 113, 114, 124, 125, 126, 129, 130, 131, 138, 141, 149, 150, 164
Thirty-third North Carolina Troops 38, 40, 68, 69, 76, 78, 79, 80, 89, 123, 125, 127, 131, 141, 164
Thomas, Lozenzo 22
Thompson, Thomas P. 58, 174
Tilton, William S. 87
Timberlake, David A. 67, 130
Tolar, Sampson B. 112
Townsend, Neill 83
Tripler, Charles S. 96
Turpin, Bob 89
Twelfth New York Infantry 46, 52, 60, 64, 99, 110, 117, 142
Twelfth North Carolina State Troops 41, 71, 76, 79, 80, 102, 130, 131, 141, 150, 154
Twelfth South Carolina Infantry 38
Twelfth United States Infantry 47, 142
Twenty-eighth North Carolina Troops 38, 50, 53, 54, 57, 58, 60, 63, 65, 74, 76, 80, 81, 86, 87, 94, 95, 103, 106, 111, 122, 123, 124, 130, 131, 133, 135, 138, 141, 147, 149, 151
Twenty-fifth New York Infantry 46, 54, 55, 56, 57, 58, 60, 69, 80, 81, 83, 84, 94, 96, 97, 100, 102, 110, 115, 117, 118, 119, 120, 122, 130, 131, 133, 134, 135, 146, 172
Twenty-second Massachusetts Infantry 46, 57, 69, 70, 72, 73, 75, 87, 102, 103, 104, 116, 134, 141, 147, 171
Twenty-second Virginia Battalion 33

Urbanna, VA 13, 35

Virginia and Tennessee Railroad 17, 26
Virginia Central Railroad 9, 12, 16, 40, 49, 72, 86, 108, 116, 120, 134, 138, 146, 147

Wade, Benjamin O. 71, 76, 150
Wadsworth, James S. 17, 18, 22
Walker, Leroy 122
Walker, Reuben L. 113
Warren, Gouverneur K. 47, 48, 49, 52, 86, 109, 119, 130, 132, 142, 146, 148
Warwick River 25
Washington D.C. 11, 14, 18, 19, 21, 22, 23, 24, 28, 29, 34, 39, 40, 42, 108, 113

Watson, Peter H. 39, 42
Waud, Alfred 116
Webb, Alexander S. 48
Weed, Hiland A. 58
Weed, Stephen H. 47, 143, 145
Weeks, Henry A. 52, 117
West Point, VA 46
White House, VA 96
Whiting, Charles J. 65, 105
Wickham, William C. 8, 64, 104, 105
Wiggin, Rinaldo B. 75
Williams, Lawrence 104, 108, 147, 148
Williams, Solomon 71
Williamsburg, VA 8, 9, 26, 46
Williamson, George W. 112
Williamsport, MD 29
Wilmington and Weldon Railroad 26
Wilson, Henry 69
Winchester, VA 17, 23, 29
Wood, Thomas F. 74, 83
Wool, John E. 25

York River 13, 28, 41
Yorktown National Cemetery 140
Yorktown, VA 13, 25, 27, 38, 39, 46, 47, 69, 154, 155, 156, 157
Young, James 84

www.ingramcontent.com/pod-product-compliance
Ingram Content Group UK Ltd.
Pitfield, Milton Keynes, MK11 3LW, UK
UKHW050527150426
5217IPUK00026B/1826